THE AIR MARSHALS

TO THE LADY
who awarded me my wings

THE AIR MARSHALS

The Air War in Western Europe

ALLEN ANDREWS

WILLIAM MORROW & COMPANY, INC

NEW YORK 1970

Printed in Great Britain

Library of Congress Catalog Number : 70-115988

CONTENTS

LIST OF ILLUSTRATIONS

Between pages 144 and 145

CHAPTER ONE

MARSHALS AND MARSHALLED

*The license to publish anything upon military opera-
tions, whether true or not, which results from the
liberty of the press, is a very great inconvenience.*

THE DUKE OF WELLINGTON

This book is about the air war in the West in the Second World
War, and the generalship of the men who fought it, all of whom
had been junior officers in the First World War. The decisive
weapon they used was the strategic bomber.

I innocently witnessed the assault on London which made it
the first capital city in the world ever to be attacked by strategic
aerial bombardment. It was a historic raid, for it largely
governed the thinking of air marshals through the critical period
which ended with the Second World War. I was too young to
go to school, and I was playing in the family garden at
Greenwich on the morning of 13 June 1917 when I saw the
hollow lozenge of German Gotha bombers moving across the
blue sky to position themselves over central London. Bugles
blown from motor cars racing through the streets were sounding
the air-raid alarm. But I did not recognize the note, and my
mother, working at a sewing-machine damaged earlier from the
Silvertown munitions explosion, was not yet sophisticated enough
in civil defence to call me in when the anti-aircraft shrapnel
began to fall – splinters which accounted for 15 per cent of the
casualties in that careless dawn of air warfare. The bombs killed
162 people and injured 432, an impressive score from only 14
aircraft, none of which was shot down by the 92 British fighters
which engaged them. Twenty-three years later I removed my
mother, and her sewing-machine, from the ruins of a house in
Greenwich destroyed when 413 bombers – at that time the
largest number of German aircraft to be put over London –
discharged a record load of high explosive and incendiaries, not
by day, but by night.

I mention these experiences – the first and the last personal anecdote to be included in this study – as an illustration of the short time in which the theory and practice of strategic "terror" air bombing was developed and came to fruition, compared, say, with the 200-years' gestation of the successful application of gunpowder. During that brief period also, the air forces, particularly in the United States, propagated the rival theory of strategic precision bombing against carefully calculated objectives. The prime of modern aerial warfare was thus developed during the working life of a sewing-machine, in the time it took, in my own case, for a boy to progress from being able to spell "air force" to being rigged in the blue uniform. In the case of the commanders who are the theme of this book, the principles of war in the air were laid down in the time it took to rise in seniority from lieutenant or captain in 1917 to general or marshal in 1940. The air marshals of the Second World War had no dead predecessors.

They were serving indeed, and fighting, when military air activity made its first advance, from observation to aggression. The Royal Flying Corps and the air auxiliaries of both the French and German armies went into war in 1914 as reconnaissance squadrons; and the United States air arm, first active against Pancho Villa in 1916, was significantly named the Aviation Section of the Signal Corps.

When the British characteristically began the First World War with a historic retreat, their reconnaissance aircraft proved of immediate value, giving accurate information on enemy positions and batteries, and directing artillery fire. Air observation on both sides became so important that counter-measures were soon pursued, and fighter aircraft were detailed to destroy the reconnaissance machines, the scouts. Then the Germans, in the first instance, established escort squadrons to protect the scouts while they were making their observations. These escort units developed their function into a trench-strafing role, attacking French and English frontline troops in their trenches by bombing. A use was found for these squadrons at night, when they were directed to fly further behind the Allied lines to bomb rest areas and communications objectives. The attempt by one side to deny to the other the tactical advantages accruing from all these army-support operations resulted in the "duels" and "dog-fights" which were regarded as the typical form of air fighting over the Western Front. But at the end of the war the American Brigadier General Billy Mitchell used massive air brigades to intervene with decision as an independent force in a ground battle, and the potential of an "air service" to act as a genuine air *force* was established.

Such operations, however, still constituted no more than intervention or support in a battle fought on the ground. The air force was being used independently only in a tactical sense. The other aspect of air power was its strategic use : could aircraft, used independently, achieve victory in war?

The object of war is to obliterate the enemy's means and will to resist. This can be done by concentration on the destruction of his armed forces, or by concentration on rendering him too weak, materially and morally, to sustain those armed forces; or by application to both these aims. Could aircraft be used to strike at enemy armed forces in a manner which armies and navies could not match? Could aircraft, by internal penetration, destroy enemy resources and morale more effectively than any blockade by land or naval forces? Could they not at least cooperate with armies and navies to produce defeat or collapse more effectively? This strategic application of aircraft depended on the use of the strategic bomber. The Royal Naval Air Service, formed in July 1914, was the most aggressive air arm of any nation in the early years of the First World War : it conducted successful strategic bombing against Zeppelin sheds in Germany and enemy bases in Belgium, besides sinking warships by torpedo. Gradually this initiative was allowed to fade, and the Germans in their turn developed strategic bombing, raiding Britain from airfields in Belgium. The effective raid on London in June 1917, which was the first of a series of attacks, so alarmed the Cabinet and the General Staff that the Prime Minister ordered a radical re-appraisal of the function of the British air services. The architect of the reorganization was General Smuts. He greatly strengthened the composite air defences of the country and, declaring that counter-attack was vital, recommended the formation of a large strategic bombing force. The establishment of such a novel arm urgently required, in his view, the creation of an independent air force. Against military opposition the Cabinet accepted this proposal and speedily embodied the new force. On 1 April 1918 the independent Royal Air Force was created, with Major General Hugh ("Boom")[1] Trenchard, formerly General Officer Commanding Royal Flying Corps in the Field, as its first Chief of the Air Staff.

Very soon Trenchard gave up the post to take command of the Independent Bombing Force in France, the strategic air offensive arm the establishment of which had been one of the principal objects in creating the autonomous Royal Air Force. The Independent Bombing Force had been planned to comprise 100 squadrons and to include 225 four-engine long-range bombers capable of bombing Berlin from British bases. Dissension within the Supreme Command, and the comparatively sudden end of the war, rendered the force ineffective compared with the achievement of the hundreds of squadrons cooperating with the Allied armies. Nevertheless, when the Royal Air Force settled down to its peace-time establishment with Air Marshal Trenchard[2] again as its Chief of Air Staff, the theme dominating the thinking of its senior officers was its function as an offensive strategic bombing force. The air arm of no other nation maintained this conception strongly. The United States Air Service, though separated from the Signal Corps in May 1918, remained an adjunct of the Army. Its war record, amazingly active for its short service, had been almost totally concerned with army cooperation : 13,000 pursuit flights and 6,600 observation flights against 215 bombing missions. There were air service theorists who were to reshape the "tactical" image of the force, but they had not spoken yet. The French had never supported the idea of any independence or strategic function for their air arm. The Germans, even before their defeat and the prohibition of a standing air force, had retreated from any great faith in strategic bombing. For the moment the British alone based their planning on this distinctive "war-winning" use of bombing aircraft; and particularly on the potential of aerial bombardment to inspire self-destructive panic among enemy civilians.

But this article of faith impregnating the creed of the British air marshals gradually came to be accepted, in lay terms, by public opinion throughout the world. Air marshals of all nations

1. An allusion to the pitch of his voice.
2. He became the first Marshal of the Royal Air Force in 1927.

perused in their professional publications the theory propounded
by the Italian General Giulio Douhet that there was no defence
against the bomber, and the bulk of an air-force budget should
be diverted to building bombers. But it was the newspaper
readers of all nations who noted that the Italian bombing of
Ethiopia swiftly ended their war there, that the Japanese bombing of Hankow and Canton opened these cities to their troops,
while from Spain the very mention of bombed Guernica
raised a peak of horrified – but *submissive* – emotion. The words
of Stanley Baldwin, uttered as early as 1932, seemed final:
"The bomber will always get through. . . . The only defence is
offence, which means you have to kill more women and children
more quickly than the enemy if you want to save yourselves."

The influence of the thought of military strategists on public
opinion, and of public opinion on policy-makers, is positive
though imprecise. In addition general staffs have individual
national urgencies which superimpose their bias on general
theory. In Great Britain the Air Staff in the 1930s had as a
powerful basis for their reliance on *offence* the knowledge, or
belief, that in their geographical position there was no effective
defence against air attack. Were they right, or had they been
jockeyed by the public panic they had in part created? Only
the onset of war would enlighten them. In the United States,
by contrast, the general certainty was that they were territorially
impregnable from the air; yet a minority influence in the Army
Staff tenaciously propagated the ideal of the aggressive precision-
attack strategic bombing force. Was the minority remote in an
ivory castle of aggrandisement, or farsightedly anticipating the
truly global responsibilities of a world war? In Germany the
advocates of independent strategic bombing had, by 1939, been
killed or dismissed. Was it nevertheless possible for the Luftwaffe
to be forced by its own success as an army-support service to
aspire to be a potentially war-winning force? A substitute Navy?
And, if the change in aim was made, would the implications of
the conversion be thoroughly followed through?

Marshals interact with the marshalled. Wars are fought by
people. People are led by commanders. Commanders are
directed by one man in each fighting arm, and his decisions are
affected by the force of the personality of his colleagues commanding other services, of his supreme commander, or of the

head of state. These men at the top in the air war are the air marshals who fought the long, intellectual, physical and finally mortal struggle between the three main air forces of the West: the Luftwaffe, the Royal Air Force, and the United States Army Air Forces. The subjects of this book are Göring, Portal and Arnold, Tedder and Dowding, Spaatz and Harris, posed against their predecessors and immediate subordinates (the great names of aviation), and inevitably reacting to the Wagnerian aura of Hitler, Churchill and Roosevelt.

The man at the top of the pyramid is still a man: but a remote man, out of touch with the reality of his rival marshal or his own men. It was one of the first exercises of a marshal to become as intimate as possible with the conditions, conditioning, aspirations and force of the marshal on the other side. But this intimacy had to be filtered through a screen of false or fallible intermediaries. Even before the battle was joined the marshals allowed themselves to be deceived by massive bluffs and elementary ignorance. And in the fog of war they groped for a death-hold against an enemy whom they could not accurately place and whose form was reconstructed from the misapprehensions of the past, only gradually corrected by experience. A marshal was remote from his own fighting men, not always through distance or freedom from danger, but through the lack of communication with 200,000 aircrew killed in battle in the German war alone and the 500,000 survivors who did not always know what they had done. He had to rely on interpreters and calculators, intelligence and gossip. He sent gladiators out into an arena too vast for even a bird's-eye comprehension of the battle, and if he had the ability to make some snatched appreciation he never had the time: the game had already moved ahead and the operations of the day had necessitated further dispositions, plans, bargaining, perhaps humiliation. For a marshal had his private war with the marshals of other Services or with production chiefs who wanted his men, matériel, potential and intelligence for their own use.

A marshal therefore studied reports of his gladiators and the destruction they had done, written by people who had not always been present and assessed by others who had rarely met the fighters. Sometimes the marshal re-interpreted the interpretation, or edited it for study by his loving-hating, allied-enemy brother marshals. Always he had to make decisions about the future based on a tentative conclusion which, for morale's sake, he had often to disguise as considered judgement.

As a result, a marshal does not know his own strength. Generally he grossly overestimates it. Göring makes a wild error and throws away the war he might have won while America was still neutral. Arnold, miscalculating the impregnability of the superb defensive formation flying he had drilled his bomber crews to practise, accepts the optimism of his local commander so disastrously that the unescorted Fortress losses in Eaker's Eighth Air Force exceed the maximum figure of butchery that the force can stand. Portal, tardily learning that the first 30,000 tons of high explosive discharged by Bomber Command have gone immeasurably adrift, sardonically challenges Churchill to publish any defection from faith in strategic bombing, and stubbornly goes on to increase his bomb deliveries fiftyfold and improve their accuracy incalculably.

This account of the role of the air marshals, and of the succession of great air battles which they directed, deals with cunning, ambition and intelligence, courage, desperation and loyalty. All these human factors are displayed in the painful evolution of air generalship that produced the victory and defeat in the West. The story cannot be solely concerned with the High Commands, for the tragedy of war is played with human spear-carriers who bleed real blood. The marshals are human, too, and the contrasts in their behaviour cannot be viewed too petulantly. Arnold and Portal go fishing together, having made disposition for the imminent death of 20,000 men. Göring plays with his train set, or surprises his guests in the dress of the Emperor Nero. Churchill watches a crazy film while London burns: "There was nothing I could do about it, so I watched the Marx Brothers in a comic film which my hosts had arranged. I went out twice to inquire about the damage, and heard it was bad. The merry film clacked on, and I was glad of the diversion."[1]

Wars are directed by marshals and fought by people. Their victims are people. People fall by human error and neglect, or as samples in political salesmanship, as well as by strategic intent. The first mother to mourn a dead British pilot weeps for a battle that never was – the so-called Battle of Barking Creek

1. Winston S. Churchill, *The Grand Alliance*, Cassell, London, 1950.

in the first hours of the war, when Spitfires attack Hurricanes falsely plotted as enemy raiders, and "Sailor" Malan's 74 Squadron registers its first kill. In Lübeck, an ancient German city assessed by "Bomber" Harris as "built more like a fire-lighter than a human habitation", 312 people die because their timbered town best suits the British Air Staff's wish to test saturation incendiary attacks against high-explosive bombing; and their deaths must be allocated as what Harris calls "commercial traveller's samples which I could show to the War Cabinet".[1] Over Europe, a high, still undetermined number of skilled aircrew die in 1943 because in 1940 the United States Air Corps Matériel Division omits to appraise the P-51 Mustang as a potential long-range fighter; and, eighteen months later, when Arnold enthusiastically orders it Portal decries it and delays British exploitation of the aircraft which the Royal Air Force was the first to develop.

One dead Briton, 312 Germans, hundreds of Americans. . . . Mistakes are a part of the record of war, and must be accepted. But the victims may echo the remonstrance of the frogs to the boys in Aesop's tale: "Though this may be play to you, 'tis death to us." It is an aspect which it is always good for marshals to remember, though it can be irresponsible for the marshalled to be over-solicitous in reminding them. Death and destruction are the powers specifically remitted to the marshals, who are delegated by the marshalled to deal out these sanctions. They train themselves for as long as possible with only dummy casualties in what the Anglo-Saxons call exercises and the Germans call games. But they learn best to fight in the course of actual war, dealing death and suffering deaths, making mistakes and bearing inevitable anguish in their successes, losing their own sons as some marshals did, losing legions of Service sons whose death was not as nothing to them, and distributing death on meek civilians in the expediency of war. It would be the height of unrealism for the marshalled, by transferred guilt, to upbraid the marshals for the severity of decisions and actions taken to win a war. But it would be the extreme of laxity not to inquire of the marshals how efficiently they discharged their commission.

1. Marshal of the Royal Air Force Sir Arthur T. Harris, *Bomber Offensive*, Collins, London, 1947.

CHAPTER TWO

GÖRING GOES TO WAR

> All the business of war is to endeavour to find out
> what you don't know by what you do; that's what I
> called "guessing what was at the other side of the
> hill".
>
> THE DUKE OF WELLINGTON

The armoured special train stood in a beech wood at Wildpark,
east of Potsdam, hard by the Luftwaffe battle headquarters
quarried out of the base of a cliff. Field Marshal Hermann
Göring, Commander in Chief of the Luftwaffe, and General
Albert Kesselring, commanding Air Fleet I, sat moodily in the
drawing-room coach. It was shortly after noon on Thursday,
31 August 1939. An aide came into the compartment with a
signal. Hitler had given his final order designating Y-Day. The
invasion of Poland was to start at 4.45 in the morning of 1
September, in about 16 hours' time. Göring read the order to
Kesselring and told his aide to get Ribbentrop on the telephone.
When the Foreign Minister was on the line Göring angrily
shouted "Now you've got your — war. It's all your doing."

He hung up, ordered the adjustment of the plans for the
dawn bombardment, then motored to Berlin to supervise the
removal of art treasures from his Prussian presidential palace
there. Two days later, on the morning of Saturday, 2 September,
with the Polish Air Force already virtually destroyed, Göring
stood in the crowded ante-room of Hitler's Chancellery. The
official interpreter Schmidt passed through to the room where
Hitler and Ribbentrop were conferring. Schmidt was carrying
a document and communicated an air of excitement. "There is
going to be a second Munich," someone confidently speculated.
Schmidt came out. "I have just handed the Führer an ultimatum
from the British Government," he said. There was a silence of
sheer incredulity. It was broken by Göring, soberly declaring
"If we lose this war, then God have mercy on us."

17

Before he died on the hangman's rope at Nuremberg, Field Marshal Wilhelm Keitel explained in animated conversation the reason for the hush of disbelief, and the immediate pessimism of Hitler's commanders. Keitel, a general in 1939, was Hitler's Chief of the High Command of the Armed Forces throughout the war. "I told Hitler just before the Polish campaign that we had ammunition for only six weeks. I said I hoped hostilities wouldn't start, because they would simply have to stop after six weeks. You see, that was why we really didn't believe Hitler meant war – especially after he had arrived at an understanding with Russia. We were sure it was all bluff."[1]

Göring, as dragon, had done his clumsy best to huff-and-puff real fire, yet simultaneously assure the British that it need not scorch them. He had to. In testimony at the Nuremberg trial General Karl Bodenschatz, Göring's adjutant, declared that the Luftwaffe was not ready for war in 1939 and Göring desperately knew it. The Luftwaffe's stocks of bombs were, in fact, enough for only three weeks' sustained operations on 1 September 1939, and if annihilation bombing of Warsaw had proved to be necessary Göring would have exhausted his supply. As it was, the panicking Air Staff had to call on the munitions industry for the manufacture of thousands of moulded concrete bombs in the winter of 1939. All that their Commander in Chief could rely on in the interim was his standing bluff that had put the fear of the Luftwaffe into the minds of statesmen, Service chiefs and civilians in Britain and France. But there were times when the risks of reality were sickeningly clear, and drained the spunk from the marshal. On the day before the war started the strain of the long gamble had reduced the volatile Göring to a fit of deep depression.

"Now you've got your — war!" was all that Göring, Hitler's deputy, could allow himself as recrimination – and that not said to Hitler. Göring had to fight the war as if that had been his intention all the time. The truth about this tantalized man was that he had considered war as a means of policy only some of the time. He found that not only was a continental strategic bluff now being tested, and consequently his own suave assurances on the Luftwaffe were about to be professionally

1. G. M. Gilbert, *Nuremberg Diary*, Eyre & Spottiswoode, London, 1948.

probed, but also his personal purpose in life was being put to question. Already the suckers of administrative power and beautiful possessions were drawing him to the consideration that peace had advantages no less substantial than war. War could not even promise promotion to him, a field marshal (but that difficulty was finally overcome by creating a higher rank). It was not that Göring's type of courage baulked at war, or that in his flamboyant bossiness he shrank from directing war. Once, during the Munich crisis, in a public row with Ribbentrop – whose crude and ignorant incitement of Hitler towards war was a twister in the stream of German leadership that span Göring towards peace – Göring had stormed : "I know what war is and I don't want to go through it again, but if the Führer orders I shall be off in the first plane." Then he added darkly "And Ribbentrop should be in the next seat."

Of all the air marshals involved in the Second World War Göring had the most at stake : mainly because until the point of outbreak he was, though a professional gambler, only a dilettante airman in the intervals he could snatch between being a dilettante economist, police chief, diplomatist and revolutionary. Oliver Herford defined a dilettante as a philanderer who seduces the several arts and deserts each in turn for the other; even within Germany Göring had proved himself not only a seducer but a fortune-hunter. Certainly his future enemy air generals were not unduly encumbered by possessions or divisive responsibilities. Air Vice Marshal Arthur Harris – with no home and hardly a possession in the world, having lately relinquished a command in Palestine – was sitting that week-end in a friend's farmhouse telephoning Air Marshal Charles Portal, Air Council Member for Personnel, to ask for a job. Lieutenant General Henry Arnold, Chief of the Air Corps, U.S. Army, was in the air with General George Marshall, Chief of Staff, U.S. Army, bound for amphibious invasion exercises on the West Coast. Because these men had no direct part in either promoting or retarding the outbreak of war, though all had had a hand in planning for it, their concern and responsibility was more concentrated. Göring, with what the U.S. Prosecutor Mr Justice Robert Jackson called later at Nuremberg "a pudgy finger in every pie" – and every pie worth millions in money – was more involved and inevitably more vulnerable. If any man had a soft underbelly it was he. But it was he, with Hitler, who had consistently exposed the belly and forced the pace of play by doubling and redoubling the stakes before the showdown.

It would be unrealistic nonsense to compare modern war with poker, and mere convention to liken it to chess. Wars have until now been directed in the dark through a thousand channels of logistics and pressure by men whom their enemies have variously called mad, crippled, drunk or drugged, whom even their friends have termed vain and bloody-minded. In the past the inevitable diffusion of effort, the inability to win fast, has had its saving grace. It has meant that the men who engineered wars have not necessarily won them. The nearer we get to push-button warfare the less likely is this to be. In future the marshals who are most intent on wars will win them.

This will only serve to make politics more deadly. In spite of the complexity with which the Second World War was waged nothing is more striking than the simplicity with which it was engineered. Many poker games have been more difficult to follow. *Post mortem*, the West can see the stages, at least from 1935, at which the bluff of Hitler and Göring could have been successively called. But if Germany had won we should not have even this enlightenment.

A purely German inside view of this was expressed in 1946 by Hjalmar Horace Greeley Schacht, Hitler's economist and director of rearmament until 1938. Discussing the difference of attitude of the West to the Weimar Republic and to the Hitler regime which succeeded it, he said :

To every little suggestion [of the Weimar Republic] the Allies said No! We asked for a colony or two – anything for trading possibilities : out of the question! We asked for a customs union with Austria and Czecho-Slovakia and they said No! We pointed out that Austria had voted 90 per cent for union with Germany. They said Nothing doing! But when a gangster like Hitler comes to power – Oh my, take all of Austria, remilitarize the Rhineland, take the Sudetenland, take all of Czecho-Slovakia, we won't say a word! Why, before the Munich Pact Hitler didn't even dare dream of getting the Sudetenland incorporated into the Reich. All he thought he *might* get was a measure of autonomy for the Sudetenland. And then those fools Daladier and Chamberlain drop the whole thing in his lap. Why didn't they give the Weimar Republic *one-tenth* of that support?[1]

As overlord of German war production Schacht, the trained economist, was succeeded in 1938 by Göring. The marshal's achievement in this sphere was solid, and must inspire considerable encouragement for any unequipped adventurer who determines to go far in politics. Göring joined Hitler as his second in command and front man in the third year of the Weimar Republic, 1922. The association would have been impossible if Göring had followed an earlier intention and become a Freemason. But, waiting for some friends who were to take him to join the Masons, he picked up a blonde and went adrift.

In those days Göring still occasionally wore the high-necked tunic of the Imperial Air Force, with the four decorations culminating in the exclusive *Ordre Pour le Mérite* which had made him a postcard hero as an ace of the First World War. It presented an image which Hitler found valuable. Göring's father was a high consular officer, and from the age of twelve the boy attended a military academy or cadet college. At the age of nineteen, two years before the first war broke out, he was commissioned in the infantry. By 1915 he was a skilled air observer and before the year was out he was a fighter pilot. After being seriously wounded he came back to command a squadron, and in July 1918 after the death of Manfred von Richthofen he took over the great "Flying Circus" squadron of the dead knight. On 19 November 1918 he disbanded the Richthofen Squadron. He reminded the officers of its historic record of 644 victories for the loss of 56 pilots, raised his glass for the last toast, "Our time will come again", and hurled the wineglass to the floor.

Göring spent three somewhat dissolute years in Scandinavia, giving aerobatic displays, selling joy-rides, touting a parachute and acting as a charter pilot. In February 1922 he married Carin von Fock, daughter of a Swedish baron and an English gentlewoman. She was at that time the estranged wife of a Swedish officer who generously gave Carin a divorce and a dowry to facilitate the second marriage. By the end of that year Göring had met Hitler in Munich and had immediately taken

1. G. M. Gilbert, *Nuremberg Diary.*

over command of the National Socialist party's S.A. storm-troopers, whom he shortly organized into a tight division of 11,000 men. Relying on a cadre of 600 men of this force Hitler, in November 1923, used Göring to make their first feint to seize power. It was the notorious beer-hall *putsch* at the Bürgerbräukeller in which Hitler bluffed a public meeting of 3,000 people including the heads of the Government of Bavaria that his armed revolutionaries had taken over the state. In this, their first essay in the medium, the bluff was so crude and un-supported that it led to disaster. In the subsequent debacle, the march of 3,000 S.A. troops on Munich next day, Hitler fled the field, but was afterwards imprisoned in a fortress where he wrote *Mein Kampf*. Göring was gravely wounded in the groin by gunfire, had to be smuggled out of the country into Austria, and was driven by the pain of his wounds to morphine, a drug to which he became addicted. Göring had to be confined in a Swedish asylum while the drug was withdrawn, and he was in any case unable to return to Germany until a political amnesty was decreed in 1927. By this time Hitler was decidedly cool towards his lieutenant. Without force and ambition the airman would not have re-ingratiated himself.

However, by the summer of 1928 Göring was one of the dozen Nazi deputies legally elected to the Reichstag. He used his position to turn "fixer" and lay the foundations of his personal fortune. Prompted by his convictions no less than by the subventions he was already receiving from the German aircraft industry, he loudly and consistently championed in the Reichstag increased support for German civil aviation. He was in fact already an adviser to Lufthansa, the German state-controlled airline.

Germany was still bound by the Treaty of Versailles, signed in June 1919, under which her aircraft and matériel had been impounded, a future military air force forbidden, and only 140 commercial machines left in the country. With tre-mendous resilience the aircraft manufacturers had kept in the running. Professor Hugo Junkers, the designer, at the age of sixty founded his factory at Dessau in north Germany in 1919, and produced a revolutionary all-metal monoplane 6-seater, the Junkers F.13fe, before the Treaty of Versailles was signed. For a decade this machine was the hardest-worked transport in the world, operating in South America, Great Britain, Sweden, Japan, South Africa and the United States. A copy of it was used as a bomber in Russia and Japan. When the Junkers planes were later banned to German ownership they were sold to a former German Air Force officer, Erhard Milch, with an address in Danzig from which he operated the planes within Germany.

In 1922 Junkers had accepted 80 million Reichsmarks from the Government and started a factory at Fili in Moscow, competing with Ernst Heinkel's factory in Sweden and Claudius Dornier's pair in Friedrichshafen and Switzerland. By 1925, the Focke-Wulf and Messerschmitt concerns were also set up. By that year, too, the German Defence Ministry, in which Kesselring, Stumpff and Sperrle were already working – they all commanded Air Fleets against England in 1940 – were running a scheme in collaboration with Soviet Russia under which the Reichswehr trained the Soviet General Staff and the Soviets trained German military aviators in secretly built German military aircraft flying from the air base of Lipesk in the Moscow region. Flying for sport and gliding were organized on a wide scale within Germany, actively supported by the Government. In 1926 Erhard Milch, then a secret Nazi, was made chairman of the monopoly German civil airline Lufthansa, which had $37\frac{1}{2}$ per cent Government capital. Lufthansa training schools were the most comprehensive in the world, particularly pioneering electronics aids to navigation. When the Government later faltered in its support for Lufthansa it was the Reichstag deputy Captain Göring who successfully challenged the change in policy, and Göring who privately assured Milch in the lobby that when the Nazis came to power the German Air Force would be reborn.

By 1930 the Nazis had increased their Reichstag membership from 12 to 107. By 1932 they were 230 strong, and Göring was President of the Reichstag. On 30 January 1933 Adolf Hitler was Chancellor and Hermann Göring was Prussian Minister of the Interior and Reich Commissioner for Aviation.

It is impossible to separate the paths of Göring the creator of the Luftwaffe and Göring the strong-arm man of Nazism, for these were his corridors of power for the rest of his life. As Minister of the Interior for Prussia (and soon to be Prime

Minister) he was virtually in command of the police of the whole of Germany. Within two months of gaining office Göring had replaced two-thirds of the Prussian police chiefs and set up the Secret State Police, the Gestapo, to replace part of the Prussian police force. By the end of the year he had instituted fifty concentration camps – he put 4,000 Communists inside on the night of the burning of the Reichstag – and had announced his credo :

In the future there will be only one man who will wield power and bear responsibility in Prussia – me. Whoever does his duty in the service of the State, obeying my orders and ruthlessly using his revolver when attacked, he is assured of my protection. A bullet fired from the barrel of a police pistol is my bullet. If you say that is murder, then I am the murderer. I know two sorts of law because I know two sorts of men : those who are with us and those who are against us.[1]

It is impossible to imagine these words issuing from any Western war leader, even at his most paranoiac. Yet they were a characteristic utterance of the man who was Commander in Chief of the Luftwaffe during its entire existence and who – whenever he had the time or mood – gave it direct and intimate orders constituting the gladiatorial Thumbs Up or Thumbs Down on the development of a war-winning plane or the lives of the crews of an air fleet. This almost unlimited personal power was a factor to be studied by any opposing air marshal making an appreciation of his enemy.

In 1933, as Milch well understood, planning a military force from a civilian office, Göring had no intention of making an equally blatant public announcement about creating a new air force. Hitler had yet to sidle into acceptance by the Western Powers. Yet precise advances were made, and it was soon no secret to any Intelligence Service that the Luftwaffe was in being. On 29 April 1933, three days after the formal founding of the Gestapo, Göring created the German Air Defence Union, a propaganda organization deliberately designed to prepare public opinion to accept German "air police" to defend the Reich against the reputed "ten thousand warplanes" massed on its borders. Within a week the Commission of Aviation had

1. Speech at Dortmund. See A. W. Blood-Ryan, *Göring, the Iron Man of Germany*, Long, London, 1938.

been upgraded into the Ministry for Air Traffic, with Göring as Air Minister at the head and Milch, still running Lufthansa, as his deputy. Göring then met some of the military pilots who had already been through clandestine courses. He announced that the secret training in Russia would now end, to be replaced by equally secret training in Italy. Milch established a full air administration and began a notable expansion in aircraft production and pilot training, at the same time laying down many new airfields.

Meanwhile Göring had to clear the decks to permit Hitler's absolute dictatorship over Germany. In 1934 all formal opposition from Catholics, Democrats or Communists had been effectively bludgeoned down, and the immediate danger to the regime came from factions within the Nazi party, battling for ultimate control of the police and the army. Göring allowed the national police and his own Gestapo to be assigned to Heinrich Himmler as Reich Minister of the Interior. This was an enormous diversion of power, since Himmler already controlled the S.S. blackshirt strongarm elite, originally formed as a personal bodyguard for Hitler. Göring's only precaution was to found yet another police force several thousand strong, based on Berlin, as a private buttress. The first task he gave it was to form firing squads.

Göring and Himmler could be relied on to destroy their enemy Roehm, head of the vast S.A., now an amorphous organization of brownshirt bullies two and a half million strong, who were threatening to swamp the army. On 30 June 1934 Hitler personally arrested his intimate friend Roehm at Wiessee, near Munich and, after some days of shifty vacillation – for Hitler was not an efficient killer – had him shot in his cell after he had refused to commit suicide. In Berlin Göring and Himmler were less hesitant. Some hundreds of arrests of S.A. leaders and surviving politicians were made, and the prisoners were hustled immediately to Göring's headquarters. The simultaneous arrests were performed so efficiently that Göring's Cadet School at Lichterfelde in the park by the Diet became blocked with the victims, whose names could not be checked fast enough against the lists which already decreed their death or imprisonment. They stood in pale groups under guard in waiting-rooms, while Göring's bull voice could be heard in the study: "Shoot him!" On the night after his arrest of Roehm, Hitler flew into the Tempelhof airfield and was met by Göring and Himmler. In the sunset they showed the long list of names, now thumbed and torn, to their shrinking master. A month later old President Hindenburg was dead and Hitler assumed his powers as head of state, styling himself officially Führer and Reich Chancellor. He was now titular Supreme Commander of the Armed Forces and a new oath of allegiance was made to him. The Luftwaffe, though it did not then publicly exist, took this oath. General Göring supervised the ceremony. His cross-bolt advancement from an honorary captaincy had been agreed by Hindenburg, though Göring himself characteristically screwed up the seniority from major general to full general – backdated two years. General Göring drew his sword and Major General Milch put his hand on it while the other officers present raised their hands. They repeated the oath, a declaration of allegiance not to a nation or a constituted government but to a person, Adolf Hitler. It was this oath, taken at this time, which became the basic defence of Göring, Kesselring, Milch and others at their subsequent trials for war crimes.

In 1934 the German Air Force was built, almost literally reconstructed in twelve months after a period of planning and tooling-up, and in the next spring it was unveiled. On 1 March 1935 the Luftwaffe was officially declared in existence with Göring Commander in Chief, Milch Secretary of State and General Wever the Chief of Air Staff.

Göring was forty-two years old. Milch was younger, a pilot of the First World War but with a less distinguished record. It was Milch's tireless reconstruction from behind a Lufthansa desk that gave the military force its first cohesion, but its earlier extinction as a Service had meant that it could not have the core of experience and application among officers of the middle rank which was the particular strength of the Royal Air Force. Milch laid down the form of the Luftwaffe more authoritatively than anyone, and if he had had a freer hand would have made it a sounder force than it was. He had used Lufthansa for the surreptitious placing of orders for the construction of aircraft and airfields, and for providing preliminary bomber and reconnaissance-training, but these were mere extempore details by comparison with his serious planning.

Milch had the sense of scale necessary in building an air force. He wanted to sow widely a strain that should be strong, even if of slow growth. He was content to mass-produce obsolescent machines on which aircrews and groundcrews could train assiduously while the new designs and production methods were being perfected for combat use – and 1935 was a year of revolution in aerial development. He wanted to breed officers of stamina. His nearest target was a war in eight years. In these aims he certainly did not get his way. He was constantly harried for quick results by Göring, and through Göring by Hitler, who listened keenly to Göring's eruptive enthusiasm and – at least until 1940 – believed it. Consequently the through-put of Luftwaffe crews was trained over-fast, yielding a quicker turn-over than Milch envisaged, while too often the aircraft were pushed into production before they had been fully tested, and were interminably adapted afterwards. This is a feature of a running war, and Britain and the United States had painful experience of it. But Milch had to suffer it with thinner justification.

Milch's clearest signature lay on the organization of industry, the early capture of factories in which he could lay down a good production plan for the future, and on the morale he built up, enthusiastically backed by Göring, in Luftwaffe personnel through the excellent conditions of service he maintained. The Luftwaffe was an elite arm; its accommodation, food and pay were the best. Werner Baumbach, who became General of the Bombers in 1943 at the age of twenty-six, described his introduction to the Air Warfare School at Gatow, Berlin, in one of the first cadet classes of the new Luftwaffe :

The moment we entered the establishment we had the impression that no trouble or expense had been spared. Our quarters, the sports ground, the gymnasium and swimming bath, the flying-ground, halls and lecture-rooms were all the last word of their kind. The whole atmosphere of the place breathed the spirit which animated Hermann Göring, Commander in Chief of the Luftwaffe, in building up the new arm. We swore by the Führer and worshipped Göring as the greatest air hero of the First World War.[1]

Alongside the material conditions went intensive "infantry"

1. Werner Baumbach, translated Frederick Holt, *Broken Swastika*, Hale, London, 1960.

discipline and training, to which Baumbach and many others took unkindly, and in addition there was quite overpowering indoctrination. The Luftwaffe was the arm of the National Socialists and was largely recruited from the keenest of the Hitler Youth. It was a privileged service of high morale.

The first Chief of Staff was Major General Wever. He had been with Milch from 1933 but was killed in an air crash in 1936. Although a former infantry officer, he had the most comprehensive view of air warfare of anyone on the German General Staff, and when he died there was no equal mind to replace him. In consequence the Luftwaffe entered the Second World War as an unbalanced force with an incomplete strategy. The British and American Air Staffs accepted a concept of air warfare which included the application of air power through continuous saturation strategic bombing; and their ultimate aircraft production was keyed to this end among others. The instrument of this policy was the long-range bomber. In 1935 the Luftwaffe, too, through Wever, commissioned long-range four-engine bombers,[1] and the prototypes were ready for trial a few months after Wever's death. But because no one else in the Luftwaffe would champion them they were deleted from the construction programme – and were consequently not available for the blitz on Britain in 1940.

Wever was succeeded by Kesselring, then by Stumpff and finally, in February 1939, by Colonel General Jeschonnek, who finally crystallized the Luftwaffe policy opposing long-range bombers. Though Jeschonnek had some solid grounds for his advocacy of light and medium bombers, particularly the already strained capacity of the Reich for producing aircraft engines, aluminium and flying instruments, he was over-enthusiastically supported in his stand by the other great influence on the development of the Luftwaffe, Lieutenant General Ernst Udet. Udet, three years younger than Göring, was a first-war pilot

1. 225 four-engine Handley Page bombers capable of attacking Berlin from British bases had been commissioned for Trenchard's Independent Bombing Force, but by November 1918 only three had been delivered and none had been in action. The Boeing prototype for the B-17 Flying Fortress flew in 1935. Long-range four-engine bombers were flown by the U.S.S.R. well before the German prototypes flew.

with a far more impressive record of kills even than Göring, under whom he had served in the Richthofen Squadron. A gay companion and a man of supreme flying skill, Udet was earning a good living as a stunt pilot and racing aircraft jockey when Göring persuaded him to come into the Luftwaffe.

Udet's first achievement was to reinforce the conviction, already widely held within the German Air Staff, that the major achievement of air bombing in the future would be effected by *Stukas* (Stuka is an abbreviation of the German word for dive-bomber). This was a concept which he himself had held since he had bought two Curtiss Hawks in 1933 and found feverish delight in the demonstration of "hell diving". After he joined the Luftwaffe the Junkers Ju 87 was put into production as the force's dive-bomber. Udet had demonstrated it and flew the prototypes; he was one of the few German first-war pilots who were familiar with modern machines – as Göring certainly was not. Udet personally took the world speed record with a top speed of 394 m.p.h. in a Heinkel He 100V3 in 1938 (though Stainforth had recorded 408 m.p.h. on one circuit in a Supermarine S6B as far back as 1931, the year when the machine took the Schneider Trophy for Britain). Udet's preoccupation with speed certainly influenced the policy of the German Air Staff in favour of the comparatively fast and light bomber, and therefore against the heavy four-engine "Ural" bomber that Wever had been advocating, following the Italian General Douhet's concept of long-range strategic bombing.

By the end of 1936 the types of German aircraft that were actually to fight through the first years of the Second World War had been decided on and their mass-production planned. There was no long-range bomber;[1] there were three medium-fast twin-engined bombers, then relatively unarmoured and re-

1. But there could have been, if a shrewder chief had ordered them. Between 1937 and 1940 four four-engine bombers were developed to the point where they could have been put into mass-production: the Ha 142, the Dornier 19, Junkers 90 and FW200. The latter two were manufactured, though at the rate of fewer than ten aircraft per month. From August 1940 to the spring of 1941 the Focke-Wulf FW-200K Kuriers operated over a 2,500-mile combat shuttle. In this period fewer than fifty of these big bombers sank or damaged several hundred thousand tons of Allied shipping.

latively lightly armed – the Dornier Do 17, the Heinkel He 111, and the Junkers Ju 88; there were the Henschel Hs 123 and the Junkers Ju 87 dive-bombers; and the highly successful Messerschmitt Bf 109 as the principal fighter. There was the Henschel Hs 126 army cooperation aircraft, and, constituting a notable failure to produce a heavy two-seat fighter, the Messerschmitt Bf 110 twin-engine "Destroyer". The emphasis in production reflected the belief of the Air Staff that the bomber was certainly an offensive weapon, but a *tactical offensive weapon*. The force was designed for comparatively short range work in support of the ground forces and it was intended that the Luftwaffe should operate precision bombing. This was one of the reasons for the emphasis placed on the Stuka, which, in daylight, was highly precise if it could hold its dive; indeed, in 1939 the Staff laid down the aim that all bombing aircraft should be able to dive-bomb.

The civil war in Spain, in which thousands of Luftwaffe personnel were blooded between 1936 and 1939 in the Legion Condor, provided invaluable experience in the development of tactics, and extremely deceptive encouragement of unescorted and unopposed bombing. Formation bombing, sometimes carried out in Heinkel He 111s from as low as 500 feet, determined the pattern of future close support of army operations. Werner Mölders, then a lieutenant but later to become General of the Fighters at the early age typical of the fast-bred Luftwaffe, evolved a system of loose-formation fighter tactics which was far in advance of the methods used by the Royal Air Force at the beginning of the war. The other great lesson learned from the Spanish war was the value of ground-staff mobility. The use of air transport to convey whole unit installations forward through the battlefield was strikingly demonstrated in the true "blitz" operations against Poland and France.

From the skill built up in these practised but, operationally analysed, severely narrow exploits of the Luftwaffe, Field Marshal Göring – the promotion came in 1938 – was to acquire massive prestige. Göring was not now an airman, but a politician in air force uniform. In a childish tiff with the then imbecile Rudolf Hess in an interval during the Nuremberg trial, Göring interrupted Hess's enthusiastic description of how he had flown to Scotland actually using instruments with a petulant "Yes, yes, I fly by instruments, too!" Few navigators would have entrusted themselves to him.

Moreover, few disinterested students of air tactics and few serious designers could have cared to maintain a long conversation with this egocentric ace who, in spite of a façade of modern jargon, fundamentally thought that air war meant dog-fights relying on the tight turns of a slow biplane. Göring undoubtedly had the intelligence to grasp a service problem or a facet of the theory of air power, but he did not have the persistence to apply himself to it for long. He was the champion, and indeed the hero, of the Luftwaffe, and, while things were going well, was extremely popular for his comradeship, understanding and encouragement of his pilots. He won for the Luftwaffe all the prestige and power he could get, but he was not the constant directing head of the Service. Nobody was – and that was its grave defect. There was no broad, professional mind governing it, and there was no long-term strategic aim. Once Wever was dead and Jeschonnek inherited the responsibility for technical drive there was no one who could evaluate technical innovations and either reject them or order them to be pursued with zeal. At the same time Udet, the first Quartermaster-General, refusing to be chair-bound, was too busy "dicing with death" at the Luftwaffe Research Centre to carry through the organization which his office demanded. One of the curiosities of the Nazi dictatorship, and a reflection on the leadership principle, is that in some spheres it was not a regime of "German thoroughness" but of astonishing inefficiency.

However, Göring used the reputation of the Luftwaffe to bolster the bluff used in the main political moves of the last three years of Nazi-tolerated peace.

In March 1935, when the Luftwaffe was unveiled, Hitler told Sir John Simon and Anthony Eden that Germany already had an air force as big as Britain's. This was not in fact true, but could not be publicly proved to be untrue. Britain at that time had a first-line force in excess of 850 aircraft (though 362 of them were in the Empire). Germany had something over 565 military aircraft suitable for first-line units, but some of them lacked engines and others lacked instruments. The 1,888 aircraft actually in the Luftwaffe were mainly trainers of newly built but second-line machines. The fabricated myth of Luftwaffe strength was sufficient, however, to permit the German reoccupation of the then demilitarized Rhineland without opposition from France.

The only air "force" at Göring's disposal for this momentous advance, made in March 1936, was one squadron of Arado 68 single-engine biplane fighters which did not even possess armament, though some carried dummy machine-guns. Adolf Galland flew the squadron in to the nearest airfield at Werl, submitted to the publicity of inspection by pressmen and foreign intelligence agents, then withdrew his machines to hangars where he hurriedly painted new squadron numbers and insignia on the fuselages. He flew on to Dortmund, repainted the identification, flew to Düsseldorf, and proceeded in this way through the Ruhr, creating a putative air fleet out of one squadron. The strategy was more than a temporary success over shivering European public opinion : it had an enduring effect on the trust in the leadership's power of *bluff* which was developed among the professionals in the German High Command. "Just imagine!" said Keitel. "We reoccupied the Ruhr with three battalions – just three battalions! I said to Blomberg[1] 'How can we do it with only three battalions? Suppose the French resist!' 'Oh,' said Blomberg, 'don't worry. We can take a chance.' And he got away with it!" Jodl testified at Nuremberg that the French could have "blown us to pieces". Galland said the Armée de l'Air "would have annihilated us".[2]

The annexation of Austria was an operation the culmination of which was left by Hitler almost entirely to Göring. For the Marshal it was a dangerously deceptive easy triumph, and it was achieved through a show of force indolently directed by telephone. Göring did not even bother to leave Berlin. He ordered his Nazi subordinate in Vienna to send the appropriate telegram which Hitler needed to justify the invasion. In twenty-seven blustering telephone conversations on one day Göring achieved the resignation of Schuschnigg, the Austrian Chancellor, the formation of a Nazi cabinet, and the complete quiescence of

1. Field Marshal Werner von Blomberg, Minister of War and Commander in Chief of the Armed Forces, dismissed January 1938, after which Hitler became Commander in Chief as well as Supreme Commander, *ex officio* as Head of State.
2. G. M. Gilbert, *Nuremberg Diary.*

the Austrian army as the German troops came in by road and air. In the middle of this armchair marathon he saw the Czech Minister in Berlin and got him to telephone Prague, securing an assurance that the Czechs would not mobilize. How easily, in Göring's opinion, the acquisition of vast territory could be secured may be deduced from the tone of one extract from Göring's telephone instructions to Vienna :

You are the Government now. Listen carefully. The following telegram should be sent here by Seyss-Inquart.[1] Write it down. "The provisional Austrian Government, which after the dismissal of the Schuschnigg Government considers it its task to establish peace and order in Austria, sends the German Government the urgent request to support it in its task and help it to prevent bloodshed. For this reason it asks the German Government to send German troops as soon as possible." Seyss-Inquart has to take over and appoint a few people : the people we recommended to him. He should form a provisional government now. It is absolutely un-important what the Federal President may have to say. Then our troops will cross the border. Look, and he should send the telegram as soon as possible. Well, he doesn't even have to send the telegram. All he needs to do is to say "Agreed !" Call me either at the Führer's or my place. Well, good luck. Heil Hitler ![2]

It is at once instructive and humiliating for ordinary re-sponsible citizens all over the world to realize that half-extemporized orders of this not notably intelligent nature, such as might have been issued by an astute master pirate, were the words that changed the maps of Europe, sent political panic coursing through the West, whipped up rearmament, started a war in which thirty millions died, and altered the record of history for ever.

The man who spoke them was issuing from time to time orders to the same fundamental effect and of the same slipshod thinking to the German Air Force, to the most powerful German industrialists – for he was now economic dictator of the country – to German diplomats, and indeed to the ambassadors and heads of state of independent sovereign countries. After Austria the next territories on the list for incorporation into the German

1. Dr Artur Seyss-Inquart, the young Catholic lawyer who acted as Nazi quisling in Austria and was appointed Chancellor.
2. Anschluss Transactions, Wiener Library, London.

Reich were Czecho-Slovakia and Poland. Throughout the spring
of 1938 Göring talked to foreign ambassadors and even the
King of Sweden in the most open way about "my intention to
liquidate Czecho-Slovakia this summer". The autumn crisis
finally matured, to be resolved by the cession and military
occupation of Germany's first instalment of Czech territory, as
agreed by Chamberlain and Daladier at Munich. At that time
Göring openly worked against an actual declaration of war,
though Hitler and Ribbentrop threatened it throughout. Göring
realized that his air force was too weak for war, though it was
an indispensable instrument for bluff.

The pilot Adolf Galland, who was working in the German
Air Ministry at the time of the Sudeten crisis, recorded the
state of the air forces brought up to menace Czecho-Slovakia
and to intimidate Chamberlain:

> The department in which I worked received the order to furnish
> two groups of aircraft for the support of land operations. Just like
> that! And, of course, at the latest the day before yesterday! ... A
> state of emergency had been declared on the Sudeten frontier. ...
> The creation of these two ground attack groups was actually
> accomplished inside the time required, thanks to the pressure of
> the tense political situation. A great deal had to be improvised.
> The young, odd assortment of recruits were given a ruthless high
> speed training and hastily equipped with second rate aircraft, a
> collection of all types: He 51s, Hs 123s, He 45s.

On 29 September the Munich Pact was signed.

> After things had taken such an unexpected and gratifying turn,
> we staged a fighter parade exercise from Freudenstadt, our new
> base in the Sudeten country, and later watched an impressive
> landing of a large force of airborne troops. ... The population was
> indescribably elated and quite unjustly looked upon each of us as
> a hero and a liberator.[1]

Behind the "liberation", and behind the open intimidation
of the aged Czech President Hacha before the final extinction
of his country in the following spring, was Göring. Göring
personally threatened the ailing president with the immediate
aerial bombardment of Prague in such a hectoring manner that

---

1. Adolf Galland, translated Mervyn Savill, *The First and the Last*,
Methuen, London, 1955.

the old man fainted in front of him, and had to be revived with a shot from Göring's own hypodermic. And when Czecho-Slovakia fell the plans against Poland were already outlined. But Göring's share in the execution of these plans was superficial. He could only switch from one to another of his massive responsibilities in impulsive taurine rushes. He was in intimate contact with every important ambassador in Berlin. He had taken over from Schacht the industrial and financial responsibility for rearmament and was directing the Four Year Plan, the achievement which, according to the post-war verdict of German experts, was his best monument. He was "directing" the expansion of the Luftwaffe, but in so unorganized a manner that the whole pace and path of its development had got completely out of hand.

Hitler still trusted him in this sphere and the disorganization was not yet recognized, but what must have been obvious to the General Staff was the happy-go-lucky optimism with which Göring wilfully deceived Hitler and was in turn deceived by his subordinates. The dictum with which the air chiefs finally cancelled the programme for long-range four-engine bombers had been "If the aircraft industry can produce three twin-engine bombers for the expenditure on two four-engine craft, go ahead with twin engines. The Führer will not ask how big the bombers are, but how many there are." Later, when Ernst Udet, a flier and not a planner, but now an unhappy Quartermaster-General in charge of Equipment and Supply, displayed new aircraft to Hitler and Göring, he was able to pass them off to both his superiors as specimens of machines now ready to come from the assembly line when in reality they were only prototypes. The business of bluff was permeating the whole of the leadership.

And so, in a great final spree churning high policy with dim detail in a senseless vortex – perhaps the most terrifying evidence of the intoxication of power – Göring moved towards the climax of his activity. His responsibilities were so vast that he no longer had the time to draft orders. An almost incomprehensible note scrawled with a huge pencil in his broad day-book was tossed to a subordinate and became a decree. It is possible that Göring considered these scraps of paper to be as ephemeral as the agreements with foreign powers that littered his way to war.

Yet they were archives, and were later produced in evidence against him. In one revealing outburst to American psychologists within his cell at Nuremberg Göring revealed the speeding, sandy opportunism of German policy : "They don't have to show films and read documents to prove that we rearmed for war. Of course we rearmed. Why, I rearmed Germany until we bristled. I'm only sorry we didn't rearm still more. Of course I considered your treaties as so much arse-wipe. Of course I wanted to make Germany great. If it could be done peacefully – fine ! If not – too bad !"[1]

But there was one treaty that Hitler and Göring had to rely on. This was the secret section of the Soviet-German Pact, signed ten days before the war on Poland, agreeing that Poland should be partitioned between the two powers. At Nuremberg the Russians initially blocked the disclosure of these secret clauses. This made Field Marshal Alfred Jodl almost frenetic with frustration as he came down from the dock : "So now they want to hide the fact that there was a secret treaty. They cannot do it. I had the advance demarcation line right among my plans and planned the campaign accordingly. The war would probably never have been risked if Hitler had not had this agreement in advance. But once he had the agreement in his pocket he said 'Now I can risk it !' Because our eastern front was secured."[2]

"Now I can risk it !" are famous last words for many a ruined gambler. The remaining risk was not some outcome of the immediate eastern campaign. The risk was what action would be taken by Britain and France. If it had been left to France alone the answer to the speculation would have been NO ACTION. The cause of the outbreak of the Second World War in September 1939 was Hitler's ignorance of the British. By a superficial interpretation they flinched at Munich, and Hitler expected them to cower a year later. In terms of the war game, Britain made a strategic withdrawal at Munich, and stiffened and stood a year later, just as the British Eighth Army fell back on Alamein in 1942, to regroup, reinforce and advance 3,000 miles after four months. Hitler came to be regarded as

1. G. M. Gilbert, *Nuremberg Diary*, and Douglas M. Kelley, *22 Cells in Nuremberg*, Allen, London, 1947.
2. G. M. Gilbert, *Nuremberg Diary*.

an inspired strategist by the German General Staff, who greatly admired his intuition and were captivated by his stamina at bluffing. But Hitler had no comprehension throughout his career of the worth of the strategic withdrawal, and certainly never practised it – his monumental failure was at Stalingrad. It is understandable that, from what he knew of them, he could not anticipate the rallying of the British in 1939.

Hitler's entourage had had no doubt for two years about his detailed plans for aggressive war. On 5 November 1937 he outlined his programme "for the improvement of the military-political position", as the conquest of Czecho-Slovakia and Austria and the neutralization of Poland were called, to clear the decks for a major struggle with France. The first two of these objectives were gained and the world turned to consider the German claim to Danzig, which would effectually strangle Poland's only outlet to any sea. But Hitler privately declared on 23 May 1939 in the presence of Field Marshal Göring, General Keitel and Grand Admiral Raeder "Danzig is not the subject of the dispute at all. It is a question of expanding our living space in the east and of securing our food supplies. . . . There is therefore no question of sparing Poland, and we are left with the decision : *to attack Poland at the first suitable opportunity.* We cannot expect a repetition of the Czech affair. There will be war. Our task is to isolate Poland. The success of the isolation will be decisive."[1]

The possibility of successfully isolating Poland was diminished by the French and British guarantee, announced by Chamberlain on 31 March 1939, promising "all support in their power" to Poland if she resisted a threat to her independence. Stalin told Churchill later that the Russians did not believe in the summer of 1939 that the British and French Governments would go to war if Poland were attacked. Indeed the British Government appreciated, in Churchill's words, that the guarantee "had no military value except within the framework of a general agreement with Russia". Hitler's major tasks in the isolation of Poland were therefore to prise Russia from the West and to weaken Britain's resolve. He had already started the operation in May 1939 when he spoke to his Chiefs of Staff.

1. International Military Tribunal, *Nazi Conspiracy and Aggression*, Nuremberg, 1947

The tension over German claims to the port of Danzig and a corridor of land through Poland to reach it was systematically heightened. On 22 August Hitler called his Service chiefs to Berchtesgaden and announced that he had now come to an arrangement with Russia and was prepared to strike at Poland. Y-Day would be in four days' time, on 26 August. On 24 August Roosevelt offered to mediate, and on the next day the British Government concluded a formal treaty with Poland confirming the military guarantee – useless as they may have considered it. On that day, 25 August, Hitler telephoned Göring and said he had called off the planned invasion of Poland. Göring asked if this were a postponement or a cancellation. Hitler said "I shall have to see whether we can eliminate British intervention."

How was Britain to be emasculated? Göring had already decided that he himself should be the instrument. Rarely does the incidence of *folie de grandeur* coincide with the opportunity to exercise such power, however inexpertly. And on 25 August Göring was reaching the climax of his amazing individual attempt to eliminate British intervention. He had a private agent in conversation with Lord Halifax, the British Foreign Minister, in the Foreign Office in London that very evening.

This agent, the Swedish industrialist Birger Dahlerus, had been prompted to bring the attention of the German leaders to the stiffened British national attitude towards Nazi policies as a result of a meeting with three British businessmen at the Constitutional Club in London on 2 July. Four days later he was in conference with Göring, who assured him that the British opposition to the German claims for Danzig and the Corridor was "sheer bluff" and under no circumstances would the British support their guarantee to Poland by force of arms. Dahlerus asked if Göring would meet representatives of British business who might convince him that the national attitude was not bluff. On 7 August this extraordinary meeting took place between Göring, the man who was Commander in Chief of the Luftwaffe, the architect of German rearmament and the virtual conqueror of Czecho-Slovakia and Austria, and seven powerful but obscure British company directors, of whom only one even appeared in the "first 25,000" of Britain's *Who's Who*, and that one possibly only because he was a hereditary baronet : he was

Sir Robert Renwick, now Lord Renwick, chairman of Associated Television in London.

Göring affably proposed a lunch-time toast to the British and to peace, and gave his hearers his "sacred assurance as a statesman and an officer"[1] that the German demands for Danzig and a corridor hid no designs for any encirclement policy against Poland and would not be followed by any further demands for new territories. This declaration was made just a few weeks after Hitler's direct statement to Göring: "Danzig is not the subject of the dispute. Attack Poland at the first opportunity. Our task is to isolate Poland." The British businessmen duly reported their conversation to Lord Halifax.

On 21 August, the day on which news of the Soviet-German understanding began to leak, Lord Halifax was told that Göring wished to visit him secretly in England. Arrangements were made for a clandestine flight. This approach was vetoed by Hitler. On 23 August, the day after Hitler had told his Staff that the war would start on the 26th, Göring telephoned Dahlerus in Sweden and asked him to come to Berlin. Next day he told Dahlerus that his recurrent fear of a war on two fronts had now disappeared by reason of the German-Soviet Agreement, and that he wanted Dahlerus to go to England to convince the British Government that an understanding with Germany was possible. Dahlerus saw Halifax in London next day, the date of the Anglo-Polish Treaty and of the postponement of the invasion of Poland. On 26 August Halifax gave Dahlerus a personal letter to Göring expressing the definite wish of the British Government to come to an understanding with Germany. Dahlerus delivered it to Göring in Berlin that evening. "Herr Dahlerus," said Göring as he puzzled at the script, "translate this letter into German and remember how tremendously important it is that every syllable conveys the correct shade of meaning."

As soon as he had the translation Göring drove Dahlerus from his hunting lodge to Berlin and woke up Hitler to present it. Hitler's behaviour during a preliminary fifty-minute harangue against England was, in Dahlerus' reserved words, "abnormal. He seemed more like a phantom from a story book than a real

1. Birger Dahlerus, translated Alexandra Dick, *The Last Attempt*, Hutchinson, London, 1948.

human being". Hitler then asked Dahlerus for "any reason for my perpetual failure to come to an agreement with England". Dahlerus suggested "a lack of confidence in you personally and in your Government". Hitler made an impulsive gesture and snapped "Idiots! Have I ever told a lie in my life?"[1] Dahlerus asked for clear details of the proposed corridor to Danzig.

Dahlerus actually conveyed these astonishing proposals to Chamberlain and Halifax on 27 August and was back the same night with the British acceptance of Germany's claim to Danzig and the Corridor. He had to report Britain's unwillingness to hand over colonies at the point of a gun, and the rejection of the "protection" of the British Empire. To Göring's astonishment, in another midnight meeting Hitler declared that he welcomed this answer. Within hours the British Ambassador, Sir Nevile Henderson, had conveyed the British attitude in an official note. Göring, up late next morning after the long night, said excitedly to Dahlerus "We'll have peace. Peace has been assured."

The only possible peace envisaged was that Britain should keep out of the war. The game had been taken as far as it would go. Poland must still be annihilated, and Britain kept as long as possible in the negotiating corner from which it would be increasingly difficult to emerge with speed. That is undoubtedly how Hitler and Ribbentrop saw the ploy : how clearly the vacillating Göring appreciated it, as he juggled the dice of diplomatic power, and weighed Luftwaffe deficiencies against martial glory, can only be guessed. When Ambassador Henderson had his second meeting with Ribbentrop on 29 August he was suddenly given the intentionally provocative ultimatum that Britain must ensure that Polish negotiators arrived on the very next day to agree the cession of the Corridor.

1. Birger Dahlerus, *The Last Attempt.* Göring tore a page from an atlas and marked the corridor territory with a red pencil. Dahlerus was then asked to memorize the terms of Hitler's proposal to Britain. He offered a pact under which (1) Germany got Danzig and the Corridor in return for guarantees to Poland; (2) Germany would have tropical colonies returned to her as sources of food and raw materials; (3) Britain for her part was to receive a pledge that Germany would "defend the British Empire with the German Wehrmacht wherever the former might be attacked".

Though Dahlerus flew once more to London and back with fresh territorial "suggestions" from Göring, scrawled on another torn page from an atlas, there was no real marrow in any further parleying. On 31 August, after Göring had already received his secret orders for war on Poland next day, he insisted on being taken to luncheon by Dahlerus at the Esplanade Hotel in Berlin. So much did he like the brandy he was given that he requisitioned two bottles and had them sent to his car.

Göring, and most of the High Command, still thought that Britain would not fight. In the nervous banter that precedes such a decision Göring deprecated to Ambassador Henderson over afternoon tea the possibility that he, Göring, would be compelled to have England bombed. Henderson said he might therefore die by Göring's own hand. Göring promised that he would fly over England and drop a personal wreath on Henderson's grave.

In this monstrous unreality of open-cockpit derring-do the last day of peace passed. When Hitler saw Raeder on the expiry of the British ultimatum he said, more embarrassed than Raeder had ever seen him, "You see, I wasn't able to keep England out after all."

But for a period in the interim, when war was already joined with Poland and had already been offered by Britain, a curious reaction transformed Göring. Dahlerus reported:

He seemed to have completely lost the power of surveying the consequences of a war. Everything was lined up according to a plan which nothing could upset. Finally he called in Körner, his aide, and Gritzbach, the Secretary of State, gave them a long harangue and presented each of them with a sword of honour which he hoped they would carry gloriously through the war.

It was as if all these people were in some crazy state of intoxication.

In this manner Marshal Göring went to war. And yet, at ten o'clock on the morning of Sunday, 3 September 1939, an hour before the British declaration of war was due, Göring agreed to a last appeal by Dahlerus that the Marshal should fly personally to London to negotiate. Moreover, he got Hitler to agree that he should leave German soil by eleven o'clock. Dahlerus made the last of many strained telephone calls between London and Berlin on a line that had been closed to ordinary traffic for a week. At 10.15 he was through to the Foreign Office. The British Government's reply was that Göring's visit could be considered only if a reply were first given to the British ultimatum. Göring once more telephoned Hitler, acting in effect as a British emissary calling the Führer's final bluff. There came a dusty answer, and Dahlerus was connected for his final call to London.

The revving aircraft standing by at Göring's Luftwaffe headquarters ticked away the last minutes of peace. At eleven o'clock the engine was cut. The complicated aspirations of the Commander in Chief resolved into a simpler theme. The map tables under the trees were folded, and the armoured train was routed for the east.

Marshal Göring had to win a multiple war in the air.

CHAPTER THREE

THE OPPOSITION

> I am certain that there is no desire in this country . . .
> to do anything offensive. But if we should be under
> the necessity of going to war, you will witness the
> most extraordinary exertions ever made by this or
> any other country in order to carry out the same with
> vigour.
>
> THE DUKE OF WELLINGTON

The air marshals aligned in the West against Göring in 1939,
either already in top command or marked to mount to the
firing-step, were Dowding, Portal, Harris and Tedder of the
Royal Air Force and Major General Arnold, Chief of the
United States Army Air Corps. In the background was the
powerful thrust of Marshal of the Royal Air Force Lord
Trenchard, Chief of the Air Staff for eleven years after the First
World War, whose offensive spirit, consistently propagated,
ranks him among Göring's major opponents. In the year before
Munich Göring had tried to frighten Trenchard : after a
banquet in Berlin he ended an impressive fireworks display with
the over-amplified sound of dive-bombers screaming in to the
attack. "There's German might for you," he shouted. "I see
you trembled." In spectacular anger Trenchard stormed back :
"You must be off your head. I warn you, Göring, don't under-
estimate the R.A.F."[1]

With the exception of Dowding, the Royal Air Force marshals
were "bright boys" favoured and advanced since 1918 by
Trenchard, the perpetually active father of the independent
British air force and the most practical world advocate of independent air power. To Arnold of America, too, Trenchard
was, in words he used later, "the patron saint of air power",[2]

1. Andrew Boyle, *Trenchard*, London, Collins, 1962.
2. H. H. Arnold, *Global Mission*, Harper, New York, 1949.

and the Englishman's ideas were of abiding influence. Arnold, Spaatz and Doolittle consulted Trenchard, then aged only seventy-two, at the end of the Second World War for a briefing before the fierce debate which led to the formation of the independent United States Air Force. But it is convenient to consider Arnold's creation of United States air power separately, (Chapter 8), while the concurrent formative years of the Royal Air Force and its "offensive" marshals may be traced here in relation to the career of the man who, as Chief of the Air Staff for five years, was to command the Royal Air Force through desolation and victory.

Charles Frederick Algernon Portal, who in spite of the ample choice made available at his christening was known at home and in the Service as Peter, was forty-seven when he became Chief of the Air Staff, after six months as Commander in Chief, Bomber Command. He was four months younger than Göring, who was nine months younger than Harris – 1892–3 produced an interesting vintage; Udet and Milch were even younger, being in the very early forties when war broke out; Tedder, then forty-nine, was five years younger than one of his recurring opponents, Kesselring; Dowding was fifty-seven in 1939.

Portal's family were originally Huguenot émigrés who had come from France to England in 1695. They were prosperous middle-class countryfolk with connections in City of London commerce, the paper industry and the law. Portal went to Winchester, the public school reputed to produce more independent-thinking intellectuals than any other gentlemanly stable : not a harsh institution, as British public schools went, though Dowding, who went to Winchester nine years earlier, was said to have "suffered cruelly". Portal usefully captained the school cricket team, a not very traumatic responsibility, which is considered in England to be character-building. Perhaps more significantly, he took an early interest in falconry, the ancient art of training falcons and hawks for the chase and kill of other birds; this is a subject in which he became an expert. Portal went from Winchester to Oxford, where he read law and was known at Christ Church not only for his intellectual pursuits but for the mastery of the motor-cycle; he won a notable road race on this machine.

Portal was called to the Bar in 1914, but two days after the outbreak of the First World War left the law for ever, became a despatch rider in the Motor Cyclist Section of the Royal Engineers, and embarked for France. A month later he was not only delivering despatches but featuring in them: as Corporal Portal he got the first of his three "mentions" in the very first despatches sent home by the Commander in Chief of the Old Contemptibles, Sir John French. Almost step by step with Göring, he was a commissioned observer in the Royal Flying Corps in 1915 and a pilot in 1916. An all-rounder in the fashion of the air service at that time, he was fighter-pilot, bomber, renaissance man and spotter. He carried out five tactical bombing raids in one night on the Western front, and on another occasion attacked five enemy aircraft single-handed and shot down three. As Squadron Leader Commanding 16 Squadron of R.E.8s he had the habit of personally ranging the artillery his aircraft were directing. He came through the war with a Military Cross and a double award of the Distinguished Service Order. He had the very rare record of a thousand hours of combat flying.

On the day that Portal took over 16 Squadron, 1April 1918, the Royal Air Force was officially created – the union of the Royal Flying Corps with the Royal Naval Air Service. It was the first independent air force in the world, and in 1918 by far the strongest. It had a strength of 360,000 men and 22,000 aircraft of which 3,300 were classed as frontline machines. In the revulsion against armies and armaments that followed the First World War its body was butchered more savagely than any comparable service except the defeated German Air Force, and in the year of Versailles the Royal Air Force had only 371 machines in the first line.

But what had been saved was its independent existence – no mean feat of endurance in the face of bitter opposition by post-war Army and Navy leaders. The Royal Air Force was initially preserved by two men: Hugh Trenchard, its first supreme Marshal, and Winston Churchill. As Secretary for War and Air, Churchill backed Trenchard's formative modelling; as Secretary for the Colonies he gave the Royal Air Force extraordinary responsibility; and even as Chancellor of the Exchequer he found opportunities to push the Service, in spite of a climate of retrenchment.

Trenchard, as Chief of the Air Staff, with an initial allocation of only £15 million a year, budgeted his slender means almost solely with an eye to future development. He built his actual force up from twelve to eighteen squadrons, each of twelve firstline machines. Of these, twelve squadrons were often on active service overseas as pacification "firemen" and the rest virtually committed to support of the Navy and Army at home. But the bulk of the money was earmarked for the continual process of rejuvenation by research, technical training and aircraft development. Above all, Trenchard instituted a particular morale : what he called "the Air Force spirit". The French very early lost this by the integration of their air force into the army and the Americans only partially and painfully maintained it against the pressure of their own army establishment. The national prestige of the Royal Air Force before 1939 was never so high as the repute of the Royal Navy or the Army – largely because, except for the backbone of First World War veterans, its officer personnel, rarely encouraged to ripen into traditional mellowness by reason of the swift turnover of short-service commissions, was regarded as *déclassé* in a period when British class distinctions were still of great national weight. But, prestige apart, in 1939 the Royal Air Force was different, special and modern.

Trenchard, with his strong and lengthy influence on the Royal Air Force, hardened Air Staff thinking on the function of an independent air force as being primarily an arm of offensive attack through strategic bombing. This shaped the balance of the force, with its preponderance of bombers, at least until the emergence of the new metal monoplane fighter and of radar revived respect in the power of air defence. (In Britain, as in the United States, fighters were regarded as instruments of strategic defence; the conception of a long-range fighter to support raiding bombers had been rejected.) From Trenchard's conception of air power as a strategic hammer derived his other great seminal belief that the direct objective of a strategic bombing offensive was the morale of the enemy civilians : that a bombing force punctured the enemy's will and means to resist by the terror it induced, through slaughter as well as through the destruction of the homes, factories and matériel of the workers and fighters. The strategic thinking was closely in line with the concept expressed by the influential Italian theorist Douhet.

This was a mode of thought which recurred in varying intensity among British war leaders, including Portal and Churchill, throughout the Second World War, but was never accepted as an openly defined objective by the Americans – neither by the politicians nor by the Air Staff of the United States. Portal first heard the theory authoritatively expounded as early as 1923 at a meeting of the Air Staff to which he, a squadron leader attached to Operations and Intelligence, had been somewhat significantly invited.[1] The "enemy" in planning thought at that time was France, and the discussion centred on the effect of heavy bombing. Portal heard Trenchard say, according to the semi-indirect parlance of the official minutes :[2]

The policy of hitting the French nation and making them squeal before we did was a vital one – more vital than anything else. The question had been asked at Camberley[3] "Why is it that your policy of attack from the air is so different from the policy of the Army, whose policy it is to attack the enemy's army, while yours is to attack the civil population." The answer was that we were able to do this while the Army were not, and so go straight to the source of supply and stop it. Instead of attacking a machine with ten bombs we would go straight to the source of supply of the bombs and demolish it, and the same with the source of production of machines. It was a quicker process than allowing the output to go on. The Army policy was to defeat the enemy Army – ours to defeat the enemy nation. The Army only defeated the enemy Army because they could not get at the enemy nation. We must avoid allowing our policy to be affected by the policy of the Army and the Navy. Our policy in strategy was totally different from that of the Army.

Not only was the strategy of the Royal Air Force different from that of its sister-services. The circumstances of its secondary,

1. Trenchard, scanning his force for future leaders, had privately marked Portal's name in the first Air Force List ever published.
2. Minutes of a Conference held in the room of the Chief of the Air Staff, Air Ministry, on 19 July 1923. Sir Charles Webster and Noble Frankland, *The Strategic Air Offensive Against Germany, 1939–1945* (*History of the Second World War*), *Appendix 1,* H.M. Stationery Office, London, 1961.
3. At the Staff College.

empire-sustaining, role tuned its officers to a rare pitch of responsibility. The squadrons serving overseas between the wars were never a "colonial force" in the French sense of specialized occupation armies or native levies. They were normal units of the Royal Air Force serving a tour of overseas duties in the normal circuit of their experience. The intermittent spells of this type of service which became familiar to officers of all ranks were a unique maturing influence in the growth of the "Air Force spirit". For, unlike any other air service in the world, the Royal Air Force exercised sole defence responsibilities in certain imperial areas and was the senior service in others. Iraq was a Royal Air Force empire from 1922 : the Air Officer Commanding British Forces had four infantry battalions under him as well as eight squadrons of aircraft and the R.A.F.'s own armoured car squadrons.[1] Aden was taken care of in the same way. The North West Frontier of India, Somaliland and Jordan, even for a time Turkey, where Tedder commanded 207 Squadron at Constantinople in 1922–3, were other areas of Royal Air Force activity, though the air commander was not supreme.

The fruit of the system was a strong cadre of regular officers with tactical experience, command appreciation and an insight into planning. It was in Iraq in 1923 that Squadron Leader Arthur (not yet "Bomber") Harris, commanding 45 Squadron, which had plenty of work against Turkish armies and insurgent tribesmen, built his own bomb racks on heavy transport aircraft, sawed a sighting hole in the nose, and initiated the prone position for bomb-aiming which was standard in later Lancasters. In Iraq, incidentally, Dowding inaugurated the practice of dropping warning leaflets on the villages of independent-minded sheikhs before the subsequent bombing. Wing Commander Portal was a keen bomber-leader, and, while commanding 7 Squadron in 1927–8, himself acted as bomb-aimer to win the Service bombing trophy in successive years. The actual tactical

1. In the Second World War Tedder believed that his prompt independent movement of these R.A.F. armoured cars, detached from the Western Desert while the soldier Wavell hesitated about his dispositions, saved the base of Habbaniya during the dangerous German-inspired Iraqi revolt of May 1941. Lord Tedder, *Without Prejudice*, Cassell, London, 1966.

experience was relatively crude, and gained against a lack of technical opposition; but, short of a cynical entry into the Spanish civil war, it was all that could fall to the Royal Air Force. The command experience was more ripening. Air Commodore Portal, Air Officer Commanding British Forces in Aden in the mid-thirties during the Italian war against Abyssinia, appreciated the refinements of responsibility during a military crisis endured by the current man at the top. Just before the Second World War Air Commodore Harris became Air Officer Commanding Palestine and Transjordan, and in his own truculent words "had a busy year teaching the British army the advantages and the rebels the effectiveness of air power".[1] Before that, as head of the Air Ministry Planning Department, he had joined with the Army and Navy planners to produce a remarkably accurate appreciation of the course of the coming war with Germany, even forecasting 1939 as the date of its outbreak. This document of 1936 was the basis of the strategy determined by the Chiefs of Staff for the conduct of the war.

War, however, is a matter of matériel as well as men. The machines which were to fight the Second World War in the air were developed and produced under constraints that were hazardous in the extreme.

In the early 1920s the British General Staff became alarmed at the military, and therefore political, strength of the squadrons of France, the country then considered to be Britain's only potential enemy in Europe. Accordingly, in 1922, the Government was persuaded to agree that a Metropolitan (or Home Defence) air force should be established "of sufficient strength to protect us against air attack by the strongest air force within striking distance of this country". Against the 600 first-line aircraft of France a home force of 14 squadrons of bombers and nine of fighters was to be established as a first instalment.

Strategic defence was thus interpreted as offensive attack, using the preponderance of bombers over fighters – the principle of a strategic bombing force which the Air Staff had nurtured from the beginning.

Later it was decided that 600 aircraft in 52 squadrons, in

1. Marshal of the Royal Air Force Sir Arthur Harris, *Bomber Offensive*, Collins, London, 1947.

the proportion of two bombers to one fighter, were to be operating by 1928. But successive Chancellors of the Exchequer –
of whom it must be recorded that, in 1927 and 1928, Winston
Churchill was not the least emasculating – insisted on economy
and deferred the completion of the 52-squadron scheme. The
politicians continually operated and extended the so-called Ten
Years Rule, the theory that a major war was impossible within
the next ten years. This was advanced from year to year, and
abandoned only in 1934. Consequently, even in 1934, when the
unadmitted existence of the Luftwaffe was well known to the
Air Staff, the Metropolitan Air Force tally stood at 316 bombers
in 28 squadrons, 172 fighters in 14 squadrons, with 15 flying-
boats and 60 army cooperation machines. In addition there
were 24 squadrons comprising 256 aircraft overseas, and 13
Auxiliary squadrons.

The great and much publicized increase in Royal Air Force
establishment decided in 1934 was intended as a deterrent to
the Germans. They converted it, however, to an incentive and
surpassed it. For the British deterrent, numbers were deemed
more important than quality. It was the case in reverse of "the
Führer will not ask how big they are, but how many." Therefore the numbers announced as intended first-line aircraft – and
actually put into the first line at the time of Munich – could not
really be put in the first line in a shooting war, since half of
them would be needed as replacements for battle casualties.
For deterrent purposes, of a psychological rather than a physical
nature, it was also decided to build half the new aircraft from
obsolescent light bomber models, because more could be produced for less money.

The period was a time of swiftly changing thought in aircraft
design, and the British had not yet commissioned a modern
medium-weight bomber for production on any effective scale.
They had made up their minds, however, on their fighter needs
– largely on experience gained from the Schneider Trophy
races; and two eight-gun monoplane fighters capable of a swift
climb and a speed of 275 m.p.h. at 15,000 feet were specified
for the industry. The prototype Hurricane was in the air in
1935 and the Spitfire in 1936.

What was ultimately to be even more important, in 1936 the
specifications of the really heavy bombers, which were to succeed

the Wellingtons and other medium bombers then coming into production, were drawn up. "Bomber" Harris has claimed credit for many facets of the final air victory, but he has never publicly mentioned the memorandum of 16 January 1935, drawn up by Group Captain A. T. Harris, Deputy Director of Plans, advocating a policy of building aircraft of maximum range and bomb capacity so that even the medium bomber would disappear. His advocacy, which was not unsupported, was effective. The clinching orders came, indeed, with a fortuitous rush. Contracts had been drawn up for the Stirling four-engine bomber and a Supermarine heavy bomber which was never built, and for medium bombers which were later upgraded to become the Lancaster and Halifax. The orders were placed in October 1937 when the Air Ministry suddenly realized that fresh funds had been released in the wildly expanding armaments universe, and that, unless they quickly made up their minds on what they wanted, the Army and Navy, who had advance knowledge of the bonanza, would leave little for the air allotment.

The pace increased. Airfields were bought. There was expansion of Service training in civilian flying schools (started by Tedder as Director of Training 1934–6). Shadow factories were laid down by motor-car manufacturers at Government expense to mass-produce aircraft if the starting-gun fired. Machines were bought in America by a Department which suddenly found itself subsidising foreign private enterprise – actually financing new factories for Americans in which they would build British aircraft.

Yet when Munich came the production line had scarcely started to move. The Royal Air Force had 1,982 first-line aircraft against 3,307 in the Luftwaffe, and there was "no real reserve, whether bombers or fighters", the Secretary for Air revealed later. By far the majority of the British machines were obsolescent. Among the 709 fighters were 43 Hurricanes and no Spitfires. The rest were biplanes that even Göring could have flown. It is small wonder, though a matter of infinite pity, that the British Air Staff wished to do absolutely nothing professionally against Hitler's threat to Czecho-Slovakia. And, with that sort of backing, Chamberlain did nothing.

After Munich, fighter production bounded forward. It was a time when the British Air Staff – and the British alone – quite confidently began to question the dogma which everyone, Service leaders, politicians and civilians, had accepted for twenty years : "the bomber will always get through." The comparative advance in the potential of fighters, and Britain's unique possession of an effective early warning radar system that would set the fighters above invading bombers before the enemy were in a position to attack – these surges in defence technique swung against the bomber.

But a deficiency far more serious, because avoidable, in bombing technique was that training had never been brought up to the standard necessary to fight a long bombing war in the dark. The fact was not yet apparent to the British or German Staffs, but the standards of navigation and bomb-aiming over distant enemy territory, and of necessity by night, were so low that any bombing force which had to venture so far afield as had the British was assured of a dismal record. The Germans, as events fell, had bombing bases just across the Channel, and consequently had far less difficulty in navigating to their targets. The British, with an air force whose theoretical justification for existence had been for twenty years to serve as a strategic bombing offensive force, not only had bombing planes technically too vulnerable against daylight fighter attack, but crews too ill-trained to find their mark at night and to bomb it decisively.

When war came the bustling but still virtually uncontrolled aircraft industry in Britain had produced a total Metropolitan Air Force of 3,860 aircraft of which 1,660 were in the first line. The 1934 force of 316 bombers now stood at 536 in the first line and 1,450 in reserve. The 156 fighters had grown to 608 in the first line and 320 in reserve. There were now 96 reconnaissance aircraft, 216 coastal aircraft and 204 Fleet Air Arm machines in the first line with reserves of 105, 125 and 200 respectively. The 1934 total of 256 aircraft overseas was now 415. These were the figures for 26 September 1939 as given by the Secretary of State for Air to the War Cabinet.[1]

In the remarkably accurate preview by the Joint Planning Sub-Committee which Group Captain A. T. Harris had signed for the Royal Air Force in October 1936 the Service planners,

1. Basil Collier, *The Defence of the United Kingdom* (*History of the Second World War*), H.M. Stationery Office, London, 1957.

assuming the outbreak of war in 1939, had agreed :[1]

The greatest danger of a rapid German success on land seems to lie either in the speed, strength and surprise of her initial attack enabling her to break through French or Belgian defences before they could be fully manned, or in the inability of the Belgian Forces to hold the whole of their northern and eastern frontiers and the failure of the French to concentrate an army in Belgium to support their Allies. Speed in giving whatever help we could would, therefore, be of the first importance and every measure we could take to delay the German attack would acquire corresponding importance.

There would be a danger that a rapid German advance might dispose of Holland, Belgium and France successively . . .

We anticipate that Germany's munition position would, at the beginning of the war, be stronger than that of our Allies, since she would start with her industries highly organized for war production and with considerable reserves of material in hand . . .

We have shown that in 1939 Germany's war preparations are likely to be considerably more advanced than will be the case in Great Britain or France. We concluded that, if war occurred, Germany would endeavour to exploit her preparedness by a rapid victory – within a few months : and that the Allies would have no means of winning quickly. . . . The Allies must, therefore, plan for a long war . . .

After Germany's initial offensive is held, we must be prepared for the war to enter a second stage during which our object must be the development of our industrial output, especially of aircraft and munitions, and to restrict that of Germany . . .

We must be prepared to face an attempted knock-out blow aimed either at ourselves or our Allies. In either case we must concentrate our initial efforts on defeating this attempt which, if in the form of air attack on Great Britain, may well subject us over a period to a strain greater than we have ever experienced. If this can be successfully accomplished, we must thereafter rely on our industrial and economic power, backed by the resources of the Empire, eventually to bring a counter-offensive against Germany.

The one fundamental assumption that seems in the light of post-war revelations to have been wrong is the anticipation that

[1]. Appreciation by the Joint Planning Sub-Committee of the Situation in the Event of War Against Germany in 1939, 26 October 1936, Webster and Frankland, *The Strategic Air Offensive Against Germany, 1939–1945*, Appendix 4.

"Germany's munition position would, at the beginning of the war, be stronger than that of our Allies." It was true of aircraft, tanks and rifles but not of fuel and projectiles. Even now it seems incredible that Germany should start a war with three weeks' stock of bombs and (on Keitel's admission) six weeks' stock of ammunition. But the fact must be accepted as an indication of Hitler's faith in short wars and as a reminder of the inept and dilettante diplomacy that took him into a long war, as well as of the astounding luck of being presented with six months' breathing space to restore the shortages incurred by Hermann Göring, director of rearmament.

The British Air Staff were prepared for a long war and relied on the gradualism of a swelling counter-offensive. But one Royal Air Force marshal decided that it really depended on him whether there would be such a recoil at all. If Britain went down under an all-out air attack, then the reserves of industrial and economic power and all the resources of the Empire were worth nothing. The primary essential was that Britain should not be knocked out. A determination to scheme like a fox and ensure that the knock-out blow should never connect on Britain became the *idée fixe* of Air Chief Marshal Sir Hugh Dowding, Commander in Chief Fighter Command and the man in operational control of Anti-Aircraft Command (including Searchlights), Balloon Command and the observer and radar chains sustaining the air defence of Britain.

By this resolve he sentenced himself to disbarment from the highest office in the Royal Air Force and to oblivion at the end of the Battle of Britain. There is no evidence that he ever regretted his decision. For a full year the air struggle between Germany and Great Britain was crystallized into the contest of Göring versus Dowding. The winner was Dowding, and he slipped from the ring virtually without a cheer. But he had never been popular before his victory and did not depend on acclaim afterwards. Years later he declared: "I myself remain under no sense of grievance. The Germans lost the battle and that was all that really mattered."

Hugh Dowding was fifty-four years old in 1936, when he left Research and Development and took over the newly created Fighter Command. Nicknamed, not over-affectionately, "Stuffy", he was a tall, gaunt and lonely man, a widower after two years of marriage and the father of an only son who was to serve as a Battle of Britain pilot. Dowding himself was the son of a schoolmaster. After four obscure years at school at Winchester he spent a year at the Royal Military Academy and took a commission in the Royal Artillery, serving in Gibraltar and the North West Frontier of India. Having taken an aviation course, he was transferred to the Royal Flying Corps on the outbreak of the 1914 war and flew on patrol over Belgium with the impressive armament of one Mauser pistol with shoulder-stock.

He was never an air ace. In France he commanded first a squadron, then a headquarters wing. On the Somme in August 1916 he asked Trenchard to rest a particular squadron – 60 Squadron – which had suffered severe casualties. Trenchard immediately suspected Dowding's own morale. He characterized Dowding as "a dismal Jimmy" opposed to the offensive spirit of the Royal Flying Corps, and replaced him. Dowding consequently spent two years on administrative work in England as a brigadier general. His permanent transfer to the peacetime Royal Air Force was at first opposed, but later grudgingly passed by Trenchard.[1] After service in Iraq he was appointed to the Air Council in 1930 (immediately Trenchard retired) as Air Member for Supply and Research, and continued with responsibility more narrowly focused on Research and Development until 1936. It was Dowding who instituted the design competition which led to the prototypes of the Hurricane and Spitfire, ordered as high-performance metal landplanes incorporating all practical war features of the Supermarine seaplane. Dowding nursed the development of these revolutionary fighters and he put his weight behind the proposal for four-engined bombers. Where he faltered was in the tardy development of the self-sealing petrol tank[2] and the ill-judged backing

1. Trenchard took twenty-six years to change his mind. During the Battle of Britain he personally told Dowding that he had gravely underestimated him. Boyle, *Trenchard.*

2. Dowding openly castigated himself for this omission in 1941 in a book which Churchill banned for five years. Rhetorically asking "Why are senior officers so stupid?" Dowding explained: "If a junior officer puts forward a suggestion the implication is that a senior officer might have thought of it, ought to have thought of it, and didn't think of it." Lord Dowding, *Twelve Legions of Angels,* Jarrolds, London, 1946.

of the short-range Battle bomber which, often armed with only two machine guns, was brushed out of the Royal Air Force in the Battle for France.[1] Pre-eminent among his successes was the energetic encouragement of radiolocation. (This was the English word for the visible recording on a cathode ray tube of aircraft reflecting short-wave radio beams, and the subsequent estimate of the aircraft's position. Since the birth of radiolocation in 1935 its name has been changed to the American term *radar*.) The Royal Air Force operated the first radar chain in the world from 1937, and by that time Dowding was exploiting the invention to the full extent of his resources in his newly created post of Commander in Chief Fighter Command.

The Royal Air Force was bomber-minded. The British Government was bomber-minded insofar as its political rearmament programme had any practical direction at all, beyond trying to deter Hitler by bluff. Prime Minister Baldwin had summed up the attitude : "The bomber will always get through. ... The only defence is offence, which means that you have to kill more women and children more quickly than the enemy if you want to save yourselves." Dowding himself was certainly not an opponent of strategic bombing. But he also argued tenaciously during his years of command for a realistic appreciation of the power of the new fast monoplane fighters, particularly for escort duties to help the bombers get through. British bombers should therefore attack enemy bomber bases, dispersed and distant though they were. But this was an incidental theory, and not Dowding's crusading responsibility. For him, British fighters were the immediate home defence against enemy bombers which got off the ground. They were the arm which could catch and deflect the dreaded knock-out blow. Dowding's dour championship of the fighters, and the ungracious severity with which he pursued all his convictions, possibly cost him the top position of Chief of the Air Staff, for which he was certainly considered. If so, it saved him for Fighter Command. Even in this post he was given four successive warnings of his imminent forced retirement. He fought the Battle of Britain on

1. The Air Council corporately and individually believed in the light day bomber, and instructed Dowding to get one. He did. But it is the lot of marshals to take responsibility for the failures as well as the successes to which others contributed.

borrowed time, with his retirement gradually extended from March 1940 to July, October and finally November. In his own phrase he commanded the battle with the status of "an unsatisfactory domestic servant under notice".

Dowding fought within the Service for adequate defence aircraft at a time when 4,000 fighters – the whole of British production in the four-months all-out effort of the Battle of Britain – cost £30 million ($120 million at that period). Those fighters could have been paid for in 1939 – and an extra £4 million set aside for pilot training – if the increase in the *five taxes* which were slightly raised in the 1939 Budget had been double what was actually proposed. The Budget of 25 April 1939, introduced not only after Munich but after the extinction of Czecho-Slovakia, raised taxation by £33,945,000 in a full year, or by about $3\frac{1}{2}$ per cent of the ordinary revenue. We are accustomed to saying that the survival of Britain in 1940 – and therefore the final defeat of Germany five years later – was accomplished by the narrowest of margins. The narrowness of the margin is nothing for Britain to be proud of. It meant that sweating air mechanics worked to exhaustion through summer nights, patching up aircraft in which nineteen-year-old pilots were to die at dawn, after only a dozen hours of solo operational flying. The narrow margin of blood and victory meant, in housekeeping terms, a penny a packet on cigarettes and three farthings a pound on sugar.

Dowding, an officer in the armed forces of the Crown, made no effort to influence the scale or allocation of public expenditure on rearmament: Churchill himself was able to do little to move the nation on this cause. The Commander in Chief Fighter Command made it his task to impress on the Air Staff the importance of backing the resurgent potential of modern fighter aircraft. By 1938 the politicians in the Air Ministry were supporting him by insisting on a swing to fighter production. But within months Dowding was fighting both politicians and professionals for the control of his own fighters in the defence of Great Britain. He was on his own against Göring.

CHAPTER FOUR

SIEG HEIL: WARSAW TO DUNKIRK

All soldiers run away, madam.

THE DUKE OF WELLINGTON

Field Marshal Göring gazed derisively at the German General Staff's *Directive No. 1 for the Conduct of the War* which had been handed to him on 31 August 1939. "What am I supposed to do with this bumf," he queried. "I've known all this for ages."[1]

Göring liked to affect a soldierly contempt for the clerks, though as the most disorganized Commander in Chief in history he depended more than any other leader on the tidiness of his staff. He had, indeed, been for months a party to the most lowly details of the preparation for war, including an initial operation of cheap infamy that stands as a brand mark of the Nazi attitude to war. Villainy on a grand scale, or a *ruse de guerre* that deceives by massive effrontery, can often be appreciated and sometimes envied in war. But the Second World War began with a gangster's trick that would have been below the dignity of a sneak-thief in the Hamburg brothel area.

It had been decided that a pretext was necessary for the German declaration of war on Poland. A false "provocative incident" was therefore engineered. It occupied its paragraph in the War Plan, and its timing had to be altered as meticulously as that of the first troop movements, in step with Hitler's last-minute postponements. The final order to proceed was promulgated. On the night of 31 August 1939 a dozen prisoners of the Gestapo, taken from a concentration camp, were dressed in German army uniforms and placed on the limit of the Silesian border with Poland. The Gestapo had shipped the prisoners forward for the operation under the code name "canned goods", and this was to be an almost exact description of their role. When the dummy German soldiers were in position a small

1. Walter Warlimont, translated R. H. Barry, *Inside Hitler's Headquarters 1939–45*, Weidenfeld & Nicolson, London, 1964.

59

detachment of Gestapo men, for their part dressed in Polish uniform, crossed the Polish border for a few yards in the dark. They re-entered Germany at the point where the "canned goods" had been posted, and shot them to death. They went on, with much noise of small arms but no further casualties, to "capture" the German radio station at Gleiwitz, whose staff had been forewarned of the operation. The Gestapo took over the transmitter and broadcast in Polish a magniloquent account of the Polish invasion of Germany, the Polish massacre of German troops and the Polish capture of Gleiwitz. The German News Agency picked up the story and used it, for what it was worth, on the morning of 1 September as justification for the great onslaught of the German Army and Air Force. As far as world opinion was concerned, the plan was a complete miscalculation. The world did not expect even a show of legality from a bandit mentality. It did not heed the news of Gleiwitz nor elevate it to propaganda level for one side or the other. The Gestapo killings achieved nothing. The first dozen unnecessary victims of a long war lay, contorted in death, on the edge of Silesia. They were political trash, hardly worth moving from the track of the advancing Panzers.

In a score of airfields surrounding Poland, from East Prussia, due north of Warsaw, to Silesia, almost due south, German fitters and armourers and instrument testers worked through the night of 31 August. The false dawn lightened. The bombers stuttered at starting, fanned their course to the runway ends, revved their engines to a scream and plunged off, to join formation and turn east. At four miles a minute 700 bombers sped over a land that did not know it was at war. The first targets were nine major Polish airfields, seven in the west and two in the east. The Russians, massing to advance, were as keenly delighted with the operation as the German Third Army in East Prussia. The Polish Air Force got off the ground and fought valiantly. It was smashed in a short while, and the wild dash of its pilots was never again exhibited until refugee Polish squadrons in Hurricanes swept into the Battle of Britain. Within two days any effective air opposition to the German advance was crushed. The bombers were switched to army support, in which the 150 Stukas and 350 reconnaissance aircraft of the two air fleets engaged were already fully committed. The heavier bombers took a week to smash the railways and road communications to the west of Warsaw. They then devoted a week to the railways leading east. Certain units picked off the principal headquarters and key depots and factories. Then all combined to harass and destroy the beaten enemy. There was so little scope for the German fighters, apart from strafing ground formations, that many squadrons were sent home to Germany. The heavy bombers, well within range of their targets, had no need for new landing grounds and worked throughout from their advanced German bases.

It was all over, bar the bombing of Warsaw, in nineteen days, and Warsaw itself fell on 27 September. The German army operations in Poland comprised a campaign of encirclement. The Reichswehr stormed through the defending formations behind nine brigades of Panzers. Then they wheeled, surrounded and exterminated. The thirty Polish divisions, including twelve brigades of symbolically futile cavalry, were crushed, cut through and destroyed. In the changing daily war maps of the German High Command the Polish Army appeared like a body in a bath of acid. It was eaten into, it was devoured, it broke up. Soon only minor masses of stubborn flesh and bone remained. And still the dissolution continued until nothing was left of the military might of Poland save the swirling scum of defeat.

Göring came home to Carinhall, perhaps in the most exhilarated mood he had ever experienced. The former open-cockpit hero, lieutenant commanding the Richthofen Geschwader, had won his first war in the space of three weeks. It was undisputed that the air power of his Luftwaffe had clinched the decision. With a four to one superiority he had conquered an air force of 500 first-line planes at a cost of 19 aircraft lost on actual operations.[1] He had bombed a country into submission in a matter of days and ripped open his first capital city. The achievement was only heightened by the chill of genuine fear he had felt during the first few days. For he had beaten the clock. The fact was that the war could not have gone on at its furious opening pace for longer than another fortnight. Germany had started the six-year war with ludicrously

1. There were severe and disproportionate losses from crashes which affected Göring's will to proceed immediately against France.

low stocks of oil and bombs. The bomb supply was a scandalous reflection on the inadequate Luftwaffe inspectorate system. The total stocks would have been spent in three weeks if a stronger opposition had demanded heavier attacks. Milch, who appreciated the situation, could not get Göring or Hitler to accelerate bomb production until the demands of the Polish war opened their eyes in a tardy panic. The heavy drain on oil stocks exerted by the mechanized ground forces and the Luftwaffe was only subsequently replaced by captured Polish reserves. September 1939 would have been a favourable time for a land attack on Germany by France and Britain, the nations with whom she was nominally at war. Churchill later gave a military reason for the omission, stating that the earliest date at which the French could have mounted a big attack was "perhaps at the end of the third week of September. But by that time the Polish campaign had ended. By mid-October the Germans had seventy divisions on the Western front. The fleeting French numerical superiority in the west was passing."[1] On the other hand Jodl declared his complete mystification that "France and England remained stationary at the Maginot Line with 110 divisions against Germany's 23, while Germany was busy finishing off Poland."[2]

Even if the Allied armies were too inert to advance, some effect would have been achieved by strategic bombing from the advance airfields in France, which were never actually used until medium bombers operated from them in 1945. But no one in France or England would countenance such a move. Only Marshal of the Royal Air Force "Boom" Trenchard, sixty-six years old and out of office, urged the Cabinet in a personal memorandum "advocating strongly hitting at German communications from the air as we had every geographical advantage. I never stopped arguing this."[3] All that happened was that Churchill (then First Lord of the Admiralty) facetiously suggested that Trenchard's nickname should be changed from "Boom" to "Bomb".

France was clearly dragging her feet, and damping down the

1. Winston S. Churchill, *The Gathering Storm,* Cassell, London, 1948.
2. International Military Tribunal, *Trial of The Major War Criminals,* Nuremberg, 1947.
3. Boyle, *Trenchard.*

élan of Britain. Perhaps the West could be persuaded to call off its war. Göring's intricate negotiations with Halifax and Chamberlain through the Swede Dahlerus had been designed to persuade Britain to do nothing while Germany took Poland. As diplomacy the intrigue had failed, but in actuality the object of the complicated manoeuvre had entirely succeeded. Britain had declared war, but she had done nothing while Germany smashed Poland. To that extent she and France had acquiesced, for it was in the certainty that all was quiet on the western front that Hitler had transferred heavy artillery from the Rhine to the Vistula for the final bombardment of Warsaw. Now that the end was in sight, surely Britain could be persuaded to make no trouble. Göring telephoned Dahlerus in Sweden once more, and had this well meaning man scuttling to Berlin on the day that Warsaw was enduring its crushing bombardment. He saw both Hitler and Göring and they discussed with him how best to persuade the British to withdraw without loss of face. Dahlerus managed to make yet another air trip to London, and saw Chamberlain. He returned to report to Göring the British Government's firm demand : the first essential was that the German Government be reconstituted. They would not negotiate with Hitler.

If Göring had been a harder man – even a more unscrupulously ambitious man – he would have recognized his chance and taken it. Dahlerus asked him outright in private "Do you serve Germany, or do you serve Hitler?" The marshal made no reply then, and seemed in a genuine dilemma, though the occasion must have recalled the fact that he had already replied on 9 September in a speech at an armaments factory in Berlin :

We are prepared for an acceptable peace and equally determined to fight to the last under the Führer, who through many years has raised up the German people. Shall we be parted from such a Leader at the wish of Great Britain? It is too monstrous to speak of it. We want peace, but peace at the price of our Führer is to destroy the German nation. Germany is Hitler, and Hitler is Germany.[1]

Six years later, in Nuremberg jail, he made in disenchantment

1. *Keesing's Contemporary Archives,* Bristol, 1939.

another answer. Kelley, the prowling American psychologist, observed casually in Göring's cell that all Hitler's followers must have been yes-men. "That may well be," Göring grunted. "But please show me a no-man in Germany who is not six feet underground today."[1] Men who are wholly seized by patriotism or ambition will risk the grave. Göring was not single-minded enough for such a cause and his weakness was recognized. There was a strong movement among the German generals to end the war in the autumn of 1939, and the only figurehead they could agree on to replace Hitler was Göring. But the marshal's genuine awe of Hitler, as well as his equally genuine fear, made him a feeble prospect and he was never offered the uncompromising choice of serving Germany rather than Hitler.

On 6 October the Führer publicly offered peace to the West from the Reichstag, and three days later, against the advice of his chiefs of staff, decreed that the attack on France must take place in the autumn. For a number of reasons, including the weather and the Luftwaffe's disinclination to use concrete bombs, the offensive was successively postponed. Göring, in the intervals between systematically sacking Poland of raw materials, machinery, produce and the first million slave workers, conserved his military strength and forbade his air force to enter engagements across the French frontier. The French on their side, with the considerable military influence they still possessed, had persuaded the British not to bomb any German objective save naval units at sea or in fortified havens remote from civilian centres. Though the struggle at sea continued with a ferocity ignored by American journalists, if never by British widows, the war on land was undeniably phoney. The Royal Air Force Staff, in a dedication to final victory rather than the prospect of immediate glory, did not complain at the inactivity, as they had not cavilled at the respite bought by Munich. They blandly ignored Trenchard as if he were a senile gaffer. The principal thorn in their side was not the intellectual vigour of the founder of their Service, but the infuriating nagging of the man they had appointed Commander in Chief Fighter Command, the curmudgeon who took the air defence of Great Britain more seriously than they did.

Dowding had been promised 53 squadrons of fighters, with

1. Kelley, *22 Cells in Nuremberg*.

which he was to assume responsibility for the whole of the islands, including Scapa Flow, the naval base in the Orkneys north of John O'Groats. By September 1939 he had been given only 39 squadrons. Four squadrons of Hurricanes were immediately lopped from this total to provide the fighter nucleus of the Air Component of the British Expeditionary Force in France. In addition, Dowding was ordered to make six more squadrons mobile for future incorporation in the force in Europe. In the critical week during which, according to the Staff Appreciation of 1936, the knockout blow could be expected he found his reliable strength reduced to 29 squadrons, only as many as he had had at Munich. Moreover, after the subtraction of the ten France-orientated squadrons of Hurricanes, the aircraft then being produced in the greatest numbers, he had only six squadrons of Hurricanes (as against five at Munich) with ten squadrons of Spitfires and the remainder Blenheims, Gladiators, and the old Hinds and Gauntlets. With his basis of 29 squadrons Dowding was urged, after the Air Staff's appreciation of the first days' operations of the Luftwaffe in Poland, to impose on the general defence of Britain the particular defence not only of London, where the panic-blow against morale was expected to fall, but of the aircraft industry centres at Sheffield, Coventry, Derby and Bristol. These were widely-set strongpoints whose defence prohibited any fighter concentration in the forward areas of Britain on the south and east coasts.

Dowding promptly engaged in a running fight with the Air Staff in which he urged "absolute priority" for the build-up of Fighter Command in the defence of Britain *before* production should be frittered away on a tactical fighting force in France or on the strategic bomber force. His polemical campaign could have been viewed by the Air Staff – who were committed by their tradition and planning to the offensive even though political decisions forbade them to attack German territory – as partisan pleading for an individual command. The Air Staff had planned to win the war by holding the first onslaught and then progressing to the offensive. Their accepted responsibility to absorb the initial German attack implied that resistance would be sustained through fighters in France, as well as in the defence of Great Britain. But the drain of Hurricane fighters sent to France was the policy decision which Dowding most vigorously

c

opposed. He argued that the departure of the first squadrons required that all replacements would be made at the expense of Fighter Command reserves – reserves were then theoretically held at 225 per cent of frontline strength. He called the despatch of the Hurricanes the opening of a tap through which the entire output of Hurricanes would eventually be drained away. He brusquely declared that the primary threat to Britain came from German bombing and the primary task of the Royal Air Force was to multiply the home fighter forces to meet it. Only the Royal Navy, he asserted in a memorable crystallization of his views, shared with Fighter Command responsibility for "the continued existence of the nation and all its services".[1]

Dowding battled tenaciously, perhaps too energetically for the sensitivities of the Air Ministry and the Air Staff. His loyalty to the Service – though never his devotion to his country – became suspect in high places.[2] Certainly, in the first nine months of the war, his views were not accepted, even if the vigour of his advocacy was not forgotten. The best the Air Ministry would promise was that of every four new Hurricanes that came into service three would be allocated to Fighter Command and one to France; which, since he needed 24 squadrons to achieve his original mark, implied that eight fresh squadrons would be sent to France. (In the event, many more were sent abroad.) Aircraft production during the quiet autumn – they were by no means all Hurricanes – allowed Dowding a nominal force of 51 squadrons at home of which only 34 were fully trained, two were destined for Norway and ten were already earmarked for France. And until the Battle of France the air defence of Britain halted at that level, with Fighter Command's existing squadrons perfecting their training, with no fresh squadrons being formed, and with the certainty that, as

1. Denis Richards and Hilary St George Saunders, *Royal Air Force 1939–1945, The Fight at Odds*, H.M. Stationery Office, London, 1953.

2. There was a revealing repercussion of this when, in 1943, three years after his removal from Fighter Command, he was kicked upstairs to the House of Lords as a sop to the public awareness of the debt Britain owed him. He was formally warned by Lord Trenchard, the only other air force peer, that his support was required in the event of adverse criticism of the Royal Air Force in the House of Lords, and no unfavourable comments on the Service should be publicly made. (Collier, *Leader of The Few*, Jarrolds, London, 1957.)

soon as the whistle sounded in France, the tap draining the Aircraft Storage Units would be turned full on.

But first there was to come the startling demonstration of German air power in Norway.

From the first weeks of the war Churchill, as First Lord of the Admiralty, had been trying to persuade the War Cabinet to sanction the laying of sea mines in what he called "the covered way" – the 1,000-mile corridor in protected territorial waters between the west coast of Norway and its fringe of islands. Down this corridor, unmolested by the blockading British warships off the islands, steamed, for seven winter months in the year, the cargo vessels carrying the irreplaceable high-quality Swedish iron ore shipped from the Norwegian port of Narvik. Only a few days behind Churchill, German naval thought had turned to the desirability of taking over the whole of Norway. Admiral von Raeder, Chief of the Naval Staff, presented this view to Hitler on 10 October 1939, stressing, as he later recalled, "the disadvantages which an occupation of Norway by the British would have for us : the control of the approaches to the Baltic, the outflanking of our naval operations and of our air attacks on Britain, the end of our pressure on Sweden. I also stressed the advantages for us of the occupation of the Norwegian coast : outlet to the North Atlantic, no possibility of a British mine barrier . . ."[1]

Hitler gave the proposal his keen attention, and on 14 December, the day Quisling had been brought to Berlin, ordered the High Command to prepare the invasion of Norway. Keeping curiously in step, Churchill after prolonged thought circulated a paper to the Cabinet on 16 December advocating immediate mining of the protective channel in Norwegian waters and by implication raising the whole question of the spurious neutrality of Norway, which was positively damaging not only the Allies but the chance of aiding Finland, against whom Russia had recently declared war. Churchill could not gain the sanction of his colleagues for the mining, though the Cabinet did instruct the Chiefs of Staff to consider reaction to a German occupation of Norway. Throughout the winter there were occasional nibbles by the Anglo-French Supreme War Council at a plan to aid Finland, which for months had resolutely resisted the Russian

1. Quoted by Churchill, *The Gathering Storm.*

attack, by sending troops through Narvik. This, a clear violation of Norway's neutrality, would achieve the strategic aim of stopping the iron ore exports at the same time as the tactical and sentimental aim of helping a small country for which much sympathy was felt. No serious work was done on the project, although the Chiefs of Staff were instructed to prepare plans for a landing at Narvik.

Ironically, the person who took the project of an Allied advance into Norway more seriously than the British or the French was Hitler. On 20 February 1940 he decided finally on the occupation of Norway :

> ... because I am informed that the English intend to land there, and I want to be there before them. The occupation of Norway by the British would be a strategic turning movement which would lead them into the Baltic, where we have neither troops nor coastal fortifications. The success which we have gained in the east and which we are going to gain in the west would be annihilated because the enemy would find himself in a position to advance on Berlin and to break the backbone of our two fronts. In the second and third place the conquest of Norway will ensure the liberty of movement of our Fleet in the Bay of Wilhelmshaven [Heligoland Bay, protecting the approaches to Hamburg and Bremen], and will protect our imports of Swedish ore.[1]

The fact was that the British had no intention of advancing into Germany via the Baltic, for a reason which, very significantly, Hitler ignored. The British were fearful of German air power in that area and had no air organization either to support their own troops and ships or to take over captured landing grounds. However, Hitler had made the decision to take Norway, and on 1 March 1940 he determined to initiate the operation a few days before his projected D-Day for the invasion of France.

The prospect, indeed the certainty, of the plunge at France, including the German advance overrunning of Belgium and Holland, was bleakly known to Britain and the countries involved, though the King of the Belgians affected not to believe it and the Staffs of the two smaller countries made no co-operating defence with the Allies. In one of the most fantastic

1. Evidence of General von Falkenhorst, *Trial of the Major War Criminals.*

incidents of the war, Major Reinberger, a paratroop officer
serving on the staff of the 7th Air Division, was, on 10 January,
offered a lift to Bonn by a brother officer. This pilot, suffering
from a hangover and flying an unfamiliar Messerschmitt Bf
108, lost his way from Munster and force-landed in Belgium.
Reinberger was carrying in a yellow pigskin case the detailed
plans for the invasion of Belgium, Holland and France. And
he was not even carrying a box of matches to burn them. He
had to borrow matches from a peasant, and the delay resulted
in his arrest while most of the plans were still legible. The
German officers were taken into military custody and the plans
were incredulously perused. On 11 January Hitler was cautiously
told of the disclosure. In one of his most memorable carpet-
biting episodes he sent for Göring and acquainted him violently
with the full extent of his contempt for the Luftwaffe. The next
day was Göring's birthday, when the massive presents from
corporations and public bodies, long ordered or approved by
his adjutant, were to be bestowed. Kesselring, then commanding
Air Fleet One, based on Berlin, went to Carinhall to convey
greetings from the Luftwaffe. It was a momentous occasion. A
humiliated Göring thundered at the silent company his detailed
abuse of the Luftwaffe chiefs. He announced that General
Felmy, commanding Air Fleet Two in the west, had been
dismissed, and turned to Kesselring. "And you," he snarled,
"will take over Air Fleet Two – because I have nobody else."
Stumpff succeeded Kesselring in command of Air Fleet One,
and subsequently took over the newly created Air Fleet Five
with the direction of the air campaign from Norway.

From 3 April 1940 the British had reliable intelligence of the
embarkation of German troops intended to advance on Norway.
On 8 April, after six months of Allied vacillation, the Royal
Navy finally laid mines in Norwegian coastal waters off Narvik,
while tardy preparations were made for British and French
forces to land in Narvik, Stavanger, Bergen and Trondheim.
But the port of Narvik at that very moment was crammed with
supposedly empty German ore-ships, in reality fully laden with
supplies and ammunition to be used for the German take-over
the next day; and the port of Bergen was similarly infiltrated.
Very early on that next morning, 9 April, the British Chiefs of
Staff were roused with the news of the Scandinavian invasion,

and they met in committee at dawn. According to Major General Ismay, who was present :

The gathering that assembled in my office at 6.30 a.m. was not exactly inspiring. I had hoped that one or other of the Chiefs of Staff would have a plan of action, but as far as I can remember not a single constructive suggestion had been put forward by the time we had to break up the meeting and join the War Cabinet at 10 Downing Street.[1]

What had happened was a further exercise in the German art of blitzkrieg. At five in the morning of the 9th, German forces swept over the Danish land frontier; others came ashore from sea transports; the Luftwaffe flew a massive demonstration armada over Copenhagen; and within twelve hours Denmark was subjugated. Simultaneously with the conquest of Denmark, 150 Luftwaffe transports unloaded paratroops over the principal Norwegian airfields and 300 additional transports hurled in troops, supplies and flak-guns on the captured landing grounds, crash-landing many on the crowded airfields in the urgency to push in their support. Long-range reconnaissance aircraft and seaplanes maintained surveillance over the intensive movements of the strong British fleet which went into action against the entirety of the German naval forces. Within a day German fighter patrols and Stuka bombers were operating from Norwegian bases, providing cover for the ceaseless traffic of air and sea transports.

The contribution of the Luftwaffe can be gauged from one operation. Resisting an attempted assault on Oslo from the sea, one Norwegian minelayer, an armed whaler mounting a single gun, and strongly fortified shore batteries, repelled a German fleet led by three cruisers and crippled the heavy cruiser *Blücher* – drowning the senior officers of the German administration coming in to take over the capital. Immediately, under an alternative plan prepared against a naval failure, Oslo was, instead, captured by airborne troops with some assistance from soldiers carried in small craft. Apart from Narvik, which was taken by 2,000 troops conveyed in ten destroyers escorted by

1. *The Memoirs of General The Lord Ismay*, Heinemann, London, 1960. Possibly influenced by this reaction, Sir Samuel Hoare, Air Minister only from 5 April to 10 May 1940, unsuccessfully tried to get Trenchard appointed Chief of the Air Staff. Boyle, *Trenchard*.

the *Scharnhorst* and *Gneisenau,* the rest of Norway was won and maintained by German air power: by the capture of airfields leading to the occupation of ports, and the consequent landing of seaborne and airborne troops under the protection of 700 operational aircraft.

In an operation entirely different from the defeat of Poland, in bad weather and on battle grounds far from home, the Luftwaffe, using bombers, transports and seaplanes with the utmost flexibility, had demonstrated that a country could be laid open for occupation by ground forces although the attackers were faced by a superior naval power. The superbly equipped Luftwaffe had virtually replaced a navy in supporting an over-sea invasion of a country far more remote from German bases than Hitler intended England to be. General Jodl said of its performance in Norway: "The Air Force proved to be the decisive factor in the success of the operation. It bore the main burden of the fight against the enemy fleet, which was numerically far superior to our Navy."[1]

By contrast, the Royal Air Force performance in Norway was a débâcle of almost Polish proportions. Gallant men were sent in insufficient numbers, often in inadequate machines, un-supported by technical services, uncoordinated into any serious plan. How warmly, for instance, the pilots of 263 Squadron would have welcomed the *bumf* of a War Plan which Göring pretended to despise. It is informative to follow the fortunes of this squadron and of 46 Squadron during the Norway opera-tions, to appreciate the muddle and improvisation over which resolute pilots were still intermittently able to triumph.

Although the fate of Norway was effectually decided on the first day of the invasion, the country's dying struggles took two months, being prolonged by the infusion of a number of British and Allied military detachments. A fortnight after the first devitalizing blow the aircraft carrier H.M.S. *Glorious* was zig-zagging 180 miles west of Trondheim in central Norway, at 64 degrees north, in the latitude of Iceland. A heavy snowstorm was blowing, providing some cover against air reconnaissance or bombing and naval attack. On the carrier's flight deck

1. Jodl, *First Thoughts on a Landing in England, 12 July 1940,* quoted in Ronald Wheatley, *Operation Sea Lion,* Oxford University Press, 1958.

eighteen Gladiator biplanes of 263 Squadron were ranged for take-off. The aircraft were not Fleet Air Arm machines. They had been flown aboard by Fleet Air Arm pilots but their own Royal Air Force pilots had never yet made a take-off from a carrier. The *Glorious* had been specially recalled from the Mediterranean to convey the Gladiators because 3,000 green British troops, whose artillery had been sunk in passage, were trying to hold the main drive of the German army and the supporting Luftwaffe northwards from Oslo. The British troops had no air cover at all, the Royal Norwegian Air Force Gladiators having all been lost in combat or on the ground. They were resisting close coordination air attacks with rifles and machine-guns alone. No established airfields remained in Norwegian or British hands, but a small frozen lake fifty miles from the sea had been selected as a Royal Air Force landing ground; and the old Gladiators were the only aircraft which could operate from so cramped a "field".

The navigational equipment of the Gladiator squadron consisted of four maps shared between eighteen pilots. With this aid they were to take off from the carrier, fly through a snowstorm, locate a lake walled between mountains 230 miles away, and land on ice. With the aid of two Fleet Air Arm aircraft to navigate them there they did all this.

The runway on the frozen lake had been cleared of snow manually by two hundred civilian Norwegians from the mountain country around. But in the spring thaw the ice was beginning to melt at the shores of the lake. The Royal Air Force ground staff advance party, which arrived by sea thirty-six hours before the Gladiators landed, had to leave most of their servicing tools and equipment on the jetty at the port of Andalsnes, for they had no transport. They commandeered two Norwegian lorries to take essential gear up the valley. Their only other transport aid was one horse-drawn sledge, which took some supplies from the lake shore to the cleared runway. They had no petrol bowser for refuelling the aircraft. Their starter trolley batteries were not only uncharged, but had no acid.

The pilots of 263 Squadron landed their Gladiators in the flat night sunglow, found beds and turned in early. They were due to fly a dawn patrol at 3 a.m. In the morning, however, when they tried to start and taxi for take-off, the carburettors were frozen, the controls were frozen, and the wheels were welded to the runway by ice. At 4.45 a.m. two aircraft managed to take off and destroyed a Heinkel He 115 seaplane. At 7 a.m. flights of He 111s tried to come in and bomb the ice-bound Gladiators. Three Heinkels did get through and destroyed four of the Gladiators. The only opposition the British could offer was fire from two Oerlikon guns stoutly manned by a handful of sailors. As the morning wore on, some of the aircraft were started by using accumulators taken from Army lorries passing near the lake. But the machines could not stay up for ever, and when they came down there was only one armourer in the party for rearming them. The time spent on the ground was far too prolonged, and during that time the raiding bombers picked them off. By noon ten Gladiators had been destroyed on the ground and the bombers concentrated on breaking up the ice of the runway itself.

In spite of the almost continuous enemy action the operable Gladiators in the squadron took off on thirty sorties during the day and shot down several German aircraft. By night-time five fighters were left. They were flown to an even rougher emergency landing ground near the coast at Setnesmoen, near Andalsnes. Next day one of the five was lost when its engine failed and the remainder were destroyed by their own pilots before they were evacuated by sea transport to Scapa Flow. Within a fortnight 263 Squadron had again sailed in a carrier, the *Furious*, remounted with eighteen more Gladiators.

Central Norway had now been abandoned. The squadron was to support operations in the north near Narvik. The second two Gladiators to take off from *Furious*, at a visibility of 300 yards, hit a mountain wall. The first two returned, landed on the carrier, and with the rest later made Bardufoss landing ground in clearer weather. There, on Sunday, 26 May 1940 – the first of the "nine days" of Dunkirk – they were joined by 46 Squadron of Hurricanes. These two squadrons, fourteen Gladiators, fifteen Hurricanes, and some Fleet Air Arm machines were the sole air support for the assault on Narvik, the great iron-ore outlet for the German armament industry.

Narvik was destroyed, and the wrecking forces were withdrawn by sea. The squadrons covered the evacuation against recurring waves of Stukas and bombers escorted by Messerschmitt "Destroyers". The British aircraft frustrated every air attack on the warships and troop transports; they brought down nine enemy aircraft and suffered no loss.[1] All this fighting – in contrast to Fighter Command's decisive intervention at Dunkirk – took place in the air space over the Army and Royal Navy, who were wildly appreciative. Lieutenant General Claude Auchinleck, commanding the land forces, despatched enthusiastic thanks.

On 8 June the evacuation of the Royal Air Force was ordered. The surviving Gladiators flew on to the flight deck of the *Glorious* and were stowed below. The Hurricanes, which were thought quite incapable of a carrier landing without arrester hooks, were to be destroyed. But Hurricanes in June 1940 were precious machines. Squadron Leader K. B. Cross, commanding 46 Squadron, requested permission to fly his force aboard the *Glorious*. Every pilot volunteered to attempt this landing – there were now nearly twice as many surviving pilots as aircraft. Permission to land was given. Every Hurricane touched down successfully. The pilots went cheerfully to the wardroom. At four in the afternoon the hunting battle cruisers *Scharnhorst* and *Gneisenau* sighted the *Glorious* and her destroyer escorts *Ardent* and *Acasta*. The German admiral, seeing aircraft already on the flight deck – they were the Hurricanes, not torpedo bombers – hurriedly opened the action at a range of over 15 miles (27,000 yards), far beyond the scope of the carrier's 4-inch guns, and the *Glorious* was hit with an early salvo. By 5.40 the *Glorious* had sunk with the loss of 1,000 men. Among them were ten of the sixteen Gladiator pilots and all the Hurricane pilots except two. Squadrons 263 and 46 were erased from the Order of Battle [2]

1. Fleet anti-aircraft fire was highly effective, and the German aircraft destroyed in combat totalled fifty.

2. One month later 46 Squadron was back in the line under Squadron Leader J. R. MacLauchlan, committed to the Battle of Britain. In particular the squadron was in action during the great battles over London of 7 and 15 September 1940. Of the thirty-five pilots who flew for 46 Squadron in the Battle of Britain alone, twelve were killed in the battle itself, twelve were killed in action later, and eleven survived. This death-roll, which takes no account of the Norwegian disaster or of the pilots who joined the squadron after 31 October 1940, is a typical casualty list for a Battle of Britain squadron.

A few minutes later the *Ardent* went down. The *Acasta* steamed at full speed away from the enemy, making smoke from every float. The captain, Commander C. E. Glasfurd, R.N., had a message passed to all positions : "The least we can do is make a show. Good luck to you all." He span round into his own smoke, made straight for the battle cruisers, and came out of smoke to fire his port side torpedoes. He hit the *Scharnhorst* abreast her after turret. He came back into the smoke. As he emerged to fire his starboard torpedoes the *Acasta* was almost blown out of the water. Motionless and listing, she fired all her operable guns, even the remaining torpedoes, until she was silenced, and sank. But the German battle cruisers were hurt and not to be available for the tentative invasion of Britain.

The campaign in Norway was a climax for German air power. The Luftwaffe had triumphed, not only by its planning, its bravery and its skilfully applied force; the bedrock of its power lay on the ground in its superb technical support, service and maintenance. The plight of 263 Squadron with incomparable pilots operating an "air force" of eighteen old planes from an improvised ice field without even a bowser or battery acid, is the bitterest commentary on British muddle and – even conceding the enormous advantage accruing to the attacker who takes the initiative – the clearest endorsement of German technical organization. Nevertheless, the Germans had had to concede air superiority to the Royal Air Force over Narvik, and had suffered heavily.

German organization was flexible enough to be effective in three widely different campaigns; for the operations in Poland, Scandinavia and France – all genuine Blitzkriege – varied greatly in their method. There were four German air fleets when the war started. A fleet was stabilized at about 1,000 aircraft, but would be reinforced to 1,500 for a special effort. The fleet was a balanced force of operational aircraft : bombers, fighters and (an outstanding feature in the Luftwaffe) reconnaissance machines amounting to one-fifth of the total force. Within the air fleet all non-flying functions of the force were removed from the operational commanders and run by separate administrations responsible only to the air fleet's commander in chief. If these varied tasks had not been handled with the greatest skill the air fleets would have collapsed as integral bodies. That they were operated with undoubted efficiency is largely due to Göring and Milch and to a lesser extent to Kesselring, a highly competent, if unpleasant, man, who helped to lay the foundations of the structure from 1933.

Airfield construction, aircraft maintenance, airfield defence, supply and medical services, were all handled within the air fleet. But what gave the fleet its strike-power was control of transport, particularly of transport aircraft, combined with a highly efficient signals service deficient only at that time in radar aids. Transport aircraft were themselves used as mobile radio stations to maintain the link between base and advanced posts. Then the machines would return, load and advance, making the base units themselves mobile. The rich endowment of transport aircraft ensured that not only ground crews, but fuel, bombs, equipment and armament were, as the general rule, shifted rapidly by aircraft. Many of the difficulties of organizing swift mobility had been experienced and overcome in Spain. In particular the Luftwaffe had become adept in the occupation of advanced landing grounds and speedily converting them for operational aircraft by airfield construction teams who were often dealing with the craters and destruction caused by their own bombs a few days previously. This constant following-up of the army, for whom the Luftwaffe had already acted as bombardment artillery, was particularly valuable in the war in France: the operational aircraft had far shorter distances to fly to the battlefront, and individual machines could carry out many active sorties in a single day.

All this was an achievement, and Göring should not be robbed of the credit for it. In addition he had the endowment that every marshal needs at a crucial point in his career – the gift of luck. The cards fell absolutely right for Göring in the first nine months. The war was waged exactly as it suited the Luftwaffe. Its strength was applied in the most effective degree and its weakness was not put to the test. For there were faulty seams even in the box-structure conception of the air fleets. They did not show until after the swift wars were won against Poland, Denmark, Norway, Holland and Belgium and the long wars against France, Britain and Russia were attempted. It is true that the war in France coasted to victory on the momentum of the original blitzkrieg. But the long wars required not only guts and drill and panache, but intellectual and administrative stamina. They demanded progressive thought in terms of strategy and production. The channels of progress existed in the specialized inspectorates – for fighters, signals, army co-operation and almost a score of other Luftwaffe functions – which theoretically linked the thinking of Göring, his chief of staff and the *Führungsabteilung* (operational staff) to the boxes of the fleets or the industry. But, as functional channels, the inspectorates were veins rather than arteries. When bold thought needed to be applied to new bombing strategy, new fighter technique, and above all to the most effective new production, there was no great tide of change. The virtually unrejuvenated Luftwaffe tended to atrophy at its 1939 level. It was impossible for Göring to be simultaneously effective as Air Minister and Commander in Chief Luftwaffe. If a vigorous Air Ministry could have pressed the development of jet aircraft, missiles and a resurrected four-engined bomber – and if the ministry had been backed by inspectors of better calibre than the jumped-up aces and specialists who were appointed – the course of the war would have been changed. This was the most telling weakness in a fast-forced Luftwaffe, which had never developed the solid strength of talented middle-echelon officers. Yet the United States Army Air Forces were developed at a far greater pace and did not show the weakness so visibly. It is not mere Western bias to observe that the fundamental difference between the two organizations lay in the stultifying *Führerprinzip* of the Germans contrasted with the uncramped, initiating enterprise of the Americans, who took intelligent men from business and from the academies, gave them responsibility with their rank, and paid them to think and even to bully.

However, in May 1940, when Göring literally did not know what sort of war he would fight at the finish, there were few doubts and unlimited laurels.

For now it was the turn of France.

The dawns of April passed. The dawns of May began. A week was gone and there was no certain sign of action. Eight days, nine days. At 4.30 in the morning of 10 May the Luftwaffe struck simultaneously at fifty-two airfields in France, Belgium and Holland, and at communications, headquarter areas and

known ammunition dumps. In gigantic leap-frog procession the
air troops jumped for the back areas. With the timing of
experience, bombers pinpointed the flak batteries of base airfields while paratroops jumped and the German fighter aircraft
wheeled in protection above. German airborne troops glided
in to occupy four key points in the Belgian defences and crashed
to surprise landings behind the lines in Holland. The Luftwaffe
dive-bombers attacked strongpoints and bottlenecks, in some
cases timed only seconds before the German armour shot forward as an arrowhead of infantry and motorised divisions. The
medium bombers returning from their first sorties could see the
columns of their own ground troops speeding down the straight
roads of enemy territory.

The speed and thrust of the ground movements blew the
brains out of the defensive reactions of the opposing generals as
cleanly as if they had been hit by a dum-dum. Their thinking
had been schooled to the tortoise-pace of the previous war,
when the ruling factor had been the murderous potential
of defensive fire-power. In the past every break-through had
involved the attacker in a double weakness from the two flanks
he created in the bulge of the line; the farther he advanced, the
greater the weakness, because the fuel, food and ammunition
for the vanguard had to be brought through a corridor made
increasingly more vulnerable. But now, though flank defence
was not a negligible preoccupation, the supply corridor was in
the air. Now, the artillery was in the air. Mastery of the pace of
the battle had passed to the air arm. And the Luftwaffe responded like a spring. Kesselring switched with the finesse of
complete control from the bombing of vital centres to the
strategic support of advancing ground troops, through the destruction of Allied communications and troop concentrations.
He sent Stukas on demand against blocking artillery or well-
held bridgeheads, and diverted them again to bomb Allied
airfields until required elsewhere. He threw fighters in great
concentration over whichever battlefield needed them along a
250-mile front. He used transport aircraft like tube trains, and
bunched 20,000 paratroops and airborne soldiers round Rotterdam in a single day before foolishly obliterating it. But the
bombardment, although a military error of bad staff coordination and inaccurate timing – since the surrender of the city was

being negotiated – proved to be a benefit to the Luftwaffe. For the object of war is to destroy the will to resist : the very speed, efficiency and ruthlessness of the Luftwaffe, *as observed throughout the world*, was therefore an important German weapon. Although Rotterdam had not ceased to resist before the bombardment, France, Britain, Jugo-Slavia, Greece and Russia – and possibly even the United States of America – had *a little less will to resist* after the terror of Rotterdam. Göring himself summed up the viewpoint, even in captivity. "It was better to kill a few thousand in Rotterdam and bring the French to surrender than to prolong the war."[1] It is the argument for Hiroshima.

It cannot be denied that the campaign of May 1940 showed the Luftwaffe at the peak of its resilience and efficiency. Yet at Dunkirk the Luftwaffe failed to follow up its victorious progress. On 24 May Rundstedt's tanks were halted twenty miles from the sea, when the northern section of the French and the whole of the British and Belgian armies were almost encircled by the German thrust to the Channel. The order was rescinded two days later, but by that time a strong British rearguard had formed to keep the German armour from the beaches. The order to halt had a strange origin. Hitler had become bewildered by the speed of his own advance. He was nervous of a final battle in the country near Dunkirk where he feared his tanks might be lost. Göring offered to finish off the retreating armies with the Luftwaffe. Hitler was amenable because, for political reasons, he wanted France, not Flanders, to be the final battlefield, and – Rundstedt said afterwards – imagined that he would be able to persuade Great Britain to accept Germany's final victory if he spared the British Expeditionary Force.[2]

Göring's motives were plain but were based on faulty information from intelligence. He wanted the prestige of the public victory yet he both over-rated the Luftwaffe and under-rated the Royal Air Force. Since the defeat of Poland the phrase "Leave it to my Luftwaffe" had become almost a catchword on his lips. Judging by his air achievements against the British light bombers supporting the Allied armies, he had justification for continuing to use the slogan. But he knew little

1. Kelley, 22 *Cells in Nuremberg.*
2. Warlimont, *Inside Hitler's Headquarters.*

of Fighter Command and was indifferent to the level of exhaustion among his own forces. On the day Rundstedt's tanks were halted General von Kleist, commanding the Panzer Group of five tank divisions and three motorized infantry divisions, reported "For the first time, enemy air superiority".[1] Kesselring complained later :

The Commander in Chief Luftwaffe must have been sufficiently aware of the effect of almost three weeks of ceaseless operations on my airmen not to order an operation which could hardly be carried out successfully by fresh forces. I expounded the view very clearly to Göring and told him it could not be done even with the support of VIII Air Group. Colonel General Jeschonnek told me he thought the same, but that Göring for some incomprehensible reason had pledged himself to the Führer to wipe out the English with his Luftwaffe. . . . I pointed out to Göring that the modern Spitfires had recently appeared, making our air operations difficult and costly – and in the end it was the Spitfires which enabled the British and French to evacuate across the water.[2]

Responsible German airmen echoed Kesselring's account of the many sorties and steady losses endured by the tired Luftwaffe crews. Werner Kreipe, later an air general, at Dunkirk commanding a bomber wing of Dornier Do 17s, was in action against Spitfires for the first time on 28 May, and ran into unexpected disaster. He reported : "On one day, out of 27 planes in one *Gruppe*, eleven were put out of action. The days of easy victory were past. We had met the Royal Air Force head on."[3]

This respect for the British defence was not shared by all the British themselves. The Luftwaffe failed at Dunkirk. In the opinion of the Royal Navy and the British Expeditionary Force, Fighter Command also failed lamentably at Dunkirk. The sailor commanding the evacuation, Vice-Admiral B. H. Ramsay, a personal friend of Churchill, reported bluntly in his official despatch to the Admiralty the Navy's "disappointment and surprise at the seemingly puny efforts made to provide air protection during the height of this operation". The soldiers responded more directly by booing and even beating up members

1. *General Halder's Diary* for 24 May 1940.
2. Albert Kesselring, *Memoirs,* Kimber, London, 1953.
3. Richardson and Freidin, *The Fatal Decisions,* Joseph, London, 1956.

of the Royal Air Force[1] through the summer of 1940. The operations of Fighter Command in May 1940 were the responsibility of Air Chief Marshal Dowding, and the Commander in Chief's conduct in the face of the enemy must be examined.

On 10 May, the day Churchill became Prime Minister, the blitzkrieg opened. On the same day four Hurricane squadrons were hastily sent to France, to join the six already there. This left 43 squadrons of which two were the Gladiators and Hurricanes lost aboard the *Glorious*. On 13 May Dowding was required to send to France 32 more Hurricanes, weeded from squadrons. On 14 May – by which time the majority of the British supporting bomber force of Battles and Blenheims in France had been destroyed – the French line on the Meuse gave way and the French Prime Minister, Paul Reynaud, begged Churchill for 10 more squadrons of Hurricanes – which, with the loss of eight half-squadrons already under movement orders, would again put Fighter Command back to the level of Munich: some 25 squadrons, which Churchill mistakenly thought would be sufficient for Home Defence.

Dowding immediately wrote to the Vice Chief of Air Staff asking to be personally received by the War Cabinet. Permission for the interview was given and Dowding attended on the 15th. He took with him a chart showing the rate of losses in five days of the Hurricanes already engaged in France. After a stilted exposition to the Cabinet he felt that he had not convinced them. He walked from his place, moved round the table, and put the chart over Churchill's shoulders on to his blotter. He said shortly: "If the present rate of wastage continues for another fortnight, we shall have not a single Hurricane left in France *or* in this country."[2]

He made his point. He won the day. But only the day. On the 16th, within hours of the Cabinet agreement not to send the 10 squadrons, the Air Ministry told Dowding that the decision did not apply to the eight half-squadrons which he had obediently released on the 15th before the Cabinet interview,

---

1. Among Army lower ranks and naval ratings there was a class-conscious dislike for the Royal Air Force, whose lower ranks conspicuously wore neckties. Airmen were called "Brylcreem boys" after a hair-oil advertisement.
2. Collier, *Leader of the Few.*

and they must go. Worse followed. On the afternoon of the 16th Churchill flew to France, and in response to a strong appeal by General Gamelin, French Minister for War, telephoned London to summon a late-night Cabinet meeting, to be held in his absence, to consider the immediate despatch of six more squadrons of Hurricanes, which he recommended. Before midnight the War Cabinet had agreed to the partial extent that three squadrons at a time should operate from French bases for half-day spells, being relieved by three other squadrons and then flying back to England.

On the next day, the 17th, when the Commander in Chief was told of the latest order, the politicians were considering a letter which Dowding had already written to the Air Ministry on the 16th, before the final blow. It read, in part:[1]

I hope and believe that our Armies may yet be victorious in France and Belgium, but we have to face the possibility that they may be defeated.

In this case I presume that there is no one who will deny that England should fight on, even though the remainder of the Continent of Europe is dominated by the Germans.

For this purpose it is necessary to retain some minimum fighter strength in this country and I must request that the Air Council will inform me what they consider this minimum strength to be, in order that I may make my dispositions accordingly . . .

I must point out that within the last few days the equivalent of 10 Squadrons have been sent to France, that the Hurricane Squadrons remaining in this country are seriously depleted, and that the more squadrons which are sent to France the higher will be the wastage and the more insistent the demand for reinforcements.

I must therefore request that as a matter of paramount urgency the Air Ministry will consider and decide what level of strength is to be left to the Fighter Command for the defence of this country, and will assure me that when this level has been reached, not one fighter will be sent across the Channel however urgent and insistent the appeals for help may be.

I believe that, if an adequate fighter force is kept in this country, if the fleet remains in being, and if the Home Forces are suitably organized to resist invasion, we should be able to carry on the war single-handed for some time, if not indefinitely. But, if the Home

1. Crown Copyright.

Defence Force is drained away in desperate attempts to remedy the situation in France, defeat in France will involve the final, complete and irremediable defeat of this country.

As a direct result of that letter and the confirmation of the worsening situation in France, Churchill, as Minister of Defence, ordered on 19 May that no further fighter squadrons should be sent to France, and that all but three of those already there should return to fight from English bases. This was the disposition of the fighter forces when the Dunkirk evacuation started. The total loss of Hurricanes alone after ten days' fighting had been 195 out of 261, of which 75 were destroyed and 120 damaged and later abandoned in the retreat.

The Royal Air Force fought the cover battle for Dunkirk with bombers in action against the German troops and artillery, as well as with the fighters. But it is the use of the fighters that has since been severely criticized. The facts of the defence operation are simple : the area behind Dunkirk was beyond the range of British radar interception and therefore no advance knowledge of German air movements was possible. The formal remedy for this was the standing patrol of fighters waiting in the air for action like duty policemen. On the first day of the evacuation, 27 May, Fighter Command put up 25 successive patrols of single-squadron strength. The solitary squadrons proved too weak for the enemy. Next day the strength of the patrols was doubled. Since Dowding initially limited the forces engaged to those which could operate from south-eastern airfields in England, this meant that there were gaps between the patrols. But the effect of the harassing and destruction of the enemy was more marked. On the 29th the strength of the patrols was raised to four squadrons, inevitably with dangerously long intervals between the patrols, since only 16 squadrons were available. During those intervals much damaging bombing and strafing was achieved against the evacuation fleet, two out of five raids managing to get through. The weather on 30 May was unfavourable, but on 31 May (the day when most troops were evacuated) the Royal Air Force held back the Luftwaffe on a fine and clear day. On 1 June the quadruple-squadron patrols were again put up to engage the bombers. Again there were tragic incidents in the intervals between the patrols as Luftwaffe bombers found their marks. By 2 June heavy German

artillery fire caused the suspension of evacuation during full daylight and Fighter Command patrolled only at dawn and dusk.
Dowding's total loss during the evacuation was over 100 aircraft
– if the Battle of France is included the overall fighter loss was
386 Hurricanes and 67 Spitfires. The Luftwaffe losses over
Dunkirk exceeded those of Fighter Command.

Well-meaning apologists for Dowding say that in the Dunkirk
operation he did as well as he could with Fighter Command. In
fact he could have done better : that he did not is the enigmatic
measure of his greatness. With a first-line force of about 600
aircraft he flew an average of 300 sorties a day. Even considering the small number of airfields within good operating distance
of Dunkirk, that was not an all-out effort, although Dowding
worked the squadrons whom he did put up until they were, in
his words, "almost at cracking point".[1] Over the month he
rotated his squadrons to give Air Vice Marshal Keith Park,
fighting the immediate battle in the south-east, a replenishment
of force.

What Dowding did *not* do was to reach out for his squadrons
in the North and the Midlands, committing them to this
tactical action which would have left the country naked.[2]

He refused to do it at Dunkirk, just as he refused during the
Battle of Britain – and the very fact that the Luftwaffe *wanted*
him then to engage all his forces is a vindication of his reluctance. Two hundred and thirty-five vessels – 142 of them
were "little ships" – were destroyed during the Dunkirk evacuation. Some of the bleeding, retching men who were lost then
were, in very clear truth, sacrificed by Dowding. But they were
sacrified for the defence of Britain, along with a hundred of his
pilots. The rate of pilot loss in May and June was insupportably
high because the combats took place over territory from which
survivors could not be rescued. Soldiers, sailors and airmen died
– but not *unnecessary* deaths. Dowding saw that this was not
the final battle of the campaign, and it was at the final

1. Collier, *The Defence of the United Kingdom* (*History of the
Second World War*).

2. Every fighter squadron except three based in Scotland saw action
during the Battle of France, but in rotation, as Dowding relieved and
rested his forces. Sixteen squadrons at a time fought in No. 11 Group
under Air Vice Marshal Keith Park.

battle that Fighter Command were to be most needed. Churchill recognized the continuation of the war as a general axiom. But he did not then see Fighter Command as the supreme factor. A week after the 330,000 survivors were home – to denigrate the Royal Air Force.[1] – Churchill saw the facts of existence with Dowding's eyes and said so nobly, although in deep distress. It was 11 June. He had flown to France for the last of his meetings with the French leaders. With Churchill were Anthony Eden, Secretary for War, General Sir John Dill, the new Chief of the Imperial General Staff, and Churchill's military secretary, Major General Ismay. General Weygand gave a desperate account of the condition of the French Army and declared that only air support from British fighter squadrons would save the day. He reiterated the old strategic maxim of concentrating all available forces at the decisive point. "Here is the decisive point," he said. "Now is the decisive moment. The British ought not to keep a single fighter in England, they should all be sent to France."

Ismay gazed at Churchill, awaiting his response. He wrote later :

There was an awful pause, and my heart stood still. The Prime Minister and the Cabinet had only recently been solemnly warned by Air Chief Marshal Dowding, Commander in Chief Fighter Command, that if any more fighter squadrons were sent to France, he could not guarantee the defence of the British Isles. That was clear enough. It was a terrible position for a man like Churchill – generous, warm-hearted, courageous with ever a pronounced streak of optimism, and I was terrified lest he might be so moved as to promise that he would ask his Government to send some additional

1. Shortly after 4 a.m. on 29 May 1940 Flying Officer Alan Deere, then flying Spitfires in 54 Squadron, was shot down between Dunkirk and Ostend while attacking a Dornier 17. He escaped from his burning machine with a wound over the eye and eventually boarded one of the evacuation destroyers. "I was escorted below decks to the tiny wardroom, already crowded with Army officers. A stony silence greeted the announcement that I was an R.A.F. officer. This caused me to ask of a young gunner Lieutenant nearby, 'Why so friendly, what have the R.A.F. done?' 'That's just it,' he replied, 'What have they done?' " Contrast this reaction to the reception in the wardroom of H.M.S. *Glorious* of the pilots of 46 Squadron, before they died with their hosts. (Group Captain Alan C. Deere, *Nine Lives*, Hodder & Stoughton, London, 1959.)

air support. Thank God my fears were groundless. After a pause and speaking very slowly, he said, "This is not the decisive point. This is not the decisive moment. The decisive moment will come when Hitler hurls his Luftwaffe against Britain. If we can keep command of the air over our own island – that is all I ask – we will win it all back for you."[1]

Churchill himself stated in his chronicle that his reply was given "in accordance with the Cabinet decision taken in the presence of Air Chief Marshal Dowding, whom I had brought specially to a Cabinet meeting".[2]

Dowding had always shown this profound foresight, if never the electrifying inspiration of his leader. Before Churchill called on the British to brace themselves for their finest hour, Dowding had declared, without flourish "I presume that there is no one who will deny that England should fight on, even though the remainder of the Continent of Europe is dominated by the Germans." Before Churchill could pay his tribute to The Few Dowding had claimed, with a noticeable absence of bias, "Only the Royal Navy and Fighter Command share responsibility for the continued existence of the nation and all its services." Before a sorrowful Churchill had declared to Weygand "This is not the decisive moment", Dowding's pugnacious, bitter and cranky presentation of his conception of the defence of Great Britain had done something to ensure that the decisive moment was delayed until he could more adequately take the strain.

"We should be able," Dowding had claimed, "to carry on the war single-handed." It was with this conviction that he accepted the Battle of Britain.

1. *The Memoirs of General The Lord Ismay,* Heinemann, London, 1960.
2. Winston S. Churchill, *Their Finest Hour,* Cassell, London, 1949.

CHAPTER FIVE

THE RELUCTANT RAVISHER

Before we begin to attack a whole people we must break their strength. This can be done only by time and the expense which always attends the operations of a large army; but if the object is sufficiently great, which for many reasons it appears to be, I put the expense out of the question, and consider only the means of bringing such a body of troops upon that point as will achieve our object.

THE DUKE OF WELLINGTON

On the evening of 7 September 1940 the British war leaders agreed that the Battle of Britain had sharpened into the all-out battle *for* Britain by direct land assault. The British Chiefs of Staff, meeting first in committee at Storey's Gate near Westminster Abbey and later with the War Cabinet in 10 Downing Street, ordered the issue of the code word *Cromwell*: interpretation – Invasion of Great Britain, troops to take up battle stations immediately. The order was issued as the red sun, seeming to hover over bombed Buckingham Palace, set straight along Downing Street, yet was outshone by a fiercer red glow from the east in the sky over the Thames. This was the reflection of a thousand major fires caused in the last two hours by the bombarding Luftwaffe. The fires were target indicators for the next wave of bombers, now approaching. Darkness never fell over London that night, neither in Downing Street, Whitehall, nor Keetons Road, Dockland.

Keetons Road is a street off Jamaica Road in Bermondsey, within smell of the Upper Pool of the Thames and less than a mile from Tower Bridge. Keetons Road had a school, a three-storeyed citadel which towered, like many schools in East London, as a comparative peak among the low and shoddy terraces of Dockland, though still dwarfed by the high reef of warehouses and the *chevaux-de-frises* of cranes on the curving river front itself. At a little before midnight on Saturday, 7 September, Police Sergeant Stevens with a brother police officer from Tower Bridge station was gingerly picking his way into the debris of Keetons Road School, from which smoke and dust clouds eddied against the copper glow of the sky. Past the grotesque bodies blown into the playground, and skirting a rough stretcher on which a fireman lay with his face skinned, Stevens clambered into the school with his companion. The policeman stooped down to pick up an object rather than tread on it. It was a small thing which, at the first touch, he thought was part of a loaf of bread. Then he perceived that it was the soft trunk of a very young baby. He put the white flesh down and the two officers went out of the school for a moment. Outside, as if in the sequence of a dream, they saw some of the bodies they had believed to be dead stir, shudder and even stand up; but most of them were rigid. The policemen, who had been working amid unaccustomed horror for six hours, sat dully watching the bodies move against the red glow overall. Then they went back into the school to bring out the living. The little baby's trunk lay awaiting the shovels, undistinguishable amongst the masonry in its drifting coverlet of soft, dense dust. If someone in the daylight demolition squad were to find a recognizable head it would be placed in the green mortuary van and some guess at its identification would be hazarded. At the least it would be entered in the Register of Civilian Dead as BABY, Bermondsey/7.9.40. Then it would be buried in the trench cut in the flat suburban cemetery, remote from the warm bedbugs and jollity of old Bermondsey.

The identifiable bodies in the space in which Baby, Bermondsey/7.9.40 was found were of people who had lived in Rotherhithe, a few hundred yards to the east. This was the part they called in Bermondsey "Down Town" – an isolated settlement based on short cross-streets ranged like a snake's ribs on the curving spine of Rotherhithe Street. It ran along the rim of the river, cut off from populous Bermondsey by the square mile of the Surrey Commercial Docks. Down Town, extending its mouldy slums from Odessa Street through Acorn Walk to Cathay Street and the inevitable Paradise Street, was a village of a thousand souls. On the Luftwaffe maps it made one serif of what the briefing officers described to their bomber crews as the *U-bend* of the Thames starting at Limehouse Reach. The U-bend pinpointed the vital docks and basins that ensured supplies to one-third of the British population throughout London and the South-East: Victoria Dock, East India Docks, West India Docks, Millwall and Surrey Commercial. The district called Down Town bounded the most concentrated target of all – the ancient lacing of basins comprising Canada Dock, Quebeck Dock, Greenland Dock, Norway Dock, Russia Dock, Albion Dock, Stave Dock, Lavender Dock, and Lady Dock. Towards this area Colonel General Johannes Fink had personally led his *Kampfgeschwader 2* on Saturday, 7 September while the afternoon sun was still high.

Fink's command was a bomber force of 81 Dornier Do17zs, which was itself the spearhead of 372 bombers of Air Fleet Two, closely screened by Messerschmitt Bf 109 fighters and Messerschmitt Bf 110 twin-engined "Destroyers", bringing the total German forces engaged to nearly 1,000 aircraft. This was the first mass raid of the war on London, a daylight attack which the Germans sensed was historic, and Göring afterwards said so several times. Fink took off from Cambrai and formed up his group, with Werner Kreipe leading one wing, over Calais. Immediately below them, near Fink's own forward command post on the cliffs of Cap Gris Nez, not only his Fleet Commander Kesselring, but the Commander in Chief of the Luftwaffe, Göring himself, watched with pride and bombast the coalescing of the formations. In this company, and on such an occasion of mass effort, Kesselring displayed his usual excitable energy but did not play the drill-square martinet unduly. At other times, he admitted, "If I saw an untidy formation I would radio an order for it to return to base." On this day, Göring himself was in personal command of the operation: he was actually to stay at the front for ten days, from 7 September until he experienced Hitler's chilly reaction to the great Luftwaffe defeat of 15 September.

Cap Gris Nez was swarming with sponsored spectators, including radio reporters who were broadcasting running commentaries on the great assault. In the thrill of the moment Göring snatched a microphone from a reporter and addressed the distant German public sitting by their sets in the Reich:

This is a historic moment. After the insolent attacks of British

bombers on Berlin the Führer has ordered a great attack on London to exact vengeance. I, Göring, have personally taken charge of the operation, and I am now listening to the roar of my Luftwaffe as its planes fly across the Channel in broad daylight on an epic mission when, for the first time, it thrusts direct into the heart of the enemy.

The German marshals – some of the twelve generals who had been promoted in July – turned away from what Kesselring called, in defeat, "an exhibition distasteful to me both as a man and a soldier". It was an odd attempt to emulate English coolness. Kesselring was notorious for the energy with which he danced on the turf and waved his men on – besides occasionally calling them back! – as they headed for England.

The bombers droned to the north-west. Fink's bomber group, in the van, was abandoned by the Messerschmitts over Sevenoaks as the German fighters reached the end of their short range. The earlier manoeuvres of convoy formation had burned fuel. Few Spitfires seemed to have been directed to combat Fink's group. The bombers were substantially unshaken by the initial attacks, and by the moderate anti-aircraft fire over London. The target was wide open. They came in keeping good formation at 16,000 feet. Their bomb-bay doors opened, and they struck the London docks heavily and repeatedly. Among the sufferers from what Kesselring called "the laws of dispersion" were the Down Town community which included Baby, Bermondsey/7.9.40, still alive at tea-time. At first the survivors had nowhere to go. But when the All Clear sounded at 7 p.m. they gathered what blankets and food they could rescue from the ruins of their houses and moved into the shelters below the warehouses on the wharfs. Enormous fires were now burning, principally in this area from acres of stacked timber, and elsewhere from oil dumps and gasworks.

Within an hour the sirens signalled a fresh Alert as the defence logged the approach of Göring's second wave, leaders of a force of 247 bombers which were to sail an undisputed course over London for the next seven hours. The beacons of burning Dockland were all the navigational aid they needed. The timber fire in Quebeck Yard, the biggest conflagration ever known in modern London, had pulled in 300 fire-engines over the three narrow swing-bridges leading to the Surrey Docks, but 300 pumps with unlimited water could not hold back the volcanic destruction. The heat from the heart of it singed the paint of fire-floats trying to slip past under the lee of the Limehouse shore nearly a quarter of a mile away. One of three ammunition ships in the area had already blown up. A lighter carrying hundreds of tons of alcohol, and others stacked with timber, had ignited : all that could be done was to hack their hawsers and send them drifting, blazing, into the river. High explosive bombs tossed into the central fire sent blazing baulks of timber arching on to ships and warehouses. A parachute mine exploded in the storage wells of a paint factory. Soon the roofs of the great Globe Wharf warehouse were blazing; beneath the warehouse sheltered many of the Down Town survivors.[1]

Police and wardens tried to organize evacuation of the whole area. Two of the three narrow approaches to the docks were impassable through bombing or the blistering fires, but the last escape route was still open. Hustling the aged, clutching babies, tearing their pockets to cram in the staple sustenance, tins of condensed milk, the Londoners were led by their wardens through grids of jagged window-frames and over smoking brick to the broader sanctuary of Jamaica Road. They scuttled without dignity, as grey as rats in the degrading pelt of the bomb-dust and wood-ash. The sick and wounded were brought out in the Council's garbage vans. Those who could stand were pushed into Keetons Road School, and standing was the only posture possible, for the school was already full. It had no relief equipment. It was not scheduled as a shelter or reception centre. It was a natural near-miss for bombing runs aimed impartially at Peak Frean's food factory or the Wapping Basin of the London Docks. At ten o'clock the doors of Keetons Road School were shut. By eleven many of the Bermondsey refugees were dead. Baby, Bermondsey/7.9.40 lay in pieces in the rubble.

> The economy of Heaven is dark
> And wisest clerks have missed the mark
> Why human buds like this should fall.

If the soul of that perplexed child was constrained to haunt the corridors of history, tapping on doors that might be opened to give an individual admission of responsibility for its fate, it is

1. Constantine Fitzgibbon, *The Blitz*, London, 1957.

haunting history still. No one has opened his door. Yet the dead baby of London represented just about as far as Hitler would voluntarily go, the extreme of his intentions for the subjugation of Britain. The child was a regrettable casualty of air bombardment. Hitler might be forced to, *but he did not want to*, kill British civilians in land warfare. The million heavily armed men poised on the north-west coast of Europe, the hundreds of invasion barges and the bunkers full of files concerned with the occupation of Great Britain – all these were real enough. They were no bluff. But they were part of an operation in which Hitler had no heart, and which he would undertake only with the greatest reluctance. Hitler did not relish the invasion of Britain as an operation. He had never included it in his simple grand strategy, and he was for long confident that his policy for Britain could be continued by other means than subjugation.

The baby was a victim, by dispersion, of a strategic bombing attack : a legitimate casualty by all the rules of war. Hitler was making a formal strategic blow when he struck at the London docks, whether he meant to hit them – as he did – or whether he did not mind if he missed – as he declared when he roared that he was conducting a reprisal for Churchill's terror-attacks. Hitler was a man who knew little about the theory of air warfare, yet in his preliminary war plans, while unhurried by the pressure of reverses, he used his air arm correctly. He was a "strategic bombing man" in his instinctive thinking, and, through his broad instructions to Göring, a far more successful one than any other air leader in the first years of the war. Indeed, he used air bombardment in every one of its then accepted roles :

1. The *auxiliary* use of air power in the furtherance of a "conventional" battle. In the Battle for France he used bombers *tactically* as artillery at Sedan, and *strategically* to destroy the relevant French railways and so prevent the transport of troops from the Maginot Line to oppose the break-through at Sedan.

2. The *temporarily independent* use of air power as a contribution to a battle strictly decided in the air, though needing the follow-up of the other Service arms for final victory. In the

Battle of Britain he used bombers *tactically* to try to destroy Fighter Command's aircraft on the ground, and *strategically* against a Spitfire factory near Southampton or the Rolls-Royce engine factory at Derby.

3. The *fully independent* use of air power as a means of procuring outright the object of the war – forcing the surrender of the enemy by negating his ability or will to resist. Hitler's targets in his independent strategic bomber offensive against Britain were :

(a) the sources of industrial production – both of military armaments and the manufactured or refined articles that were necessary to the means of life of the population;

(b) the actual means of life of the country – food and shelter (the food could be in transit from abroad or within the country, or in depots in the country);

(c) the main arteries of a nation, which, if cut for long, would reduce an intricately organized community to a dislocated shambles lacking water, fuel, communication or sewerage;

(d) the theoretically simple sapping of the will to resist by inducing sheer paralysing terror among the population so that in their shock they would become passive;

(e) the elimination of a nation's leadership by physical or psychological means.

The baby who died in Bermondsey, born in an explosive area of essential production, scorched by the furnace of a burning Rotherhithe grain store, deprived even of water to mix with its tinned milk, inarticulately sharing the terror of its mother, and finally extinguished, represented an attempt at all these targets except the last. Hitler's fifth aim was generally (though inadequately) pursued by the psychological warfare of such agencies as the German clandestine radio; although there is no doubt that the bombs directed at Buckingham Palace (as at Hitler's Chancellery) were deliberately, if opportunistically, aimed, and if Göring could have known Churchill's precise whereabouts at a given moment he would have gone for him.

Göring, unique among all the marshals, though he only intermittently assumed intimate control of the Luftwaffe, seriously attempted for one period victory through air power alone by the conduct of a strategic bombing offensive, and this accorded perfectly with Hitler's aim.[1] Hitler had no urgent wish to become the Conqueror of Britain in the context of William of Normandy.

He would corrode the country, but not ravish it. In the event of the armistice which he strove for – rather than a grovelling capitulation – it was unlikely that he would ride in triumph through the capital. It is a detail pregnant of speculation that he not only hated the sea, but there is no record of his ever having crossed the sea in his life.

Hitler wanted to force Britain to his will by blockade and the fear of invasion, and not by invasion. The nation was Germany's only enemy for a year after the fall of France, and not only the sole enemy but the principal enemy yet encountered. As early as November 1939 Hitler declared: "England has shown herself to be the animator of the fighting spirit of the enemy, and the leading enemy power."[2] The Naval High Command referred expressly to England as "the main enemy". Just before the evacuation from Dunkirk – at a time, that is, when the German leaders believed that the British Expeditionary Force of 300,000 men would be captured or killed – Hitler's directives for *naval and air* attacks on Britain in the further conduct of the war were warmly welcomed by the Naval Staff precisely because they indicated clearly "the object of this war, the annihilation of the main enemy, England. The way to her defeat lies through the destruction of France, her continental sword, to the starvation of the British island empire and to the ruination of her economic fighting power."[3]

Hitler wanted to destroy Churchill, but not Great Britain, and above all not the British Empire. On 18 June 1940 he met Mussolini with Count Ciano, the Italian Foreign Minister, to accept the French surrender. Ciano noted in his diary Ribbentrop's assurance that the Führer "does not desire the destruction of the British Empire" and Hitler's own expressed

1. But in 1940 the German Naval Staff frequently complained of Göring's preoccupation with an independent bombing offensive. (Wheatley, *Operation Sea Lion*.)

2. H. R. Trevor-Roper (ed.), *Hitler's War Directives 1939–1945*, Sidgwick & Jackson, London, 1964. Directive No. 9, Berlin, 29 November 1939.

3. German Naval Staff (Operations Division) War Diary, 27 May 1940, quoted Wheatley, *Operation Sea Lion*.

view that the Empire was "even today, an important factor in world equilibrium". Three weeks later, on 13 July, Hitler discussed British stubbornness about a settlement with his Chief of Staff Army, General Franz Halder, and General Walther von Brauchitsch. Halder recorded :

> The Führer is very much preoccupied with the problem of why England does not wish to come to terms. Like us, he sees the answer in the fact that England still places some hope in Russia. He therefore expects that he will have to compel her by force to make peace. But he does not do this willingly. Reason : if we crush England by force of arms, the British Empire will fall to pieces. But this would be of no advantage to Germany. We should spill German blood only in order that Japan, America and others might benefit.[1]

Even towards the end of the Battle of Britain, on 26 September, in a private interview with the fighter pilot Adolf Galland after the award of a decoration, Hitler declared with the utmost mildness to Galland that he had "the greatest respect for the Anglo-Saxon race. It had made it all the more difficult for him, he said, to decide on waging this life-and-death struggle which could only end with that total destruction of one or the other. He called it a world historical tragedy and said that it had been impossible to avoid this war, despite all his sincere and desperate attempts. If we won the war, a vacuum would be created by the destruction of Great Britain which it would be impossible to fill."[2]

Because he did not wish to create this vacuum Hitler had long relied on reducing Britain to tractability by blockade – which included the air attack on sea traffic and the bombing of food repositories. When he reviewed his plans for the future wars on 23 May 1939, having quickly polished off Poland on paper he turned to the conquest of Holland, Belgium and northern France as the preliminary to the attack on Britain. He emphasized then that it was no longer necessary to invade her in order to defeat her, it was only necessary to cut her lines of ocean supply. Once the Channel coastline had been gained, he declared, "Britain can then be blockaded from western

1. General Halder's Diary, 13 July 1940.
2. Adolf Galland, *The First and the Last,* Methuen, London, 1955.

France at close quarters by the Luftwaffe, while the Navy with their submarines can extend the range of the blockade."[1]

By November 1939, though aware that the depletion of armaments caused by the Polish campaign was not yet restored, Hitler was still relying on a naval and air war "within the foreseeable future" against Britain's ports, shipping, storage depots and industries. His advisers were propounding a strategic air attack on morale. The emphasis on terror was gradually heightened. By 30 June 1940 Hitler was studying the written advice of his personal military adviser, General Alfred Jodl, which recommended air attacks on imports at sea and in the ports, and on supply depots, and went on: "Allied with propaganda and periodic terror attacks, announced as reprisals, this increasing weakening of the system of food supply will *paralyse and finally break the will of the people to resist, and thereby force the Government to capitulate.*"[2] (Jodl's emphasis.)

Jodl advised that a token landing would probably be necessary at about the end of August (in only two months' time) after the total collapse in morale, but that this would not be a contested invasion. After considering this paper, Hitler ordered, on 2 July, Staff studies on the project "on the basis that the invasion is still only a plan, and has not yet been decided upon". Five days later Field Marshal Wilhelm Keitel, nominally Chief of the High Command of the Armed Forces, actually Hitler's military yes-man, revealed Hitler's thinking to Ciano.[3]

The landing was considered "extremely difficult" and it seemed "easier, and in any event necessary", to wage a large-scale bombing offensive in spite of the power of the Royal Air Force.

Hitler's teetering reluctance to commit himself to invasion is clear in the extraordinary directive No. 16 he signed on 16 July 1940 headed "Preparations for a Landing Operation against England".

It began with the customary military statement of the object of the exercise:

1. Document of 23 May 1939, *Trial of the Major War Criminals*, vol. 37.

2. Jodl, *Continuation of the War Against England*, Document of 30 June 1940, *Trial of the Major War Criminals*.

3. Malcolm Muggeridge (ed.), *Ciano's Diplomatic Papers*, Odhams, London, 1948.

D

Since England, in spite of her hopeless military situation, has so far shown no sign of willingness to come to any compromise, I have decided to begin to prepare for, and if necessary to carry out, landing operation against England.

The aim of this operation is to eliminate The English Mother-land [*das englische Mutterland*] as a base from which the war against Germany can be continued, and, if it should be necessary, the country will be occupied completely.

This statement is amazing as a military document of Hitler because it contains at least five qualifications in ifs and buts to underline the uncertainty of his resolve. The Directive of 9 October 1939 on the invasion of Holland, Luxemburg, Belgium and North-West France began with a stout trumpet-blast :

The purpose of this offensive will be to defeat as much as possible of the French Army and of the forces of the Allies fighting on their side, and at the same time to win as much territory as possible in Holland, Belgium and Northern France to serve as a base for the successful prosecution of the air and sea war against England and as a wide protective area for the economically vital Ruhr.[1]

In all other directives by Hitler outlining the opening of a war – and there were many – a note of strong resolution is struck.

A striking phrase in the July directive is the use of the words "the English Motherland" to denote Great Britain. It would be an interesting psychological speculation to determine the difference in significance to Hitler of the words Motherland and Fatherland; the point may be considered that Hitler was still thinking of Britain as the Motherland of the Empire, and still regretting the apparently necessary collapse of that empire. And, continuing this thought, Hitler made a "last appeal" in the Kroll Opera House on 19 July on the occasion when he made Göring the Reich Marshal of the Greater German Reich and twelve generals field marshals. He called "once more to reason and to common sense, in Great Britain as much as else-where. I consider myself in a position to make this appeal since I am not the vanquished seeking favours, but the victor speaking the name of reason. I can see no reason why this war must go

1. Trevor-Roper, *Hitler's War Directives*.

on. . . . Mr Churchill ought for once to believe me when I say that a great Empire will be destroyed – an Empire which it was never my intention to destroy or even to harm."[1] Though the appeal was ridiculed in Britain, it did not represent a notable bluff on Hitler's part, though possibly it denoted faulty intelligence. Hitler believed at that time that strong personalities, including the veteran former Prime Minister, Lloyd George, and the Duke of Windsor were urging on King George VI a change of Government that should effect a negotiated settlement.

Although, therefore, the invasion of Britain was planned with a certain prudence, Hitler showed an astonishing reluctance to push it ahead. The most that could then be said was, in Halder's words, that it was "not impossible that we shall be compelled to land in England". There was certainly nothing final in Hitler's words "I have decided to begin to prepare for, and if necessary to carry out, a landing operation against England." Two days after his "last appeal" Hitler told Brauchitsch, Raeder and Jeschonnek, representing the Army, the Navy and the Air Force, that if Britain did not accept his offer of peace he had not yet decided what should be done. On the last day of July, when the British believed that the Battle of Britain was in full swing, he made a firmer decision: "The air war will start now. . . . If the results of the air war are not satisfactory, [invasion] preparations will be stopped. But if we deduce that the English are being overcome and the air war promises to be effective, we shall attack." He went on to consider Russia and America, in whose potential he believed Britain still rested hope. If there was no invasion, he declared, Germany must destroy Russia. Halder noted his conclusion: *If Russia is smashed, Britain's last hope will be shattered.*" Therefore, Hitler said, he would attack Russia in the spring of 1941 since it was no longer possible to do so in 1940.

Again the determination against Russia is clear, the purpose against Britain is irresolute. Hitler really said "If I do not invade Britain I shall attack Russia, and I am attacking Russia." In the middle of August, the time when, according to his directive, the invasion should be ready to start, he told Grand Admiral Erich Raeder that he would invade "only as a last resort, if Britain cannot be made to sue for peace in any other way".

1. Keesing's Contemporary Archives, 1940.

Three weeks after that, on 6 September, Raeder noted "The Führer's decision to land in England is still by no means settled, as he is firmly convinced that Britain's defeat will be achieved even without the landing."[1]

On 13 September he declared over luncheon in Berlin with Brauchitsch, Göring and Jodl that he had no intention of running the risk of invasion. Next day, over tea, he declared that an invasion would be the shortest course to eliminate Britain and he would invade, but not yet. On the 17th he formally postponed a decision on invasion. On the 18th he ordered that the invasion barges and transports should be dispersed – inconspicuously, he hoped. On 12 October he issued a directive abandoning the invasion for 1940. Such monumental irresolution could not escape notice and comment among his marshals. Deploring the "planlessness" of the invasion operation, Kesselring said : "Anyone who knew the scrupulous care with which Hitler checked preparations before every other campaign and prognosticated the probable outcome must arrive at the conclusion from his hesitancy in the case of England that he wished to avoid an open conflict with her."[2]

Kesselring's conception of an open conflict clearly did not include a blockade, which had been Hitler's intended weapon from the time of his formal preview of the war in May 1939. If Britain was to be beaten by blockade in 1940, the German Navy was in no state to do it. The Norway invasion, so successful in every other sphere, had cost it almost half its strength in sinkings alone; with the *Scharnhorst* and *Gneisenau* both damaged, with the two pocket battleships, two light cruisers and six destroyers also under repair, the effective strength of the German surface fleet in June 1940 was one heavy cruiser, two light cruisers and four destroyers. Apart from the submarines, there remained only the Luftwaffe.[3] It was a chance that Göring seized with joy. "Leave it to my Luftwaffe" rose naturally from his lips again, and the opportunity which he had muffed

1. Naval Staff (Operations Division) War Diary, 7 September 1940, quoted Wheatley, *Operation Sea Lion.*

2. Kesselring, *Memoirs.*

3. As Jodl appreciated: "In the Channel we can substitute command of the air for the naval supremacy which we do not possess." (*First Thoughts on a Landing in England,* 12 July 1940.)

at Dunkirk was presented to him but a few days later. Hitler may possibly have thought, remembering Göring's birthday again fiasco, "because I have nobody else".

Göring had known since 23 May 1939, when the whole anticipated course of the coming war was sketched as far as the defeat of Great Britain, that vital blockade duties against England were expected of the Luftwaffe. A year and a day later, simultaneously with halting the tanks outside Dunkirk to enable the Luftwaffe to destroy the British Expeditionary Force, Hitler signed a directive for the next stage of operations, after the elimination of the British Army. He gave the Luftwaffe "unlimited freedom of action" against metropolitan Britain – the economic strongpoints of the country – as soon as forces could be built up. There was, however, a period of delay which cannot be accounted for by mere regrouping. On 5 June 1940, the day following the conclusion of the Dunkirk evacuation, Göring had moved on in his train to the Channel coast and then and there Milch proposed to him an intricately planned sequence of strong parachutist descents on the English fighter stations. The idea was passed to Hitler, but nothing came of it. Possibly he thought it savoured too nearly of invasion, and certainly Göring had divined Hitler's wish for an inoffensive compromise with Britain. But, under interrogation after the war, Göring gave a more grandiloquent explanation of the delay. Claiming entire responsibility for the air war against England he declared that the pause after the fall of France was due not only to the need to regroup but also to his personal indecision whether to tackle first "the invasion of England" or the conquest of the Mediterranean, starting with the capture of Gibraltar.

By mid-July, however, the air attacks on England were growing more intense, and Kesselring was making personal reconnaissance of the fighter bases across the Channel, though he was soon forbidden to fly over England. On 21 July, two days after the distribution of the batons, Göring took his new marshals, Milch, Kesselring, Sperrle and General Stumpff, to Carinhall and lectured them on his requirements. In addition to preliminary attacks on shipping and certain factory areas, he needed, in order to facilitate the invasion, the wiping out of Portsmouth and Dover as bases of the Royal Navy, but the sparing of other named quay and harbour installations on the south coast, which had originally been put on the target list but were now earmarked for the landing of German troops. Finally he called for detailed planning by the operations staffs of the three air fleets engaged for the concentrated assault on Britain. He wanted a meticulous priority list prepared of targets in the areas assigned. Air Fleet Two, under Field Marshal Kesselring, with its headquarters at Brussels and advanced headquarters at Ghent, took the east of England from a line drawn roughly from the Isle of Wight to Carlisle. Air Fleet Three, under Field Marshal Sperrle, based on St Denis, Paris and Deauville, took the west of England : Birmingham and the Black Country were on the centre line and therefore Tom Tiddler's Ground. Air Fleet Five, under General Stumpff, based on Norway and Denmark, took Scotland and a small area of England north of the Humber.

With Britain so painstakingly parcelled out for studious bombardment, Göring's commanders could share the complacency of his cry : "Leave it to my Luftwaffe!"

CHAPTER SIX

DOWDING vs GÖRING, AND OTHERS

All that I can say upon that subject is, that whether
I am to command the army or not, or to quit it, I
shall do my best to insure its success; and you may
depend upon it that I shall not hurry the operations,
or commence them one moment sooner than they
ought to be commenced, in order that I may acquire
the credit of the success.

THE DUKE OF WELLINGTON

Göring engaged himself totally to the air assault on Britain
from 1 July 1940. For the next three months until the end of
September he was committed to a personal struggle with
Dowding. It is one of the most clear-cut encounters between
two antagonists that is ever likely to emerge in the history of air
warfare. It is possible to assess the qualities and punishing power
of the two contestants as closely as boxers are analysed before a
fight.

Göring was self-confident and always dominant in his own
Service. There was no one between him and Hitler. The Führer
bore him no immediate grudge for the Luftwaffe failure at
Dunkirk, and at that time had complete trust in Göring's
direction of the air force, pronouncing only those strategical
modifications which were demanded by changes in his overall
plan of war. Dowding, by comparison introverted and withdrawn, was responsible to the Chief of the Air Staff, who from
September 1937 until October 1940 was Air Chief Marshal Sir
Cyril Newall. Newall had been the man whom Trenchard had
put in to replace Dowding as officer commanding the Headquarters Wing on the Somme in 1916, when Trenchard had
characterized Dowding as a "dismal Jimmy" unwilling to bear
the cost of offensive action. Newall's Deputy Chief of Air Staff
in 1940 was Air Vice Marshal W. Sholto Douglas, who finally
succeeded Dowding as Commander in Chief Fighter Command.
Dowding, single-mindedly intent on the defence of Great Britain,
had had fierce brushes with the Air Staff on policy and was to

103

have other differences on tactics : his immediate retirement had been suggested and he considered his status, as he said, as of "an unsatisfactory domestic servant under notice".[1] However, during the Battle of Britain he had the full confidence of Churchill, whom he usually visited at Chequers at the week-end.

Göring had the advantage in destructive power. He possessed what was then the largest air force in the world, though it was very soon clear that, considering the opposition, he was damagingly deficient in fighters. He could put over Britain about 1,000 bombers and over 250 Stukas, covered by over 1,000 fighters. Against this force Dowding had only 331 Hurricanes and Spitfires on the completion of the Dunkirk evacuation. But, under the whip of Lord Beaverbrook, the new Minister of Aircraft Production, the trim fighters were sent out from the factories and Civilian Repair Units at the rate of over 500 a month.

Everyone who experienced the lash of Lord Beaverbrook has testified to its sting, and some who wished later to avoid the lash made exaggerated propaganda for his production achievement. There is no statistical evidence to show that his appointment as Minister notably accelerated the supply of *new* fighter aircraft. He began his service on 14 May 1940, when fighter production was steadily rising by 40 per cent per month. The figures of the monthly output of new Hurricanes and Spitfires delivered thenceforth were : June, 412; July, 432; August, 414; September, 427; October, 481. There is strong ground for attributing the thrust for this steady total to Air Chief Marshal Sir Wilfrid Freeman, Air Council Member for Research and Development, later Development and Production, from the time he succeeded Dowding in 1936 until he was superseded by Lord Beaverbrook in the new Ministry of Aircraft Production : and Freeman was back again as Air Member for Aircraft Production within three months. There is, however, convincing statistical evidence that Lord Beaverbrook revitalized the salvage drive and the Civilian Repair Organization for the restoration of damaged aircraft. Its output rose from 20 a month during February to 160 aircraft repaired during the *week* ending 19 July 1940 : it had, of course, far more damaged aircraft to work on after Dunkirk. During the Battle of Britain

1. Basil Collier, *Leader of the Few*, Jarrolds, London, 1957.

one third of all aircraft issued to fighter squadrons were replacements from the Civilian Repair Organization. Sir Winston Churchill's tribute to Lord Beaverbrook's worth during the Battle of Britain is enthusiastic and precise :

At all costs the fighter squadrons must be replenished with trustworthy machines. . . . His personal force and genius, combined with so much persuasion and contrivance, swept aside many obstacles. Everything in the supply pipe-line was drawn forward to the battle. New or repaired aeroplanes streamed to the delighted squadrons in numbers they had never known before. All the services of maintenance and repair were driven to an intense degree.[1]

Dowding started the Battle of Britain with about 700 operational frontline fighters and the fair certainty of his reserves being maintained. What he lacked was pilots, and indeed it was destined that he would never have enough : the flying training schedule could not produce the skilled men in time. A Battle of Britain pilot, so much rarer and harder to shape than a Spitfire, needed to have begun his training in peace-time, and The Few were mainly young volunteers who had made their decision in 1939 or earlier. The Royal Air Force lost 435 pilots in France, and in June Dowding had a deficiency of one quarter of his establishment. At the beginning of the battle he had nominally 1,200 pilots fully trained. At the height of the battle he was losing pilots at the rate of 300 a month and receiving an intake of 260 – doomed men, for the expectation of life for a fighter pilot was then 87 flying hours.

The material advantage was clearly Göring's. On the other hand, the intellectual superiority was with Dowding – both in the plan of battle and the means to carry it out. Göring should at least have had the planning advantage of the initiative; but he possessed it only in tactical detail – Fighter Command never knew from day to day what particular assault or deception would be practised on the morrow. Strategically there was little surprise to be achieved. The subjugation of Great Britain depended on the extinction of the Royal Air Force.

Against this contingency Dowding had devoted all his thought for four years. Göring did not put his mind to it before the summer of 1940. When he did plan, with occasional jolts from

1. Churchill, *Their Finest Hour*, Cassell, London, 1949.

Hitler to start him thinking, he planned extemporarily. Whereas the attacks on Poland, Norway and France had been perfected in detail and alternative over the previous months, the battle for Britain was not given the same careful thought. There were two reasons for this : the Wehrmacht's success in north-western Europe surprised even the General Staff by its speed; and, more so than for any other operation, the intended conquest of Britain was Göring's own responsibility. The supporting roles of the naval and land forces could be worked out. But the operation was in reality being left to the Luftwaffe and depended absolutely on the success of the Luftwaffe. In supreme self-confidence Göring sketched a plan that was to be the same as all the other conquests, depending on the extinction of the home air force and its supporting aircraft industry. And he handed it to his air fleet staffs to implement in detail, even though he almost casually accepted further obligations.

The extra tasks were those passed across by the German Navy for the refinement of their invasion plans, and additional operations suggested by Hitler's conception of an aerial blockade of Britain. Both ought strictly to have been deferred, or remitted as secondary targets, until the Royal Air Force had been knocked out, if the Luftwaffe was to be used at its most effective concentration. Göring saw, for example, possibly earlier and more clearly than the British defence authorities, the importance of Liverpool as a vital centre of food replenishment in Britain as well as of manufacturing potential. But it was a blockade target, and he should have given it secondary precedence. Instead, on his personal orders – given to please Hitler – he diminished his primary attack by sending many bombers on the long haul to Merseyside in raids that were exhausting to the British civilians but not of the most direct military value. In particular he sent 629 raiders to Liverpool and Birkenhead on the four nights from 31 August at the height of his most damaging day-time offensive against the faltering sector stations of Fighter Command, a period when every bomber over the vital south-eastern airfields in daylight was of the utmost value.

Dowding's supreme advantages over Göring lay in his military intelligence and an extremely skilled capacity to handle his small forces to the best advantage. Both were personal triumphs, but they were also the fruit of the apt employment of technical skills which the Royal Air Force had exploited and the Luftwaffe had not. The Luftwaffe had not only neglected these skills, but they had made no allowance for their use by the other side.

Fighter Command *knew* with reasonable certainty where their raiding enemies were massing. They knew in time for their squadrons to take off and secure (though not always) enough height to engage; and they could *direct* their squadrons once they were airborne to areas on which the raiders were advancing. They thus controlled their forces with the maximum economy and efficiency. British intelligence was derived from radar, in the use of which the Royal Air Force led the world. The detailed direction was effected by *fighter control*, a system which in 1940 was also unique. It was a highly intricate coordination of radar, radio-telegraphy, telephony, radio-telephony, cerebral calculation and fighting resourcefulness. Radar, radio-telegraphy and physical observation were the means of detecting the position of all airborne machines, friend or foe. The radar stations on the coast indicated enemy machines approaching Britain and their approximate force; tellers in the Royal Observer Corps reported the numbers, position, course and estimated height of those aircraft they could see or detect acoustically; an electronic direction-indicating device in all home aircraft identified them as friend, not foe, and gave their bearing. Information from these three sources was coordinated and expressed as symbols on a huge map in an operations room, giving the complete picture of the situation in the air from moment to moment.

The action essential to meet attack was ordered according to the information concerning approaching raiders. Squadrons were put into the air, and followed while in the air. A fighter controller in a subordinate operations room kept in touch with the leaders of his squadrons by radio-telephone. Dead reckoning plotters in the operations room calculated the courses necessary to set for the fighters to intercept the raiders. The controller passed on these recommended courses and heights, and maintained authority until the fighters saw the enemy. During the action he followed the battle by listening out on the radio-telephone. If fresh enemy forces were detected near the battle area he would warn his fighter leaders. When the battle was

over he resumed command and either directed his formations
to further action or nursed them back to base.

This immediate tactical direction was operated from the
lowest echelon of control, for there was a hierarchy of operations
rooms. At Fighter Command Headquarters in Bentley Priory,
Stanmore, Dowding had a complete picture of all air movements
around Britain. Not only the Commander in Chief and his
deputies worked from this information, but the operations room
was manned by liaison officers of the anti-aircraft General,
other defence services, and the Ministry of Home Security,
which had responsibility for public air-raid warnings. Within
Fighter Command were four fighter groups of which the vital
one, covering London and the south-east, was 11 Group at
Uxbridge. Air Vice Marshal Keith Park, Air Officer Commanding 11 Group, had on the map in his operations room all
the information possessed by Fighter Command which was
relevant to his own group area. In turn, 11 Group was sub-
divided for tactical control into seven sectors, each with an
operations room dealing with its own sub-area, and controlling
the three squadrons of aircraft sent up from the airfields in its
manor. Park, through his controller, would order the individual
sectors to put up squadrons in accordance with his own swiftly
conceived plan of battle, and the sector controllers would direct
their individual squadrons from that moment. The key men of
this defence system were the group and sector controllers, all
experienced pilots. They had not only to assess attacks, and
forecast feints, but to estimate the fuel and ammunition remaining to machines after action, bring their aircraft in for
replenishment at convenient intervals during the running fight,
and either retain or throw in their reserves.

The result of all this complicated endeavour was, that for all
battles over Britain – though not at great distances from the
shore – the defending fighters were placed with growing precision
where they could most effectively go into action. Initially this
precision was a complete surprise to the Luftwaffe. The core of
the system was technical equipment long built up and coordinated – a network of radar detection and telephone and
teleprinter wires which could never have been extemporized in
a midsummer panic. It had taken years of careful construction
during the time that Dowding led Fighter Command. The

system was open to arterial disruption through attacks on radar stations and sector stations and the destruction of telephone line links (which was inevitably frequent during the intensive bombing of airfields). Though crippling damage was done to the land lines, Göring never appreciated the vital importance and the extreme vulnerability of the radar points and sector stations, and never concentrated on them sufficiently to blot them out of the pattern of defence. The effect of radar inter-ception and fighter control from the ground – which made un-necessary the exhausting and relatively inefficient police patrols, as flown at Dunkirk and over East Coast convoys – was equivalent, according to later German calculations, to in-creasing the strength of Fighter Command by a multiple of three. That was the measure of the importance of Dowding's early work in Fighter Command.

Göring's commanders had to freeze their day-to-day battle plans at the moment of briefing the crews for any particular assault. Once their forces were in the air there was little that could be done from the ground to adapt the sequence of opera-tions to the reactions of the defence, and matters had to be left to the commodores of the airborne groups. To this extent Dowding and Park controlled the Battle of Britain with greater tactical effect, though it was impossible, at the critical moments, to withstand the shock of the sheer weight of numbers put up by the other side. German physical superiority told. But the threefold effectiveness of the fighter defence meant that, because quick concentration could be made on a danger point, the raiding bombers encountered an opposition which would have been offered otherwise by a much stronger force. Consequently they needed a fighter cover of their own far more numerous than the planned balance of the Luftwaffe would allow. At all later stages of the battle the strength of raiding bombers had to be kept down to a level that could be protected by the now proved insufficient German fighter force. This robbed the attack of fullest concentration. But it did ease the strain of some bomber crews and permitted the despatch of others on the night raids which kept the British – including the exhausted pilots of Fighter Command – at a markedly lower morale than their optimum, even during the stimulation of the battle.

Göring's intention was to achieve victory over Britain by

intensive air assault alone. He never seriously believed that an invasion would be mounted, except possibly as an administrative occupying force. He did not want an invasion and did not plan for it, though he occasionally diverted attacks to objectives requested by his Navy and by Hitler, who put the British food supply second to the Royal Air Force in Göring's target priority from 1 August. Göring knew that even the German High Command estimated that a conventional blockade of Britain by air and sea might entail a war lasting two years. He rejected in principle that form of war. But in his superficial fashion he did not completely clear his mind of the implications of blockade, and allowed spectacular blockade objectives to take on some of the significance of all-out assault.

In so far as his mind was clear, he planned the decisive Battle of Britain to take four days and the ensuing pulverization of Britain before surrender a further four weeks. The four-day Blitzkrieg was to knock out Fighter Command, and the subsequent hammering, which the British in their insular ignorance came to call "the Blitz", was allocated a further month. This time-table went ruinously wrong: but it is necessary to see the struggle from the German point of view, and in the opinion of the Luftwaffe the Battle of Britain did not start until 13 August. All that went before was preliminary skirmishing.

For the five weeks beginning on 10 July 1940 this skirmishing consisted by day of attacks on supply ship convoys approaching or passing through the English Channel and bombardment of a number of Channel ports, with probing night raids for navigational training and the cumulative exhaustion of the defenders. The coastwise trade of Britain – an important and economical substitute for the railway system in any island – was principally concerned with the transport of food and fuel, first-rate objectives in any blockade. The Channel traffic also included large merchant ships bringing supplies from abroad direct to the Port of London (but these imports were diverted to Glasgow, Liverpool and Bristol soon after the German seizure of the French coast). The blockade was, however, only an incidental objective of the day-time attacks. Göring's purpose was to secure air superiority over the Channel and while doing so to engage Fighter Command in an informative and debilitating sparring match.

Göring won the first round on points. He made virtually no difference to Britain's supply stocks – he sank 30,000 tons of coastwise shipping out of the five million tons of shipping which was in transit in the area over the period; but he did, as incidental largesse to the German Navy's invasion interests, knock out four British destroyers in four days and close the port of Dover as a Royal Navy base. At least temporary day-time air superiority over the Straits of Dover had at least been achieved by the Luftwaffe. What was more important, Göring had forced a clash in the British Command, as a result of which Dowding, at the insistence of the Air Staff, unwillingly pushed his fighters out to their forward coastline airfields to engage in a number of battles over the sea where the majority of British pilots who crashed or parachuted into "the drink" could be presumed lost. The German air-sea rescue service was far superior to the British.

In fact, over the five weeks, Dowding lost 150 fighter aircraft of which 74 fell in three of the last days of action : on 8, 11 and 12 August. The pace was hotting up from the early insignificant daily losses and the pattern was beginning to change. Twenty British fighters were lost on 8 August during three strong Stuka raids on one Channel convoy. On the 11th Göring made a far more subtle move to wound Fighter Command by feinting at Dover, drawing off four squadrons of British fighters, and striking hard at the west in Portland and Weymouth, where seven British squadrons – some 80 aircraft – were finally sent to deal with 150 enemy aircraft. As a result of the double engagement 32 Hurricanes and Spitfires were lost against 38 German aircraft, of which only 15 were bombers. It was not Dowding's policy to trade fighters for fighters at this weakening rate and, apart from the heavy damage to docks and supply stocks in the south-west, the day's tally spelt defeat. On the next day, 12 August, there was a heavy raid on naval installations at Portsmouth (to which the Royal Navy destroyers from Dover had been withdrawn). But the main Luftwaffe effort was a widespread series of destructive raids on Fighter Command's forward airfields and the essential radar stations. Six radar stations were attacked and one, the all-important long-distance "eye" at Ventnor in the Isle of Wight, was put completely out of action.

Fortunately, owing to the speedy operation of a stand-by transmitter which sent out a ceaseless chatter of simulated signals, though it was giving no information at all, the German monitoring service did not realize that Ventnor was unserviceable and thus gain an appreciation of the vulnerability of the radar system. Ventnor was out of action for a fortnight and crippled Fighter Command's hold on the situation during a critical period. But the wound was concealed, and counterintelligence was not perceptive. A further instance of faulty German intelligence occurred on 12 August. The forward Kentish airfields at Manston, Hawkinge and Lympne were severely bombed, but not so decisively as the bomber crews reported on de-briefing. The Luftwaffe staff, however, credited the reports of their crews, crossed off five British airfields altogether as untenable, and paid them less attention in the immediate future than they deserved – for the fighters were flying from the Kent coast next day. The error was corrected to some degree by blundering German staff work which omitted to transfer the conclusions to the operations map; and Manston in particular was to receive further punishment. Intelligence appreciation was not improved when Göring finally came to the front. As a former air observer of the First World War he gave impetuous interpretations of photographs of British fighter airfields, declaring authoritatively that certain aircraft visible there were dummies, and hacking at the map with his thick pencil to erase one more field from the enemy's order of battle.

The 13 August was to Göring's mind the start of the Battle of Britain. He was not dissatisfied with progress so far. He believed he had destroyed three times as many British aircraft as he actually had. He had closed the port of Dover in daylight and attacked the ports of Swansea, Falmouth, Portsmouth, Avonmouth, Plymouth, Harwich, Newcastle, Hull, Portland and Weymouth. He had made an initial lunge at the radar stations and "wiped out" five airfields. He had perturbed the British by sending a few bombers every night on wide-ranging raids against industrial centres as far afield as Glasgow and Belfast, and against the strategically acceptable objectives of aircraft factories at Yeovil, Weybridge, Norwich, Crewe and Birmingham. These were not massive bombardments as yet but, in his own words, "essentially dislocation raids, made so that the enemy defences and population shall be allowed no respite". His actual losses in action were 286 aircraft against Fighter Command's 150 (reported to him as 450). Even the true figure was no bad score, since an attacker must expect the heavier losses.

Göring's plan for the Battle of Britain was to destroy the Royal Air Force in the air, on the ground, and in production. That was Hitler's clear directive: "Attacks will be directed primarily against the flying units, ground organization and supply installations of the Royal Air Force, and, secondarily, the air armaments industry, including factories producing anti-aircraft equipment."[1]

Unfortunately Göring argued with Kesselring and Sperrle about the interpretation of this directive – principally whether the Royal Air Force should be mainly destroyed in the air or on the ground – and also nominated additional targets. Sperrle believed that British fighters should be tempted into punishing battles by putting up raiding bombers with moderate fighter cover and ambushing the British fighters with high-flying in-dependent fighter groups. Kesselring advocated direct bombing of airfields, headquarters and aircraft storage units on the old Polish model. This was the form of a basic strategic offensive, but Göring inclined to Sperrle's judgement – not, however, wholly vetoing Kesselring's. In theory the battle was advancing from the south coast of Britain to assault the vital centres of British air power. Göring increased the dilution of effort by adding harbour and shipping targets to the detailed programme for the first day of the battle, already known for a long time far beyond Luftwaffe staff circles by its code name of *Adler-Tag*, Eagle Day.

On Eagle Day there was an illuminating contrast between the disposition of the principal marshals concerned with the defence and with the attack. Dowding fought the day from his operations room at Stanmore and Park from his, nearby at Uxbridge. Churchill, with his insatiable urge to be in on a battle, had discovered that he could spend one or two after-noons a week in Kent or Sussex when the south-east was under heavy attack, bundling his secretaries on to his very modest train and moving into the forward sectors. For Churchill, Eagle

1. War Directive No. 17, 1 August 1940.

Day was therefore the dateline of such bread-and-butter business as minutes on the stocks of coal held by the railways and the training of civilians in the handling of the Molotov cocktail for use in invasion, as well as being an occasion when the Prime Minister could draw his necessary inspiration from participation in the day's battle.

Göring, however, was still conducting the Battle of Britain from his home at Carinhall, by the shrine of his first wife, to which he summoned the Luftwaffe General Staff from their headquarters at Potsdam in Prussia. Hitler, on the other hand, designedly moved away from his own private temple. He had spent some days doing his military thinking, as was his custom, in the seclusion of his richly ornamented house, the Berghof, on the Obersalzberg above Berchtesgaden in the Bavarian Alps. Here was his own shrine, a room dedicated to the only woman to whom he had expressed utter devotion, his blonde niece Geli Raubal, who had killed herself in his apartment in Munich in 1931. Her room at the Berghof was maintained as she had left it, even when the rest of the house was completely rebuilt; and he kept there, like Göring, a portrait of his true love painted from photographs after her death. On 13 August Hitler expressly returned to Berlin, considering his presence "necessary for the opening of the air offensive". Towards Berlin were also travelling the Commanders in Chief of the three air fleets which were to attack Britain that day: Kesselring, Sperrle and Stumpff. Their absence from the front gives some illustration of the rigidity of the Luftwaffe plans compared with the fluid defence conducted from the British operations rooms.

Eagle Day dawned, and everything went wrong. The weather was absolutely unfavourable for the German pouncing tactic of strong fighter groups flying high over a bait of bombers and fighters. A cloud layer at 4,000 feet meant that the bombers would fly mainly beneath the cloud and the ambushers well above, quite ignorant of what was going on below, while the defence would attack the bombers at their leisure. When Göring was told in his bed of the weather at 4.30 a.m. he telephoned an order to delay the attack until the afternoon. But General Fink, in his usual position in the van of Kesselring's bombers, was already airborne and did not receive the signal to return. His fighter escort did observe the order at 5.30 a.m. and vainly tried to convey it to Fink over the French coast by wing-waggling and other gestures : the fighters and bombers were not in radio contact – Adolf Galland admitted "Radio or radar guidance for such an assembly was not yet available, and even our intercom did not work most of the time."[1]

Failing to distract the Dornier Do 17Zs, the Messerschmitt Bf 110s simply returned to base and landed. Deprived even of his close escort, Fink still determined to press on to his objectives in Kent, keeping his 74 Dorniers above the cloud layer. Meanwhile one of Sperrle's bomber groups (Junker Ju 88s), having also failed to receive a recall signal, was crossing the Channel farther west in two sections, both escorted, one bound for airfields in Hampshire and another for the naval base of Portland. A further force of nearly 90 dive-bombers, with a strong fighter escort, was forming up to cruise off the south coast, having no set objective except the luring of Park's fighters into a battle over the sea.

Park, in the group operations room at Uxbridge, could "see" through radar the approaching formations. But errors on the part of the radar operators and the inability of the Royal Observer Corps to sight through cloud resulted in a serious underestimation of Fink's force. Park had been bitten on the previous day by the feint against Dover, and he did not intend to trade fighters for fighters in another round of attrition.

If he had had more accurate information of the forces above the clouds – radar could not then differentiate between fighters and bombers – he would have known that the 74 unescorted bombers in Fink's group presented his best target of the war. But he put up only eight of his 21 squadrons, and dispersed them widely against the three approaching formations. Fink, navigating beautifully by dead reckoning, brought his group down through the clouds right on his principal target, the airfield at Eastchurch, and bombed it effectively against last-minute opposition from 74 Squadron of Spitfires led by Squadron Leader A. G. ("Sailor") Malan. This was by far the most successful bombing of the morning. A small part of Fink's force had been detached for an attack on Sheerness but they were sighted by one of Park's squadrons. In the mêlée they jettisoned their bombs, killing people in Sheppey, and scrambled back into cloud cover

1. Galland, *The First and the Last.*

as soon as possible. At the same time four more of Park's squadrons were guided by ground control on to the separate Junkers formations as they crossed the coast of Sussex. They forced them far off their targets with heavy losses. The British squadrons, under orders, studiously ignored the baiting dive-bombers off the coast, and the Stukas were obliged to return to base without action. To complete the dossier of muddle, 80 Messerschmitt Bf 110 Destroyers which had been detailed to escort the Junkers 88 formations assigned to Portland, but had lost them in the cloud, flew direct to Portland, under British radar surveillance all the way. There they were "jumped" by three waiting squadrons and sent home, less six aircraft down in the Channel in five minutes.

With admirable fortitude, the deputies of Sperrle and Kesselring determined to save something from *Adler-Tag*. The weather had not improved, but Göring's order from Carinhall had delayed the formal inauguration merely until the afternoon. Air Fleet Two sent 50 escorted bombers to attack the Kentish airfield at Detling, and Rochester, where there was important aircraft production. The escorts were intercepted but the bombers got through. One section wrecked the airfield at Detling but the other could not find Rochester in the bad weather and, engaged over Kent on their return, bombed Canterbury at random merely to decrease their load. Air Fleet Three sent 40 bombers to attack airfields in Hampshire and the docks at South-ampton. Again the British interceptors mixed prematurely with the fighter escort and the bombers bound for Southampton got through. The other force – they were Junkers Ju 87 dive-bombers – was harried by Spitfires who shot down nine from one formation. The survivors caused some havoc at Andover airfield and minor damage at the important sector station of Middle Wallop.

In a day of severe fighting the Luftwaffe had put up its greatest strength to that date, flying 1,485 sorties of which one third were by bombers. They had lost 45 aircraft against Fighter Command's 13, and from his 13 machines written off Dowding had salvaged six pilots. The actual destruction wrought at the expense of the Royal Air Force had been minimal. By fantastically inefficient target appreciation none of the airfields intended to be attacked was in the orbit of the Luftwaffe's primary enemy arm, Fighter Command, save Middle Wallop, which was hardly scarred. On the other hand, the British fighters had been tempted during the afternoon engagements into action against escorts, to the relief of bombers, and a small amount of pawn-swapping had been done. The Luftwaffe General Staff believed that it had achieved fairly satisfactory results, recording that night that five more airfields had been rendered totally useless to the enemy, serious damage had been done to docks and warehouses in Southampton and, according to their figures, 134 British aircraft had been destroyed. A large proportion of the German losses were Junkers Ju 87 dive-bombers and the Luftwaffe commanders were beginning to cherish active doubt about the life expectancy of Stukas in a war involving Spitfires. There was also a reappraisal of the target priority list; it was difficult to justify an attack on Southampton as a current strategic necessity. That night the bombers of Air Fleet Three began their concentration on aircraft factories, and put eleven direct hits on to the Nuffield factory at Castle Bromwich near Birmingham, which was making Spitfires. The orders from Potsdam for the next day, 14 August, were for bombing attacks on the British aircraft industry and the Royal Air Force ground installations.

Air Fleet Three put out a number of small bombing formations which attacked eight airfields, inflicting by dive-bombing rather more serious damage at Middle Wallop than on the previous day. Parallel orders were given for attacks on railways, and at Southampton again heavy blockage was caused: but this was a raid which was valueless at that stage unless followed up. Air Fleet Two feinted in the heavy clouds over the Kentish airfields, and during fighter diversions got in a quick thrust at Manston with twelve Messerschmitt Bf 110 fighter-bombers, of which two were shot down. But it was a comparatively quiet day with fewer than 100 bombers out and eight British fighters down. Through the night the staff of the Fighter Command operations room, particularly the officers of Guns and Home Security, were alert and apprehensive. German radio messages had been intercepted indicating a heavy raid on Liverpool. It did not develop and the night passed without significant pressure. The German bomber strength was not extended. The decisive day was to come on the morrow.

By Göring's calculations, since he conveniently discounted periods of bad weather or recuperation, 15 August was the second day of the Battle of Britain. The prepared plan was for constant diversionary attacks throughout the day to mount into five effective points of pressure. These five major onslaughts were to attempt the elimination of a score of British airfields. It was an aim that might not have been impossible if Göring had thrown in every serviceable bomber and Stuka he possessed in the three air fleets – an operable frontline force after battle casualties of about 1,000 machines; and the bombers based in France could make more than one sortie in a summer day. But it had become clear from previous actions that the fighter protection needed by 1,000 daylight bombers was about 3,000 aircraft; and, even allowing for duplicate and triplicate missions by some forward-based fighters, this was over twice the force in Göring's hands. In consequence the Luftwaffe could not put up all its bombers, but only 520, some of them entirely unescorted. As Commander in Chief, Göring might claim that this was unavoidable bad luck, militarily, although, as economic czar, Göring himself could be blamed for sheer bad management. There was, however, a more blatant failing in the day's plan. The offensive was not concentrated on Fighter Command. Undoubtedly a number of air battles would be provoked, and these battles would play their part in decimating[1] Fighter Com-

1. The Battle of Britain was one of the few occasions when this overworked military word could be used with exactness. Fighter Command was *decimated every fortnight* during August and September, losing 615 pilots killed, captured, wounded or missing in those two months. If Göring believed the Luftwaffe Staff returns he calculated that Fighter Command was decimated on many single days during the battle, including 13 and 15 August. The Luftwaffe was decimated repeatedly in battle sequences, particularly in the periods 13 to 18 August (the true Battle of Britain), 24 August to 3 September, and 7 to 24 September. The Luftwaffe force of fighters and bombers available in the three air fleets ranged against Britain was kept up to about 2,300 on any given day. During July, August, September and October the Luftwaffe lost 1,883 fighters and bombers destroyed, and 612 damaged on operations. The total of 2,445 shows that the Luftwaffe had a complete turnover in the Battle of Britain. A double turnover is the record of Fighter Command which, having an average daily total of under 750 aircraft available for operations, suffered from July to October the battle casualties of 1,149 aircraft total loss and 707 damaged but capable of repair.

mand. But the attacks on ground installations were ludicrously sparing of the airfields of Fighter Command. The *intended* targets of the Luftwaffe on 15 August included eight fighter airfields, at least four bomber airfields, three naval and other airfields, two centres of the aircraft industry and four radar stations – a concentration of little over half the Luftwaffe bombers against Fighter Command.

The day of 15 August began with early-morning reconnaissance. In mid-morning Kesselring's forces put up a feint against Channel convoys in the Thames Estuary which occupied one of Park's squadrons. At 11.30 forty escorted Stukas attacked the fighter airfields on the Kent coast at Lympne and Hawkinge. The force was ineffectually engaged by four British squadrons sent to intercept them, and Lympne was put out of action for two days. A typically fortuitous result of the dive-bombing, but an incident which Fighter Command had always to expect, was that three radar stations were made temporarily unserviceable when the main electric power cable was severed by a bomb. And fresh enemy forces were continually threatening. From the Lympne engagement three defence squadrons had to be detached almost immediately to cover further lunges by German formations over the Channel; but the movement was again a diversion. For the next heavy attack was scheduled to fall on the north of England, where it was hoped that Dowding would have dropped his guard in order to send fighters to the hard-pressed south.

Dowding had not dropped his guard. His forces were thin but he had not diminished them. Air Vice Marshal Richard E. Saul, commanding 13 Group, had only three squadrons of Spitfires and three and a half of Hurricanes in his sectors defending northern England and southern Scotland. On this day the 75 operational aircraft held a 200-mile front against 99 raiders, repulsed them without allowing any military damage to the territory they were protecting, and shot down 15 (of which a maximum of two can be claimed by flak fire) without any loss to themselves. It was a notable success and it could never have been achieved without radar.

General Stumpff, temporarily commanding from Berlin his Air Fleet Five based in Norway and Denmark, had sent in the whole of his forces in two main assaults, and they were detected by radar when they were a hundred miles off the coast. Saul, in the 13 Group operations room, was informed shortly after noon of the northern attack – a force of 65 Heinkel He 111s covered by 34 Messerschmitt Bf 110s. He got a dozen Spitfires of 72 Squadron into the air fast enough to intercept them thirty-five miles from the coast. He brought 605 Squadron of Hurricanes 80 miles south from their base at Drem on the Firth of Forth to patrol the coast as a second line of defence. The Spitfires closed with the raiders and broke up the formations in the battle. Some of the bomb-load was immediately jettisoned in the sea. The remaining Germans reformed into two main streams. One was engaged over the coast near Newcastle by 79 Squadron of Spitfires and some of the Hurricanes from Scotland, and again bombs were uselessly jettisoned. The other stream, caught over Sunderland by the Hurricanes of 607 Squadron, was forced off its target, the inland fighter airfield at Unsworth, and attempted to bomb Sunderland and Seaham Harbour.

Meanwhile the rest of Stumpff's forces, 50 unescorted Junkers Ju 88 bombers, were speeding on a parallel course a hundred miles to the south, and had been detected by Air Vice Marshal Trafford Leigh-Mallory, commanding 12 Group, shortly after Saul had had intelligence of the northern horn of the attack. Mallory pushed out Spitfires, Hurricanes and Defiants to intercept. They were seen too early for a surprise attack to be made. The Junkers converted the engagement into a running fight during which 30 of the bombers slipped through. They found their objective, the bomber airfield at Driffield, and hit it decisively, destroying ten Whitley bombers and four hangars. Six Junkers had been shot down in the engagement.

At the same time Manston in the south had been sharply attacked in a Bf 109 fighter raid which destroyed two Spitfires on the ground. In the afternoon another simultaneous double-blow was struck. The right hook was aimed at one of Park's fighter airfields at Martlesham Heath, where 80 defending aircraft did not stop a determined Stuka and fighter-bomber attack. The straight left hit a vital area of the south-east. Here, heavily outnumbering the seven squadrons converging for the defence, the Luftwaffe hit the Coastal Command fighter airfield at Eastchurch and four covering radar stations, and accurately bombed two aircraft factories at Rochester; one was making Spitfire components, the other, Short Brothers, was the key factory for the construction of one of Britain's bombing hopes, the four-engined Stirling, whose production was seriously set back.

Still more attacks were mounted. To the south-west 250 aircraft from Air Fleet Three, each bomber covered by three fighters, swept in towards the Isle of Wight. Eight of the tiring defence squadrons were put up to meet them. Many of the British fighters had been in action three times that day – a few flew as many as seven sorties – and it was then only 5.30 in the afternoon. The attackers split formation to carry out a series of raids, of which the least successful was the bombing of the important airfield and sector station at Middle Wallop, covering Southampton. The Luftwaffe lost 25 aircraft in this particular assault but Fighter Command, giving some indication of exhaustion, had its biggest losses of the day with 16 aircraft going down. The attack was not over when fresh radar blips indicated that Kesselring's air fleet was coming in punching while the defences were still reeling under Sperrle's attack. Seventy enemy aircraft were detected approaching from above Calais. When the warning reached Park he realized that many of his squadrons were just landing after the last fight, and his nearest intercepting force was 501 Squadron of Hurricanes which had been airborne for three-quarters of an hour and had fought two actions already. Nevertheless he directed the Hurricanes towards the raiders, brought in four squadrons from the east, sent up three of his right-wing squadrons again after swift refuelling and rearming, and scraped up another squadron and a half-squadron. (Park's maximum force was twenty-one squadrons, with which he had to defend London and south-east Britain, from Norwich in the north to Southampton in the west, through seventeen hours of daylight every day.)

The first fighting attack of the Hurricane pilots of 501 Squadron unsettled the raiders to such an extent that they broke formation and wandered over the country, unable to fix bearings for their allotted targets, the fighter airfields and sector stations at Biggin Hill and Kenley. However, they sighted the minor fighter station at West Malling and the more important Croydon airfield and bombed both. They made West Malling unserviceable for days and did serious damage at Croydon by destroying two aircraft factories, an aircraft radio factory and many trainer aircraft. The 80 civilian casualties caused at Croydon by this raid were the first to be recorded in Greater London. Within a month the lists were to run at 1,700 casualties a day.[1]

The weary fighter pilots came in to land, not knowing yet if this was the last operation of the day. On cornfields and downs smoking aircraft were being cut apart to release the human jetsam of the contest, of whom some half were breathing still, though many of those would never fight again. Churchill had spent much of the day at Uxbridge in Park's operations room, travelling the short distance from London by car; he was to be there again a month later on the Sunday that is now celebrated as Battle of Britain Day. On this Thursday Major General Ismay accompanied Churchill. Ismay recalled :

There had been heavy fighting throughout the afternoon; and at one moment every single squadron in the Group was engaged, there was nothing in reserve and the map table showed new waves of attackers crossing the coast. I felt sick with fear. As the evening closed in the fighting died down, and we left by car for Chequers. Churchill's first words were : "Don't speak to me; I have never been so moved." After about five minutes he leaned forward and said, "Never in the field of human conflict has so much been owed by so many to so few." The words burned into my brain.[2]

Five days later, with one small emendation, this requiem passed into history in a speech Churchill made in the House of Commons :

The gratitude of every home in our island, in our Empire, and, indeed, throughout the world, except in the abodes of the guilty, goes out to the British airmen who, undaunted by odds, unwearied in their constant challenge and mortal danger, are turning the tide of world war by their prowess and by their devotion. Never in the field of human conflict was so much owed by so many to so few.[3]

1. 60,447 British civilians were killed by bombs and rockets in the Second World War, over half of them in London.

2. Ismay, *Memoirs.*

3. Churchill, in *Their Finest Hour,* describes an incident during a visit to Uxbridge when Park, after asking Dowding for three squadrons to be made available by Leigh Mallory's 12 Group, declared to Churchill that he had nothing in reserve. This was on 15 September. Churchill's speech to the Commons was made on 20 August.

On the night of 15 August ten towns were bombed, the most successful operation being against an armaments factory in Birmingham. During the day Göring had put up 1,786 aircraft, some of them on second missions, against 974 sorties by Fighter Command. Göring lost 75, Dowding lost 34 aircraft. The British claimed at the time that they had shot down 182 German aircraft, but it was not a figure that Dowding accepted. Beaverbrook told Churchill that "upwards of eighty" German machines had been picked up on British soil by his Ministry salvagers after that day's battle. On the other hand, Göring was informed that Fighter Command had lost 101 machines, and he accepted the figure more credulously. The Intelligence Branch of his Luftwaffe Operations Staff were busy computing, and by next day they had evolved their appreciation of Dowding's plight. They declared that the number of British fighters, including Beaverbrook's replacements, had been reduced to 430, of which only 300 were serviceable. Actually the figure exceeded 700.

Göring had passed all the day of the 15th at Carinhall in conference with Kesselring, Sperrle, Stumpff and their corps commanders. They were to remain within call of Göring for five days, and as a result of their discussions the battle took a significant emphasis. On the 15th Göring was already drawing dogmatic deductions from the reports on Eagle Day. He began soundly by suppressing any emphasis on targets introduced by Hitler in connection with the blockade, or targets urged by the German Navy to ease invasion :

Until further orders operations are to be directed exclusively against the enemy air force, including the targets of the enemy aircraft industry allocated to the different air fleets. Shipping targets, and particularly large naval vessels, are only to be attacked where circumstances are especially propitious. For the moment other targets should be ignored. We must concentrate our efforts on the destruction of the enemy air forces.

Göring was seriously anxious over two crises of men and matérial, the high losses of dive-bombers and the damaging aircrew casualties being experienced in the ill-defended heavier bombers. He decreed that three fighters should escort every Stuka and that bomber crews should never have more than one officer in the complement. His dismay at the crippling casualties being recorded amongst the bombers was deep and sincere, but with his elephantine mismanagement of men he expressed it by castigating the fighter pilots. Both Werner Molders and Adolf Galland were present at Carinhall. They were the fighter aces of the Second World War, already acknowledged professionally in every air force, with a far more impressive record of individual kills than any British pilot (though it was rarely acknowledged that their astronomical scores had been notched mainly against the second-rate machines of the Polish, the Dutch and the French, and their arithmetic was sometimes suspect). Molders and Galland went to Carinhall in mid-August merely commanding wings of about 30 fighters. At the end of the conference Göring promoted them to be commodores commanding groups of about 90 aircraft, as the first step in his policy of removing chairborne officers from middle-echelon commands and putting in young giants who would lead their forces into action in the air – as Fink was already leading his Dorniers.

Molders and Galland felt out of place among the generals in the "cultured and luxurious atmosphere of Carinhall". Ostensibly they had been summoned to the Commander in Chief to receive the award of the Gold Pilot Medal with Jewels. But after a perfunctory expression of appreciation for their work Göring proceeded to bash them. "The Reichsmarschall," Galland reported, "let us know quite plainly that he was not satisfied to date with the performance of the fighter force, particularly with the execution of fighter protection, and energetically called for greater efforts."[1]

In a final misjudgement, not only of human relations but of the strategic situation so many miles away, Göring reprieved the British radar stations which had taken so heavy a pounding only that day – while the station at Ventnor was still in the process of complete replacement. "It is doubtful," he said, "whether there is any point in continuing the attacks on radar sites, in view of the fact that not one of those attacked has so far been put out of action." The actual score of unserviceable stations at that moment was four, though all but Ventnor were back in operation next morning.

---

1 Galland, *The First and the Last.*

Before Göring's orders for the protection of his own Stukas and the enemy radar stations could be translated into effect, on the next day, 16 August and the third day of the Battle of Britain, a flight of five dive-bombers completely destroyed what remained above ground of the Ventnor site and necessitated the introduction (a week later) of a mobile station as substitute. Putting up almost as many sorties during the day as on the 15th, the Luftwaffe heavily hit three Fighter Command airfields at West Malling, Manston and Tangmere and five other airfields, including Brize Norton in Oxfordshire, where 46 trainer aircraft were destroyed in the hangars. Tangmere, the important airfield and sector station covering Portsmouth, scrambled its three Hurricane squadrons to meet a mass of 100 aircraft screened as approaching Portsmouth. The German force split into four sections which attacked Ventnor, the naval air stations of Gosport and Lee-on-Solent, and Tangmere itself. The Hurricanes could not tackle every formation, and a strong force of Junkers 88s made a clear run through to the airfield. In one fast, low carpet-strike on Tangmere, like the old days in Spain, they destroyed every hangar, workshop and store, cut off the power, water and sewage, and hit 14 aircraft on the ground. Into this airfield, black with flying earth and petrol smoke, which had been his home ground for the short time he had been flying in action in England, slithered Pilot Officer Billy Fiske, himself wounded and his Hurricane blasted, with no alternative but to make a wheels-up belly landing.

Pilot Officer William M. L. Fiske was an American, the son of a banker, who had volunteered for the Royal Air Force on the outbreak of war. He had completed his training and been granted a commission, and was one of the first of the non-professional airmen to come forward to the front line of Fighter Command. Flying for 601 Squadron, he claimed his first probable when the Tangmere squadrons mixed with the Junkers over the Hampshire coast on the morning of Eagle Day, and he had been in virtually continuous action for the two following days. Now he had finished his time. His smoking Hurricane skimmed like a gull on to the airfield, sparked as it zipped a scar in the surface, and exploded into flames. They got Billy Fiske out of his machine, but he died from his injuries two days later. The British put up a tablet to his memory in St Paul's

Cathedral, near the bust of George Washington. The inscription reads :

PILOT OFFICER WILLIAM MEADE LINDSLEY FISKE III
ROYAL AIR FORCE
AN AMERICAN CITIZEN WHO DIED THAT ENGLAND MIGHT LIVE
AUGUST 18th 1940

The 16 August had proved an effective day for the Luftwaffe, which damaged three fighter airfields and five others, shot down 22 British fighters and destroyed aircraft on the ground. Fighter Command, flying 776 sorties, had had no chance to recover from the exertions of the previous day. But the action had been wearing for the Luftwaffe too, and their loss of 45 aircraft with other crews injured was not something they could continuously endure. In an effort to allay fatigue and to integrate replacements into the worst-hit squadrons the Germans let a fine day pass on the 17th with only minor activity. The last day of the Battle of Britain was deferred until the morrow, after which the process of obliteration was timed to start.

But Dowding, who had no allegiance to the enemy's formal schedule, recognized that, unless emergency measures were taken, he faced disaster almost instantly from the sheer lack of pilots to fly his established squadrons. His actual figures of pilot losses in the eleven days from 8–18 August were 154 pilots killed, missing or severely wounded against 63 new entries from the training units. In desperation he got the Air Staff's agreement for 53 volunteer pilots from bomber and army cooperation units to be rushed through the swift conversion course. To transfer quickly from Battles and Lysanders to a Spitfire was no facile conversion. In addition the actual operational training of all new men was halved, and pilots were programmed to go into action after not more than twenty hours' solo flying.

On Sunday, 18 August the Luftwaffe delivered what was intended to be its last direct blanketing of Fighter Command. A finely executed raid on Kenley, with two high-flying fighter-covered formations of Dorniers alternating with a low bomber sweep of nine aircraft from only 100 feet, put both the field and its sector operations room out of action, besides destroying ten hangars and eight aircraft on the ground. A similar attack on another sector station guarding London, Biggin Hill, was less carefully timed and cost seven of the nine Dorniers. There were heavy raids on Sussex airfields and, in the last attack on a radar site before Göring's order to ignore them became operative, the station at Poling was blotted out for ten days – a serious blow, though the action entailed the lost of twelve Stukas. West Malling and Croydon fighter airfields were again damaged. In all the Royal Air Force lost 27 fighters in the air and 71 Luftwaffe aircraft were destroyed. After the day's heavy losses of Stukas the Junkers Ju 87 dive-bombers were withdrawn from the battle – a diminution of the German force by 220 of the 280 remaining machines of this type.

Göring and his marshals were still in conference at Carinhall. On 19 August Göring ordered : "Until further notice the main task of Air Fleets Two and Three will be to inflict the utmost damage on the enemy fighter forces." Bombers were to be sent over only in numbers sufficient to tempt the British into action. It was an admission that the four-day onslaught on Fighter Command which was all he had allocated to the Battle of Britain had failed. The initial struggle must go on. Göring actually moved to the forward headquarters of Air Fleet Two at Cap Gris Nez. He surveyed England through binoculars. The most outstanding landmark was the grid of the Dover radar station whose reprieve he was continuing. He did not stay. The weather was unfavourable, and activity was slight for five days. It was a lull which provided Fighter Command with an influx of some fifty new pilots without equivalent losses.

But the August slaughter still left Dowding short of 41 pilots until the seasoned men from bombers and army cooperation completed their conversion training, and these fliers were a windfall he could never expect again. The graph of pilot losses in Fighter Command's operational research office was curving into a fatally deep dive. Dowding reassessed the situation with Park at 11 Group, from which the 21 crucial frontline squadrons were commanded. They perceived that Göring's intention was to extinguish the fighters and their bases. That day Park ordered his controllers only to engage the enemy "over land or within gliding distance of the coast. During the next two or three weeks we cannot afford to lose pilots through forced landings in the sea." Above all, he emphasized that the function of his fighters was to protect the airfields, sector stations and armament industry from bombing, not to engage in the sterile combat against German fighters which Göring wanted. "Against mass attacks coming inland despatch a minimum number of squadrons to engage enemy fighters. Our main object is to engage enemy bombers."[1]

Park was now exceedingly anxious over the quality of his battered squadrons. The under-trained pilots he was getting as replacements for his dead were blunting the edge of his attack. He asked Dowding to send him veteran replacements handpicked from those squadrons in the other three groups of Fighter Command which were taking less daily strain. The Commander in Chief refused to do this; he feared the effect on morale of the squadrons so combed, and instead of priming 11 Group with individual veterans he relied on his old system of rotating whole squadrons while he rested the battle-weary. He maintained his principle of keeping an effective *overall* defence of Great Britain, even though every squadron engaged was necessarily diluted by the enormous losses incurred since the start of the campaign. As one concession, he confirmed that Park could call on a minimum force from his neighbouring groups – No. 10 in the west and No. 12 in the north – to protect the outlying airfields during a big engagement.

With Air Vice Marshal Sir Christopher Brand commanding 10 Group, covering southern England west of the line Southampton–Oxford, Park had had the most cordial cooperation. But in his relations with 12 Group, active north and east of London, there were the seeds of the intrigue which was soon to topple both Dowding and Park from their commands.

This was the controversy over the "big wing" theory of fighter tactics : the belief that a concentration of force expressed in mass formations of fighters was the most effective way in which to use the fighter arm. The principal protagonists for this theory were the Deputy Chief of the Air Staff with special responsibility for defence, Air Vice Marshal Sholto Douglas, Air Vice Marshal Trafford Leigh-Mallory commanding 12 Group, and Squadron Leader Douglas Bader, the legless pilot

1. Park's Instruction No. 4, 19 August 1940, quoted by Derek Wood and Derek Dempster, *The Narrow Margin*, Hutchinson, London, 1961.

commanding 242 Squadron of Hurricanes, who generally led 12 Group's so-called "Duxford wing"[1] of up to five squadrons in formation.

The most vigorous advocate was Bader, a man who throughout his distinguished career propagated his convictions without respect of persons.

As yet the controversy was not heated, and pressure on Park to defend south-east England with big wings was not strong. But on 29 July, when the Luftwaffe had gained air superiority at Dover, the Air Staff had urged Dowding to meet the enemy "with superior forces and large formations".[2] Dowding disagreed with the Air Staff then because their suggested method of using the forward coast stations increased his pilot losses over the sea and tended to defeat the stated object – for big wings need time and rearward distance from the target in order to form successfully, as was the experience of the Duxford wing. Park himself had a strong battle-founded objection to the use of big-wing tactics in defending southern England. He had been forced to fight the battle over Dunkirk in this fashion, gradually doubling the strength of his formations until they were sixteen squadrons strong – and he had been severely criticized for the unavoidable intervals between these strong patrols, when the troops and ships below were at the idle mercy of the Luftwaffe. His radar could not pierce through to Dunkirk, though his squadrons could form as they flew forward. But the very nearness of the enemy air bases in France during the Battle of Britain, while they allowed his radar to mark the build-up of German formations, demanded that 11 Group's fighters should scramble in immediate take-off and gain height to intercept, rarely allowing time for squadrons to assemble in formation. It was also true that, in only three months of active war, British fighter pilots had had to be individual in order to kill and survive; they had had to unlearn the cumbersome attack formulae of the peace-time drill books and abandon the tactics of tight air-display formation which the big wing advocates seemed to wish to revive.

As far as Dowding and Park were concerned, all this controversy was permissible after-dinner discussion as soon as they

1. Duxford, south of Cambridge, was the principal airfield in 12 Group.
2. Collier, *The Defence of the United Kingdom.*

E

could spare time for a banquet. For the moment they had a battle to win.

On 24 August Göring's assault was renewed. Manston was put out of action permanently as a forward fighter field. Hornchurch and North Weald, both fighter sector control stations, were bombed. Park called on 12 Group to protect these two bases, but the Duxford wing was flown in too late to affect the attack. A strong force of Sperrle's fleet attempted to bomb Portsmouth Dockyard, but were forced off its mark by ack-ack fire and killed 100 civilians in the town when it jettisoned its bombs.

At night the then large force of 170 German bombers was sent against Royal Air Force installations and aircraft factories all over England. Twelve crews were assigned to bomb aircraft factories at Rochester and Kingston and oil refineries at Thameshaven – all easily distinguishable by their riverside positions and around 20 miles from the Metropolis. The crews either got hopelessly lost or wilfully disobeyed Göring's strict orders not to bomb central London, and indiscriminately hit ten boroughs in the inner ring. The effect of this raid was historic. Churchill ordered Bomber Command to Berlin on the next night, and they went again on the 28th and the 30th. The psychological reaction of the Germans was a tremendous blow to Göring's prestige. Long ago he had promised that not a single enemy bomber would be able to penetrate even to the Ruhr; "If an enemy bomber reaches the Ruhr, my name is not Hermann Göring : you can call me Meier!" Now the attack had reached Berlin. William L. Shirer, the American newspaper correspondent then in Berlin, wrote in his diary after the first raid : "The Berliners are stunned. They did not think it could ever happen. When this war began, Göring assured them that it couldn't. . . . They believed him. This disillusionment today therefore is all the greater. You have to see their faces to measure it."[1]

After three raids Hitler was forced to make a public response. In a speech at the Berlin Sportpalast on 4 September he coupled the coming invasion with the extermination of metropolitan Britain. With the characteristic infantile hyperbole which often marked his emotional public thinking he jeered :

1. William L. Shirer, *The Rise and Fall of the Third Reich*, Secker & Warburg, London, 1960.

In England they are filled with curiosity and keep asking "Why doesn't he come?" Keep calm. Keep calm. He is coming! He is coming! ... German planes are over English soil every day. ... When the British Air Force drops two or three or four thousand kilograms of bombs, we in one night will drop 150, 250, 300 or 400 thousand kilograms. When they declare that they will increase their attacks on our cities, then we will *raze*[1] their cities to the ground.

Next morning he initialled plans for the struggle for Britain to be forwarded by an all-out attack on London on the 7th.

His figures were accurate enough. During the night of 7th September, calculated apart from the heavier day-time attack, German bombers switched their target and dropped 400,000 kilograms of bombs on London.

It was a mistake. For the Luftwaffe was within sight of victory. Between 24 August and 6 September the German Air Force had discovered the key to conquest and inflicted tremendous damage on Fighter Command through sustained attacks on its sector stations and airfields. The British defence was failing, not only through exhaustion but also through the loss of technical efficiency due to the battering of its prized systems of fighter control. Moreover, aircraft losses had risen on the British side so that whereas in the beginning of the battle they had been taking three aircraft for one they were now exchanging one for one, a rate they could not maintain if they were to survive: on 31 August they endured heavy damage at five fighter stations, flew over a thousand sorties, and lost 39 planes against the Luftwaffe's 41. Not only were fighters being lost in action, but the Germans were making increasingly successful attacks on the aircraft factories. The heavy night bombing of Liverpool induced the fatigue of long night alerts throughout wide areas on the route of the raiders. Air Vice Marshal Park's 11 Group – still taking the full strain on its establishment of 21 squadrons out of Fighter Command's 52 – was reeling. Park harboured some bitterness that airfields assigned to 12 Group cover had been heavily bombed. Some of his own sector commanders, disturbed at the rate of pilot loss, asked that bigger formations should be used, and he agreed

1. Hitler's phrase has been translated by the colloquial "rub them out".

that squadrons should act in pairs whenever events allowed time to form. The situation was grave. Between 24 August and 6 September 466 British fighters were shot out of the battle and 231 pilots lost to combat by death or serious wounds. Park later admitted that after 23 major assaults on his bases "the enemy's bombing attacks by day did extensive damage to five of our forward aerodromes and also to six of our seven sector-stations. By September 5th the damage was having a serious effect on fighting efficiency. The absence of many telephone lines, the use of scratch equipment in emergency operations rooms and the general dislocation of ground organization was seriously felt in the handling of the squadrons." Dowding himself gave the most serious indication of the pilot crisis. On 8 September he finally acceded to Park's request to detach pilots from fighter squadrons outside 11 Group, and categorized his squadrons into three classes: virtually frontline, reserve, and training duties. It was a sour fate for those fighting squadrons allocated to the third category.

One further week's absolute concentration on the south-east sector stations, with not even a bomb diverted to the factories, could have caused the fragmentation of 11 Group and forced Fighter Command to make a critical territorial retreat of 100 miles, abandoning the south coast of England and exposing London. Instead of ordering the concentration, and clinching the victory, Göring declared that he had already won the battle. He sat down in conference at the Hague to umpire an amazing argument between Kesselring and Sperrle on the current strength of Fighter Command. Göring gave the verdict unquestioningly to Kesselring and chose to believe that the fighter frontline was extinguished. He assumed that the assaults on the London sector stations had driven Dowding on a clear retreat to the north, and that the last effort necessary to expose and overcome the British reserves was to conduct a massive daylight raid on one objective: London. This would bring up all the fighters for the final massacre. He passed Kesselring's plan for the London raid to Hitler, who gladly endorsed it and the night attack on the city that was to follow the military slaughter. Jodl's recommended paralysing weapon of "periodic terror attacks, announced as reprisals" could be given its first trial. Bomber Command unwittingly dovetailed into the scheme by bombing

Berlin on 6 September. On the morning of the 7th the German High Command announced that reprisals would be taken. The "reprisals" had in fact been planned on the 5th before the commission of the offence they were to avenge.

Göring's error was twofold : in fact and in psychology. First, Dowding's defence had not yet been beaten away from the south-east, and he would come out fighting. By the irony of day-to-day error, however, Fighter Command did not engage effectively on 7 September and there was little opportunity for widespread butchery between the fighter forces. Second, Dowding's character was sterner than Göring judged it to be. He would not sacrifice his fighter reserves, nor more than half a dozen of his 31 squadrons flanking the central bastion of 11 Group, even for London. Rather would he sacrifice London for Britain. If the choice lay between the annihilation of Fighter Command and the aerial sacking of London, he would offer up the Londoners, as he had offered up the angry soldiers at Dunkirk, along with the vanguard of his pilots. More realistically than any other war leader he accepted the new axiom that in modern war civilians are in the front line. He was determined on this from the start, though he never admitted it until he had been removed. He gave only one clue. Very shortly after the Dunkirk evacuation he observed to his staff : "The nearness of London to German airfields will lose them the war."[1]

Even then he perceived the carrion which at the last the hunted could throw to the hunters. The Luftwaffe could snap and worry over the sprawling body of London, so deceptively open, yet so primitively absorbent and indestructible. In the time bought by the sacrifice Britain would resharpen her hacked sword.

Fighter Command failed tactically on 7 September – for the destruction of 41 German aircraft *after* most of them had bombed was failure. London listed 2,643 civilian casualties next morning, including more than one baby in Bermondsey. On 7, 9, 11 and 14 September the daylight assault on London was re-peated, and during the week of mourning below Dowding lost 94 of his own men in the air. On Sunday, 15 September Göring sent in every baiting bomber he could cover in a last effort to subdue Dowding. The challenge was accepted, though still by

1. Collier, *Leader of the Few.*

Dowding's local fighter forces, not his reserves or his distant squadrons. At the end of the action which the British now call Battle of Britain Day only 26 of the defending pilots were down, and of those only 13 were dead. Both Göring and Hitler recognized defeat. Göring saw that he had erred, and he must take on Fighter Command all over again at its forward line of airfields, radar sites and sector stations – if the British weather would ever allow it. Hitler knew that the English Motherland was not eliminated and the invasion he had irresolutely begun to prepare could not now be carried out, and perhaps he had a traitorous relief in his heart that the ravishing was not to be.

The tactical defeat of Dowding's fighters on 7 September led to a far stronger outcry from the supporters of big-wing tactics and to open disagreement between Leigh-Mallory and Park. Sholto Douglas of the Air Staff was now on record as saying "it does not matter where the enemy is shot down, as long as he is shot down in large numbers",[1] and he made his view incontrovertibly clear later when he said : "I have never been very much in favour of the idea of trying to interpose fighter squadrons between enemy bombers and their objective. I would rather shoot down fifty of the enemy when they have bombed their target than ten forward of it." Such an attitude was, to Dowding, a complete reversal of Fighter Command's duty, for Dowding's instructions from the Air Staff were to defend from enemy air attack primarily the centres of air forces industrial production : to try to prevent factories from being bombed rather than to fight the bombers after their mission was accomplished. Clearly the ground of dissension was broadening. Sholto Douglas also clashed with Dowding over the allocation as nightfighters of three squadrons of Hurricanes – which Dowding held would be useless for the task since single-seater aircraft could not then be fitted with airborne radar. When the Chief of the Air Staff finally ordered Dowding to transfer these squadrons[2] the Commander in Chief obeyed, but protested his strong disagreement.

By this time the Battle of Britain was won, but it was clear that Dowding had had his time. On 25 November 1940 Air

1. Collier, *The Defence of the United Kingdom.*
2. One of the units was 85 Squadron commanded by Squadron Leader Peter Townsend.

Marshal Douglas, soon to be Air Chief Marshal Sir Sholto Douglas, succeeded Dowding. Douglas's first major posting was to appoint Leigh-Mallory to succeed Park. Enthusiastically backed by the Air Staff, Fighter Command began to go over to big-wing offensives, escorting bombers over France and making sweeps and forays. At the time it was thought that the tactics had achieved extraordinary success – it was claimed that 731 enemy aircraft were destroyed from 14 June to 31 December 1941. When the figures were researched after the war it was found that in that period Fighter Command destroyed 114 German fighter aircraft over France, the Low Countries and the United Kingdom at the cost of 426 British pilots killed, missing or prisoners : a greater loss than the toll of the Battle of Britain.

The man who sacked Dowding was the new Chief of the Air Staff, Air Chief Marshal Sir Charles Portal, who took the post on 25 October 1940 and saw Dowding out within a month. Portal was an "offensive" airman of the type Trenchard and his school had always liked, and it was natural that, inheriting a conflict between the "offensive" Douglas and the "defensive" Dowding and Park, he should favour the more positively spectacular function. It may well have been time to edge out Dowding, but it was unnecessary to make his exit so shabby : it was suggested that he could make himself useful by investigating Service waste. Park was sent to a flying training group. Churchill professed no part in Dowding's removal, indeed he expressed surprise at it; and later he summed up the air generalship of the banished Commander in Chief :

The foresight of Air Marshal Dowding in his direction of Fighter Command deserves high praise, but even more remarkable had been the restraint and the exact measurement of formidable stresses which had reserved a fighter force in the North through all these long weeks of mortal combat in the South. We must regard the generalship here shown as an example of genius in the art of war.[1]

1. Churchill, *Their Finest Hour.*

CHAPTER SEVEN

PORTAL: FAITH WITHOUT WORKS

> You must keep your ground, my lads.
> There is nothing behind you.
> Charge! Charge!
>
> THE DUKE OF WELLINGTON

During the Christmas holiday period of 1940 the air Marshals and their pseudo-military superiors diverted themselves according to their characters. Hitler, Supreme Commander of the German Armed Forces, was in the front line of the Luftwaffe, who had converted the Battle of Britain into the Blitz on Britain but had been given some days off duty. In Abbeville on Christmas Eve Hitler gave a half-hour inspirational or auto-suggestive speech to officers of 26 Fighter Wing. Marshal of the Greater German Reich Göring had awarded himself home leave in order to be available for the sumptuous Christmas presents which, under pressure, were "traditionally" made to him at this season by corporations, institutions and sycophants. He had passed a busy December, first acquiring paintings in Rotterdam and Paris, then uplifting the Luftwaffe morale by improving both the skiing resorts and the brothels specially maintained for them; with a conference or two on strategy and the war economy: time-demanding, but not a more arduous programme than the normal diary of a multiple company director. Now he relaxed with a house party at Carinhall, his most intimate home, named after his first wife. It was an inflated Citizen Kane style shooting-box, built in a 100,000 acre estate in the weald of Schofheide, thirty miles north-east of Berlin. In the grounds was Carin's mausoleum in which he ostentatiously prayed, to the occasional embarrassment of his guests if not of his second wife; the enormous pewter coffin there was intended to receive his own body when the time should come.

In the vast playroom-attic, eighty feet long, at Carinhall

Göring put on his favourite show. When his guests were assembled he sat in his red armchair and pressed buttons in a complicated control panel by its side. He could not hide his glee at the immediate response. Before his eyes a squadron of aircraft appeared over a mountain, dipped to plant bombs on a stationary train, and curled away on the fixed wires which held them.

The little bombs bounced on the tin roof of the train and came to rest in the narrow streets of a miniature village. Göring relished the delight of his guests, reminded them of the time the Duke of Windsor had enjoyed the same spectacle, and allowed a servant to pick up the bombs and reload them in the racks of the model bombers. He pressed other buttons to operate different features of the delicate unreal world laid out in the playroom. The Commander in Chief of the German Air Force was absorbed in his diversion.

Field Marshal Kesselring, Commander in Chief of German Air Fleet II based on the English Channel, gave orders that no operational aircraft should go into action over Britain. He later expressed, with the petulant righteousness of a man who had been condemned for crimes against humanity, his disappointment in the British for failing to extend the same courtesy. He snatched a few days' leave from his battle headquarters at Cap Gris Nez but complained "It did not bring me the rest I hoped for because of heavy bombing raids on German towns in my administrative area."

A marshal's definition of a *heavy bombing raid* varies interestingly according to whether the marshal is giving it or receiving it. The British attacks were in fact extremely light, and Kesselring was getting far less than he was giving. Air Chief Marshal Portal's records showed that in the whole of December 1940 his bombers dropped only 992 tons[1] on Germany. Kesselring knew that he had exceeded that total in his last four nights of activity: battering Merseyside on 20 and 21 December, burning Manchester on the 22nd and 23rd, he had diminished his stocks by 952 tons of high explosive and 3,626 canisters of incendiary bombs.[2]

1. Webster and Frankland, *The Strategic Air Offensive Against Germany*, Appendix 44.
2. Collier, *The Defence of the United Kingdom*, Appendix XXX.

Portal, only two months in the top job of Chief of the Air Staff, was a worried man who betrayed his strain to colleagues more sophisticated in anxiety. On 20 December he had received a kindly minute from Churchill:

Prime Minister to Chief of the Air Staff 20.12.40 I hope you will try to take a few days' rest, and seize every opportunity of going to bed early. The fight is going to be a long one, and so much depends on you. Do not hesitate to send your deputy to any meetings I may call.

Pray forgive my giving you these hints, but several people have mentioned to me that you are working too hard.[1]

Winston Churchill, Prime Minister and Minister of Defence "with overall responsibility for the conduct of the war", did not extend such solicitude to himself. Throughout the Christmas holiday he busied himself with details of mustard gas stocks; drop-forging deficiencies; the homeless bombed-out; the inadequate issue of George Medals to civilian heroes of the bombing; the German acquisition of iron ore from Sweden; the prison conditions experienced by Sir Oswald Mosley, the British Fascist, and Pandit Nehru, the Indian nationalist; Australian concern at the Japanese threat to the Far East; secret staff talks with the French General Weygand; the proper use of merchant shipping; vermin and sanitation in air-raid shelters; the Import Programme for 1941; the shortage of anti-tank ammunition; the size of the prison population in relation to the fresh crimes introduced by a war-time regime; the occupation of Jibouti; and the cold storage of meat.

It was certainly a working holiday, and Portal, too, was at his desk all through the following week-end. By the Sunday after Christmas he was receiving fresh minutes from his Minister of Defence, and on the next day he got a corker.

One corner flared with the red sticker marked "Action this Day". The missive read:

Prime Minister to Secretary of State of Air Chief of the Air Staff and *Minister of Aircraft Production*[2] 30.12.40
(Secret)

1. I am deeply concerned at the stagnant condition of our

1. Churchill, *Their Finest Hour.*
2. Lord Beaverbrook.

bomber force. The fighters are going ahead well, but the bomber force, particularly crews, is not making the progress hoped for. I consider the rapid expansion of the bomber force one of the greatest military objectives before us ...

3. The figures placed before me each day are deplorable. Moreover, I have been told on high authority that a substantial increase in numbers available for operations against Germany must not be expected for many months. I cannot agree to this without far greater assurance than I have now that everything in human wit and power has been done to avert such a complete failure in our air expansion programme.

4. ... We must ... increase our bomb deliveries on Germany ...[1]

When the Chief of the Air Staff received this minute he had certainly not seized "every opportunity of going to bed early" as he had been bidden. On the previous night, Sunday, 29 December, London had endured what was then its most devastating raid and Portal had interrupted his work, not to shelter from it but to watch it, at the suggestion of his then Deputy Chief of Staff, Air Vice Marshal Harris. Harris wrote afterwards :

I watched the old city in flames from the roof of the Air Ministry, with St Paul's standing out in the midst of an ocean of fire – an incredible sight. One could hear the German bombers arriving in a stream and the swish of the incendiaries falling into the fire below. ... The Blitz seemed to me such a fantastic sight and I went downstairs and fetched Portal up from his office to have a look at it. Although I have often been accused of being vengeful during our subsequent destruction of German cities, this was the one occasion and the only one when I did feel vengeful, and then it was only for a moment. Having in mind what was being done at that time to produce heavy bombers in Britain I said out loud as we turned away from the scene : "Well, they are sowing the wind."[2]

Portal also commented that the enemy would get the same and more of it. But his mind cannot have been entirely serene on the assurance. Like every *effective* Commander in Chief – and one may withdraw that adjective from his opposite number,

1. Churchill, *Their Finest Hour.*
2. Marshal of the Royal Air Force Sir Arthur Harris, *Bomber Offensive*, Collins, London, 1947.

Göring, with certitude though not with contempt, for Göring had many other responsibilities – he knew too much. He was fighting four air battles: a contest in the Western Desert, at present comparatively localized but which could lead to the loss of Africa and the rich oil of the Middle East, even though local victory could never win the war; a defence against the long winter bombing of Britain by the Luftwaffe; a sea war which was not yet named the Battle of the Atlantic, absolutely vital to Britain's existence but, again, a defensive campaign; finally, the offensive bombing of Germany, still a feeble endeavour, but the only action of the armed forces of a solitary Britain which shot in a positive direction towards final victory.

The whirlwind which Harris had in mind as the future harvest of Germany was the onslaught of British bombers – Portal and he were already determined on a frontline force of 4,000 heavies, and Arnold was soon to be told so in Washington. Churchill still strongly supported them. But on the night when Portal climbed down from the Air Ministry roof and next day when he read the Prime Minister's minute naming "the rapid expansion of the bomber force one of the greatest military objectives", he knew – as Churchill did not – facts about his present bomber force which, if indiscreetly communicated, might wreck any hopes for the future of Royal Air Force Bomber Command, and even, by extension, of the United States bomber force.

The role of the Royal Air Force as a war-winning arm depended on two basic factors: faith in Bomber Command, justified by works. Faith in the bombers fluctuated wildly even in the High Command. Only Harris "sold" them consistently and unreservedly, while Portal, with more subtle advocacy, adapted his evangelism to the authoritative mood of the moment. The achievement of Bomber Command, on which all else depended, was decided by a correct contemporary assessment of their accuracy in precision attack. If they were accurate they could be despatched against precise material targets; if they were inaccurate they would have to be used to engender indiscriminate civilian terror, and the arguments for bombing as an essential weapon against German morale would need to be convincingly put. The first eighteen months of Portal's leadership of the Royal Air Force were bedevilled by utterly confusing

reports on the accuracy of the bombers, which made their
initial achievement nugatory. Yet the retention of faith was
necessary for the ultimate success both of Bomber Command and
the United States Eighth and Fifteenth Air Forces.

By a decision taken in February 1936, before Germany's
reoccupation of the Rhineland, it had been British Government
policy to have the Royal Air Force equipped with 990 bombers
by March 1939. The bombing force was to have adequate
reserves, and four-engine aircraft were to be in production. But
this paper intention was never fulfilled. From 1937 the Government knew that their omission to pre-empt factory space and
skilled workers was whittling away the total of aircraft actually
produced. Moreover they had failed – and, more damningly,
were continuing to fail – to start training sufficient skilled crews
to fly the bombers. Nevertheless, in October 1937, the Air
Ministry tried to use a belated increase in its Treasury allotment by proposing a still greater theoretical enlargement of
Bomber Command, to 1,442 aircraft by March 1941. The
Ministry was, however, steam-rollered out of the arena by the
new Minister for the Coordination of Defence, Sir Thomas
Inskip. He successfully suggested to the Cabinet that bomber
production should be retarded, and that light bombers could be
used as defensive fighters.[1] Only after the occupation of Austria

1. This truly armchair strategist, empowered with a virtual veto over
defence expenditure, proposed to knock out the German bomber force
mainly over London. He wrote to the Air Minister, Lord Swinton: "Please
do not think for a moment that I am driving my ideas to the extreme
logical conclusion that we ought to have nothing but Fighters at the outset of a war. That would be an absurdity. My idea is rather that in
order to meet our real requirements we need not possess anything like
the same number of long-range heavy bombers as the Germans. ... They
[the Germans] must come to this country to damage us. They are
likely to concentrate on great centres, such as London, which provide an
irresistible target. In fact, it would seem in accordance with strategical
principle that the decisive place and the decisive time for the concentration of our own air forces would be somewhere over our own territory at
the outset of a war. Have you considered the possibility of using our
own bombers to supplement our fighters in this respect? ... I seem to
have seen suggestions in some of the proceedings of the Technical Committees that special light bombs might be designed for aircraft to use
against aircraft." (Aide-Memoire by Sir Thomas Inskip, Minister for the
Coordination of Defence, for the Secretary of State for Air, 9 December
1937, Webster and Frankland, *The Strategic Air Offensive Against
Germany, 1939–1945*, Appendix 5.

in March 1938 did the Cabinet authorize an expansion of the bomber force to 1,352 frontline aircraft by March 1940. Yet on the outbreak of war eighteen months later the actual size of the bomber force, intended to be, under the minimum plan, well over 990 frontline aircraft, was 33 operational squadrons. Of these 10 squadrons of short-range and ill-designed Battles were sent to France for Army support and were never a part of Bomber Command's offensive. Of the rest, six squadrons of Blenheims could not effectively penetrate Germany from England and were forbidden by the French to bomb Germany from France. There remained 17 squadrons of what were then called heavy bombers: in all, 77 Wellington aircraft, 61 Whitleys and 71 Hampdens – 209 machines, only 80 per cent of which could be provided with crews on any one day.[1] For a nation whose Government, tardily awakened, had been on the qui vive for three and a half years and in actual panic for eighteen months, this 20 per cent fulfilment of the minimum plan is an appalling performance.

But it was not the full account. Bomber Command was designed as an offensive force which would attack the strategic centres of the enemy in the day-time with precision bombing from a high level, moving in self-defending tight formation. The average bombing error under these conditions, said Bomber Command, was 300 yards, but the contrasting inaccuracy of night bombing meant that they could not yet undertake any night attacks on precision targets. If war was joined the most effective blow against Germany would be a daylight precision attack on the Ruhr. That was the theory. In practice, the poor strength and training of Bomber Command, the fear of reprisals, and the even grosser fears of the French on that account, led to a banning of any attack on the Ruhr by day or night. The early strategic mass attack on Germany, still fiercely advocated by Trenchard, was never tried. On the night war broke out, the British effort was to fly night bombers over Germany releasing propaganda pamphlets, which the Whitleys of 4 Group continued to do for the next six months. Next day ten Blenheims and nine Wellingtons bombed German warships near Wilhelmshaven, ten other aircraft having failed to navigate

1. Webster and Frankland, *The Strategic Air Offensive Against Germany, 1939–1945*, Appendices 7, 38 and 39.

to the target. The Blenheims attacked gallantly from 500 feet and half their force was shot down. They hit the pocket battle-ship *Scheer* three times, but none of the bombs exploded. The Wellingtons scored no hits and lost two aircraft. Three months passed before the next attack on German warships, by 24 Wellingtons. They sank one minesweeper with a bomb which passed straight through it without exploding, but they lost no aircraft. In a similar action eleven days later half the Wellington force was lost. Four days after that, 22 Wellingtons over Heligoland were bitterly engaged by Messerschmitt fighters and Destroyers. The tight defensive formation of the bombers was broken. The Luftwaffe shot down or fatally damaged twelve aircraft and caused three of the ten survivors to force-land away from base. As a result of these four actions – virtually the total experience of the Royal Air Force as a strategic bomber force, and conducted without any penetration of the German main-land with its improving radar, concentrated anti-aircraft artillery and fighter defence – the Air Staff abandoned its whole concep-tion of Bomber Command as a daylight precision-attack force directed against strategic targets in Germany. The casualty rate had mounted to ten times what the force could bear, and the basic principle – still favoured by the United States Air Staff – of tight tactical bomber formations relying on defensive fire-power was seen to be negated.

Royal Air Force Bomber Command was a negligible force, not trained, nor equipped, nor allowed to perform the only function envisaged for it. When Portal became its Commander in Chief on 3 April 1940 it was a sterile arm operating solely at night, and its only missiles were leaflets. But, for want of a better activity, it was converted into a night-bombing force.

At the beginning of Portal's command the force's staff officers were realistic about its inefficiency at night bombing. They believed that, only under the best conditions, half of the crews could identify and attack a target at night, and if the target was not conspicuous few inexperienced crews could find it.[1] Nevertheless, with the spread of the war into the Battle of France and the putative invasion of England, the Air Staff instructed

1. Bomber Command Reports of 19–20 March 1940 and 10 April 1940 quoted by Webster and Frankland, *The Strategic Air Offensive Against Germany, 1939–1945.*

Air Chief Marshal Sir
Arthur Harris, KCB,
OBE, AFC (IWM)

Reichsmarschall Hermann
Göring, Commander-in-
Chief of the Luftwaffe
(KEYSTONE)

(*Above*) Sector station operations room (IWM)
(*Below*) German Dornier 17 shot down by a Lewis gun
(FOX PHOTOS)

(*Above*) Steel-helmeted electrical engineers at work on broken
cables following German air attack 3 December 1940 (IWM)
(*Below*) Vapour trails above Chatham (KENT MESSENGER)

(*Above*) Air Chief Marshal Harris (left, standing) with bomber crew (IWM)
(*Below*) Men of the County of London (No. 601) Fighter Squadron running to their planes (FOX PHOTOS)

Lt General Arnold, Chief of the United States Army Air Forces,
arriving in Britain with the American Military Mission

(*Above-left*) Air Chief Marshal Sir Arthur Tedder (left),
Air Vice Marshal H. Broadhurst, Marshal of the RAF, Sir Charles
Portal, and Air Marshal Sir Arthur Coningham (right) visiting
a front line fighter wing in Italy (AP)
(*Below-left*) Major-General C. Eaker (left), Allied air commander
in the Mediterranean theatre, and Lt General C. Spaatz, leader
of the American strategic bombing force, arriving at US
headquarters in London (AP)
(*Above*) Fighter planes escorting Flying Fortresses on a raid over
Europe (KEYSTONE)

Flying Fortresses of the US 8th Air Force bombing a Nazi fighter
base in France, September 1943 (IWM)

Portal to attack such precise targets as oil plants, aircraft factories and shipping: the only dispersed target offered was railway marshalling yards. Portal was personally dubious of the effect of the bombing of individual oil plants, and asked for the services of an oil expert to assess Bomber Command's efforts. Portal complained of the isolation of the targets he had been given as priority, saying that the bombs which missed them would hit nothing, whereas a near-miss on a marshalling yard, for example, would strike at enemy morale by causing death and destruction in the surrounding workers' homes. The Air Staff insisted that the moral effect of bombing must be a secondary objective. It was a conception that Portal, as a "Trenchard man", could not accept, and he was gratified to find that Churchill rapidly moved to his side. After the first bombing of London Churchill, "much in the mood to hit back", proposed to Portal that Bomber Command should bomb German cities as amply as possible.

The Air Staff opposed such a policy. There is no doubt now that its views were coloured by a false appreciation of the accuracy of night precision bombing – a view which, ironically, was sustained by the enthusiasm of Bomber Command officers, notably Air Vice Marshal Harris, commanding 5 Group.[1]

But, for whatever reason the support was given, ministers and military were united that Bomber Command should be nurtured, even if for the moment Churchill was more a Trenchard-style thinker than Trenchard's successors. "The Navy can lose us the war, but only the Air Force can win it. . . . The Fighters are our salvation, but the Bombers alone provide the means of victory." With extraordinary intellectual courage the Prime Minister told the War Cabinet this while the Battle of Britain was still in the balance, on 3 September 1940 urging a supreme effort to expand the bomber force. Eight days later Portal proposed to the Air Staff that, to affect "the will of the German people to continue the war", twenty German towns

1. In January 1940 Harris told Bomber Command that so long as three bombers were in company in daylight the pilots "considered themselves capable of taking on anything". Of night navigation he said in July 1940 "the majority of aircraft can be expected to arrive within a few miles of their objective on D.R. and W/T [dead reckoning and wireless telegraphy]." Webster and Frankland, *The Strategic Air Offensive Against Germany, 1939–1945.*

should be listed for indiscriminate reprisal bombing after any German attack on a British city.

Next month Portal left Bomber Command to take over the direction of the Royal Air Force as its Chief of Air Staff. His first directive to the new Commander in Chief Bomber Command, Air Marshal Sir Richard Peirse, showed a significant change in policy emphasis. In the past the principal precision targets assigned to the bombers had been individual oil installations. Oil targets were still to be the primary objective during the eight to ten nights of moonlight each month. But enemy morale was promoted to twin priority. The directive instructed :

> ... the time seems particularly opportune to make a definite attempt with our offensive to affect the morale of the German people.... If bombing is to have its full moral effect it must on occasions produce heavy material destruction.... Regular concentrated attacks should be made on objectives in large towns and centres of industry, with the primary aim of causing very heavy material destruction which will demonstrate to the enemy the power and severity of air bombardment and the hardship and dislocation which will result from it.[1]

This directive of 30 October 1940 held the balance as fairly as was practicable at that date between the demand for precision attacks on vital production and haphazard bombardment of populated strategic areas. But still the false belief, particularly among civilian ministers, in the efficacy of British precision bombing persistently clouded the true perspective. On the very next day after the directive was issued the Air Minister, Sir Archibald Sinclair, minuted the Prime Minister : "Our small bomber force could, by accurate bombing, do very great damage to the enemy's war effort, but could not gain a decision against Germany by bombing the civil populations."[2]

It was then within Portal's knowledge that, contrary to Bomber Harris's optimistic belief, Bomber Command already suspected that 65 per cent of their crews failed even to find their

1. Webster and Frankland, *The Strategic Air Offensive Against Germany, 1939–1945*, Appendix 8 (xi).

2. Minute, Sinclair to Churchill, 31 October 1940, quoted by Webster and Frankland, *The Strategic Air Offensive Against Germany, 1939–1945*.

precision targets, let alone hit them. On the basis of this suspicion a Photographic Reconnaissance Flight of Spitfires was formed on 16 November 1940. The first reports of this unit were enough to blast any Service optimism about the accuracy of precision night bombing, or even the theoretically easier "concentrated attacks on objectives in large towns and centres of industry". A large town, Mannheim, became the first German city to be deliberately "blitzed" by the Royal Air Force when 134 bombers were sent there on the night of 13 December. The aiming point given was simply the centre of the town, which was to be showered by picked aircrews with incendiary bombs, the rest of the force aiming at the fires so raised. The conditions were perfect "bomber's moonlight". The number of aircrews claiming to have reached Mannheim and to have bombed its centre was 102. Yet photographs taken on 21 December showed remarkably little damage.

An even more striking report was given to Portal and Peirse, of Bomber Command, on 28 December. This contained the conclusions drawn from the photographic reconnaissance, on Christmas Eve, of two separate oil plants at Gelsenkirchen in the Ruhr. They were recorded as having been bombed by 162 and 134 aircraft respectively. The crews concerned reported that they had dropped 262 tons of bombs accurately on target. Neither plant showed signs of any major damage. Even the number of bomb-craters visible, which should have been about 1,000, was negligible.

This was the clearest report to date of the effect of the British bomber offensive against German oil production, the destruction of which was then confidently expected to end the war within a year. Photographic surveys, however liable to misinterpretation, were the most solid evidence available to Portal of the real effect of his bombing. But at that moment he also had in his hands an intelligence appreciation of the strategic offensive against Germany which indicated an almost incredible success. This report, presented to the Cabinet on 18 December, was a direct outcome of Portal's request for an oil expert to assist Bomber Command in assessing the results of its attacks on oil plants. It said that, estimating "on a conservative basis", German synthetic oil production had been reduced by 15 per cent for the expenditure of only 539 tons of bombs.

The photographic survey and the expert report were diametrically contradictory. Portal chose to adopt the theoretical appreciation. On the day after he received the photographic report, on the Sunday of the London fire blitz, Portal assured his fellow Chiefs of Staff, who were finalizing policy on continuing the strategic assault on oil, that on 36 clear nights during the next four months Bomber Command could pinpoint and destroy the 17 major synthetic oil plants in Germany, about a potential half-yearly production of 1½ million tons of oil, and thus possibly end the war with Germany that year. On the basis of that declaration the Chiefs of Staff recommended to the War Cabinet on 7 January 1941 : "The primary aim of our bomber force during the next six months should be the destruction of the German synthetic oil plants. We emphasize the importance of adhering to this aim until it is achieved." The secondary aim, for moonless nights and wandering aircraft, was to be "the lowering of enemy morale, particularly in industrial areas. This object can be conveniently furthered by allotting industrial areas and railway yards as alternative objectives to all aircraft detailed for the primary aim, and by making periodical heavy concentrations against industrial towns on nights which are unsuitable for the attack on oil targets."[1]

The foundation of this authoritative policy report by the triumvirate directing the British armed forces was Portal's pledge to paralyse oil production. Portal personally repeated this assurance to Churchill on 13 January, and two days later Bomber Command was directed to wipe out the 17 oil plants. If it was faith that was sublimely necessary to sustain the bombing offensive, Portal was surely demonstrating the faith that moves mountains, the substance of things hoped for and evidence of things not seen. At the most realistic appraisal Portal was using a double-think that he would have despised in Göring, deceiving himself and others in the grim effort to bolster the diminishing prestige of Bomber Command which, without the most determined advocacy, would never be allowed the production priority necessary to build a massive front-line force.

The reality of events during the next few months battered

1. Report by the Chiefs of Staff on Air Bombardment Policy, 7 January 1941, Webster and Frankland, *The Strategic Air Offensive Against Germany, 1939–1945*, Appendix 9.

Bomber Command harder than its most apprehensive protagonists feared. On 6 March 1941 the Prime Minister directed: "The Battle of the Atlantic has begun. . . . We must take the offensive against the U-boat and the Focke-Wulfe [long-range aircraft] wherever we can and whenever we can. The U-boat at sea must be hunted, the U-boat in the building yard or in dock must be bombed. The Focke-Wulf and other bombers employed against our shipping must be attacked in the air and in their nests."[1] There was an immediate and cumulative debilitation of Bomber Command, mainly through the transfer of crews and aircraft to Coastal Command. The force finished 1941 numerically only equal to its strength at the start of the year and physically, through the dilution of its veterans, weaker – like a pugilist who has maintained his weight only by dangerous wasting. Theoretically the actual defensive diversion of Bomber Command effort to Atlantic targets meant that they must relax their offensive on German oil. But they had never started it. At that time they had made only two raids on the 17 vital oil plants: in the three months ending on 31 March only five per cent of their activity (221 sorties out of a total of 4,375) was directed against the primary target laid down. This priority was now changed. However, the active dislike which the Commander in Chief Bomber Command increasingly felt for vainly "pouring high explosive into Brest harbour", or against the Focke-Wulf factory at Bremen, encouraged a more realistic appraisal of *all* bombing accuracy. The Directorate of Bomber Operations had previously carried over unchanged, from day-time operation to night operation assessment, the peace-time assumption of an average aiming error of 300 yards. Now, conceding "an unconscious lack of honesty on our part to recognize and admit our operational limitations under certain conditions", they doubled this assumed average error to 600 yards[2] which postulated the necessity of more than twice the number of attacks to wipe out the oil plants than Portal had previously suggested.

In fact, even this assumed bombing error was wildly

1. Winston Churchill, *The Grand Alliance*, Cassell, London, 1950.
2. Directorate of Bomber Operations (1) Review, 5 April 1941, Webster and Frankland, *The Strategic Offensive Against Germany, 1939–1945*, text and Appendix 45.

optimistic, but it diminished confidence in the vulnerability of the precision target. Portal, perhaps not unwillingly, while still obeying the Atlantic Directive reverted in his thinking to his fundamental conception of strategic bombing as a direct offensive against enemy morale. He was strongly buttressed by Trenchard, who in May 1941 submitted to Churchill a memorandum very strenuously urging that the primary bombing target for the Royal Air Force should be German morale, and an enormous bomber force should be built up to accomplish it. Churchill circulated the paper to his Chiefs of Staff, and Portal commented :

1. I agree with Lord Trenchard's main thesis that the most vulnerable point in the German nation at war is the morale of her civilian population under air attack, and that until this morale has been broken it will not be possible to launch an army on the mainland of Europe with any prospect of success.

2. I also agree that to exploit this weakness the main weight of our air attack should be directed against objectives in Germany, so situated that bombs which miss their target will directly affect the morale of the German civilian population. I share Lord Trenchard's view that absolute priority should be given to the building up of a bomber force of decisive strength equipped with aircraft capable of reaching all parts of Germany. I would add, however, that this should be done after the minimum force of aircraft (e.g. fighter, general reconnaissance, Fleet Air Arm, etc.) essential for our security has been provided.[1]

Trenchard's paper was extravagantly written and was joyfully attacked on that account by the Chief of Naval Staff, Admiral Sir Dudley Pound. General Sir John Dill, Chief of the Imperial General Staff, in his comments skilfully restored the priority of the Battle of the Atlantic. But Trenchard had done a useful thing for the Royal Air Force. He provoked Pound and Dill, leading the rival services, to admit to Churchill in their written comments their agreement with Trenchard's thesis and Portal's advocacy that the war could not be won, and Europe could not even be re-entered, until the Royal Air Force had built up massive air superiority. They were less generous in their estimation of the degree of priority which

1. Webster and Frankland, *The Strategic Air Offensive Against Germany, 1939–1945,* Appendix 10.

ought to be established for the building of the bomber force. But Bomber Command was being accorded encouraging abstract favour by professional military men, and the Air Staff's demand for a frontline force of 4,000 heavy bombers seemed nearer acceptance. However, it was the politicians who had to pass it, and the Cabinet was unconvinced. Ministers were "reluctant to commit themselves to so big a concentration of effort upon one means of winning the war".[1]

If only Bomber Command could have demonstrated some outstanding achievement, the persuasion would have been easier. No such propaganda was provided. The bombers were switched to a short-term assault on the Ruhr-Rhineland transportation system and on the morale of the industrial workers in that region. When Russia was brought into the war on 22 June 1941 it was thought that the disruption of the western German railways would be the best immediate strategic aid that Great Britain could give to the Soviets. It was also considered that a diminution of German fighter strength in France might permit the resumption of daylight bombing – on French factories, submarine pens and harbours as training preparation for the day-bombing of Germany: but the bomber formations which were sent across in day-time were severely mauled. Bomber Command could produce no striking success. Nevertheless the Chiefs of Staff grew firmer in their advocacy of the 4,000-bomber force. They declared: "It is in bombing, on a scale undreamt of in the last war, that we find the new weapon on which we must principally depend for the destruction of German economic life and morale. . . . We give the heavy bomber first priority in production, for only the heavy bomber can produce the conditions under which other offensive forces can be employed."[2]

But, almost immediately, Bomber Command suffered its most wounding blow, witnessed at the highest policy-making level where its future was to be decided.

For over a year Churchill had been becoming increasingly suspicious of the bombing achievement, and he had urged his

---

1. Minute from the Air Minister, Sir Archibald Sinclair, to Portal, 16 June 1941, quoted by Webster and Frankland, *The Strategic Air Offensive Against Germany, 1939–1945.*
2. Chiefs of Staff Memorandum, 31 July 1941.

scientific and statistical adviser Professor Lindemann (later Lord Cherwell) to investigate. In August 1941, Mr Butt, a member of the War Cabinet secretariat, produced an analysis of photographs taken from night bombers in June and July. Butt recorded his conclusion : "Of the total sorties only one in five get within five miles of the target, i.e., within the 75 square miles surrounding the target." Over Germany and particularly over the Ruhr, Butt said, the proportion was much less.[1]

Churchill viewed these conclusions with extreme gravity. Yet he did not immediately withdraw his faith in the bombers : he urged that the developing scientific aids to navigation and to target-identification should be expedited. By September he had over-ridden any Cabinet reluctance, and accepted the principle of the 4,000-bomber force. He increased the national effort to achieve this. He wrote to Sir John Anderson, Lord President of the Council and one of the nine members of the War Cabinet :

In order to achieve a first-line strength of 4,000 medium and heavy bombers, the Royal Air Force require 22,000 to be made between July 1941 and July 1943, of which 5,500 may be expected to reach us from American production. The latest forecasts show that of the remaining 16,500 only 11,000 will be got from our own factories. If we are to win the war we cannot accept this position, and after discussion with the Minister of Aircraft Production and Sir Charles Craven, I have given directions for a plan to be prepared for the expansion of our effort to produce a total of 14,500 in the period . . .[2]

Nevertheless, while continuing to stress the principle of massive air superiority, Churchill became irritated by the parallel persistence of his principal air marshal. Portal, after the revelations of Butt, had no other immediate card to play but the advocacy of undisguised area bombing directed against German morale. He presented to Churchill a plan to devastate "beyond all hope of recovery" 43 named German towns with a total population of 15 million. The plan required a minimum of 4,000 bombers.

1. Report by Mr Butt to Bomber Command on his Examination of Night Photographs, 18 August 1941. Webster and Frankland, *op. cit.*, Appendix 13.

2. Minute, Prime Minister to Lord President of the Council, 7 September 1941, Winston Churchill, *The Grand Alliance.*

As Churchill recorded it, "I was forced to cool down the claims which some of our most trusted officers put forward in their natural ardour."[1] The so-called cooling down was of a freezing nature. He told Portal:[2] "It is very disputable whether bombing by itself will be a decisive factor in the present war. On the contrary, all that we have learnt since the war began shows that its effects, both physical and moral, are greatly exaggerated." He cruelly emphasized Bomber Command's inaccuracy: "Only a quarter of our bombs hit the targets.[3] Consequently an increase in the accuracy of bombing to 100 per cent would in fact raise our bombing force to four times its strength. The most we can say is that it will be a heavy and I trust a seriously increasing annoyance."

An "annoyance" was perhaps the most humiliating description of Bomber Command that could be given to Portal. This was a time of personal crisis for him. He was, in Trenchard's words, the Founder's "favourite disciple",[4] but to anyone outside the high command of the Royal Air Force he had not been an obvious choice as Chief of Staff, and not solely because he was a dozen years younger than the other Chiefs. Sir Archibald Sinclair, the Air Minister, had had great difficulty in winning his acceptance by the War Cabinet. Churchill, looking back on his appointment, referred to him, perhaps with studied non-commitment, as "the accepted star of the Air Force".[5] Churchill's military secretary, General Ismay, noted that "his

1. Winston Churchill, *The Grand Alliance.*

2. Minute, Prime Minister to Chief of the Air Staff, 27 September 1941, partially quoted by Webster and Frankland, *The Strategic Air Offensive Against Germany, 1939–1945.*

3. Even this was an optimistic reading of the Butt Report, unless by "target" was understood the 75 square miles around the target.

4. Boyle, *Trenchard.* Portal, known in the Royal Air Force as "the Big Thinker", was groomed from an early age. In 1923, after a course at the Staff College, he served in the Air Ministry's Directorate of Operations and Intelligence. Here he first came to Trenchard's intimate notice. In 1930, after a course at the Imperial Defence College, Portal served with the Plans Division of the Air Staff. In 1937, after his Aden command and a period as R.A.F. instructor at the Imperial Defence College, he became, as an air vice marshal, Director of Organization at the Air Ministry. He went on to the Air Council in 1939 as Air Marshal, Air Member for Personnel.

5. Winston Churchill, *Their Finest Hour.*

selection over the heads of many older and more senior officers was universally acclaimed by his Service",[1] but there is no indication of immediate acclaim by anyone else. As long as Portal's confidence in the aggressiveness of the bomber force chimed with Churchill's hopes there was little likelihood of grave friction. But when Churchill's faith faded Portal had to work his passage all over again.

He fought back. He challenged Churchill to produce a new strategy if he was rejecting the principle of the attainment of massive air superiority. In reply Churchill emphasized that he envisaged air superiority as a precursor to "simultaneous attacks by armoured forces in many of the conquered countries which were ripe for revolt". But, in a somewhat avuncular fashion, he extended the comfort of simple advice to the troubled marshal :

We all hope that the air offensive against Germany will realize the expectations of the Air Staff. Everything is being done to create the bombing force desired on the largest possible scale, and there is no intention of changing this policy. . . . It is the most potent method of impairing the enemy's morale we can use at the present time. . . . Even if all the towns of Germany were rendered largely uninhabitable it does not follow that the military control would be weakened or even that war industry could not be carried on. The Air Staff would make a mistake to put their claim too high. . . . It may well be that German morale will crack, and that our bombing will play a very important part in bringing the result about. But all things are always on the move simultaneously. . . . One has to do the best one can, but he is an unwise man who thinks there is any *certain* method of winning this war, or indeed any other war between equals in strength. The only plan is to persevere.[2]

A month later Churchill virtually banned bombing for a period of three to four months. Shocked by a ten per cent casualty rate on 400 bombers sent to Germany on the night of 7 November, he ordered that, to conserve Bomber Command's still-static strength, only small forces should be sent out, and not to distant targets, until the next spring. It was a bitter year's end for Portal. Bomber Command, switched inconsistently from

1. Ismay, *Memoirs.*
2. Minute, Prime Minister to C.A.S., 7 October 1941. Winston Churchill, *The Grand Alliance.*

one target-system to another, its striking power painfully evaluated only by despairing elimination, had the reputation merely of a paper tiger. No glory had accrued to its Commander in Chief, and none to the Chief of Air Staff. Peirse was soon to be relieved of his command. In logic, should the man who dismissed him, Portal himself, expect that he should stay? The question began to be asked, not always silently : Would this air marshal achieve anything?

CHAPTER EIGHT

H. H. ARNOLD, AIRMAN

Possible? Is anything impossible? Read the news-
papers!

THE DUKE OF WELLINGTON

The power of the United States Army Air Forces in the Second
World War was the product primarily of two solitary men, one
a superb but naïve professional airman, the other a patchy
politician, a supreme manager in home affairs but a dilettante
abroad, who had either the luck or the instinct to make the
right military decision at the right time. That time was the
month of September 1938.

An insecure generation was convulsed in the savage climax
of a week of seemingly unendurable tension. Three hundred
million adults in the Europe west of Warsaw were, in following
years, to become emotionally saturated against the sheer physical
friction and nauseous reaction of mass excitement : the adrenalin
could not be pumped continuously. But the thirty days of
September 1938 were their baptism of fire. The heart of the
hysteria lay in Nuremberg. There, at the beginning of the
month, the last great party rally of the Nazi regime was being
manipulated, with the utmost skill, to brainwash a quarter of
a million picked National Socialists, and, in an expanding shock-
wave, Germany and the world. Using every technique of modern
communication except television, with particular reliance on the
radio and fast-printed news film, the masterly assault on the
credulity of the people was begun. Day by day the nerve-strings
were tightened. One hundred and eighty thousand uniformed
party leaders marched by torchlight in frightening precision
to hear a speech from Hitler. Merely to make the physical
dispositions for such a *corps d'élite* was a colossal task : the
formations were the equivalent of ten divisions of British infantry, or more than the armies of Blücher, Wellington and

157

Bonaparte at Waterloo. But the stage-management was superb. During the long trooping the million spectators in and around the stadium which formed their Circus Maximus were cumulatively pulsed towards abandon by the controlled admixture of sight and sound and passion : an irresistible pageantry of the power and the fervour of youth, of tossing standards and smoking torches, massed bands, Germanic emblems, laurels for the martyred dead, and intolerably evocative hymns. "I had spent six years in St Petersburg in the best days of the old Russian ballet," confessed Sir Nevile Henderson, British Ambassador to Berlin, "but for grandiose beauty I have never seen a ballet to compare with it." When Hitler finally appeared, and in a sudden blinding blaze 150 searchlight beams converged to form a canopy of blue light over the arena, the Führer took two full minutes to pass down one avenue in the ten columns of statuesque brownshirts, each column 200 yards long. The men stood silent and still, but the crowd in the dark on the terraces, their flesh penetrated by the tingling march-beat of a regiment of brass and drums, screamed their sanity away. And then the divisions in the centre joined in with the drilled deep, staccato bay : *"Sieg Heil! Sieg Heil! Sieg Heil!"*

This was but the halfway rise in the tide of persuasion and intimidation. On the night after Hitler, Göring was to speak, and on the next climactic night Hitler again. The immediate object was to terrorize the Czechs, on whose borders the Wehrmacht was now massing. But the ultimate objective was the world – listening, as the world did then, to the direct broadcasts sent out by every German transmitter. When Göring's hour came he roared a naked diatribe unparalleled in present-day standards of diplomatic controversy against "this miserable, pygmy race" of Czechs behind whom lay "Moscow and the eternal mask of the Jew Devil".

On the evening of 12 September, the last night of the Nuremberg rally, households over Europe hushed as the radio needles were tuned to the German station. With some services there was a native-language commentary to set the scene. The storm-troops were massed in an enclosed congress hall. Military bands played the Badenweiler March while Hitler strode the length of the assembly. There was the flurry of heavy silk and the glitter of eagles as the standards round which each contingent had stood square were carried to the rear. A symphony orchestra played the Meistersinger overture. Rudolf Hess announced "The Führer will speak." Hitler stood with his head framed against the Blood Flag which had been carried at the Munich *putsch,* its staff now held by a soldier in a steel helmet. The speech began. Quickly it reached the heights of passion. The excitement began to explode. There were periods of many minutes when nothing could be heard except the shrieks of the crowd's ecstasy and the billowing of *"Sieg Heil!"* Hitler, always among the first to surrender to the intoxication of the event, was at times totally incomprehensible in the swamping seas of his own emotion. But the basic message was clear :

God has not created seven and a half million Czechs to torture three and a half million Germans [in the Sudetenland]. Behind our triple and fourfold lines of fortification stands the entire German people in arms. The Germanic Empire is nothing new. It existed 500 years before the New World was discovered, and to remind the world of this I had the insignia of the old Empire brought to Nuremberg. Dynasties change but people remain. The world must realize that the Italian and German States are old historic phenomena. No one is obliged to love them, but no power under the sun can remove them. We shall never bow to foreign will. So God be our help.

Above the last perfunctory call on God the howl of the audience buffeted the microphone into a distortion of sound. It was carried, crackling with the static of short-wave transmission, into a sunlit railroad car standing stationary under secret guard 5,000 miles away in a clearing near Rochester, Minnesota. It was a site handy for access to the Mayo Clinic, where James Roosevelt was undergoing an operation. His father, President Franklin D. Roosevelt, who, understanding German, had followed Hilter's speech, snapped off the switch and spoke across the car to Harry Hopkins. He told Hopkins, then Roosevelt's emergency relief Works Progress Administrator, to go prospecting on the Pacific Coast to find opportunities to expand the aircraft industry for war production. Hopkins noted later : "The President was sure then that we were going to get into war and he believed that air power would win it."[1]

1. Robert E. Sherwood, *The White House Papers of Harry L. Hopkins,* Eyre & Spottiswoode, London, 1948.

The date was 12 September 1938, and Roosevelt made his judgement without waiting for Munich. The Air Corps stood at a strength of 1,650 officers and 16,000 enlisted men, an excess of only 134 personnel over its strength in 1920. The fact that it had been allowed to remain at this level even through the German and Italian "civilian" air penetration of South America is a measure of Roosevelt's monumental aloofness from foreign events throughout his first five years of power. But when he did design a foreign policy, he rammed down the foundations at top speed. On 28 September he summoned his civil and military war chiefs into his office. Among the dozen in the room there were two who were attending such a conference for the first time, of whom the junior at least was naïvely delighted to have made the top grade. They were Major-General Henry Harley Arnold, Deputy Chief of the Air Corps and its acting (though unconfirmed) commander, and Lieutenant-General George Catlett Marshall, newly appointed Deputy Chief of Staff for the Army. Neither of them was *persona grata* with Roosevelt, and the President was to maintain his antipathy for a long time. But by Roosevelt's side was the man who had persuaded him to promote them : Harry Hopkins. Hopkins had met Arnold only a few days earlier, on his return from the West Coast. But in this short time he had had many long conversations with Arnold. He had sized up his character and abilities, and he had digested Arnold's ideas and passed them on to the President in capsules of energy. So complete was this brief assimilation that Roosevelt astonished the army, navy and treasury representatives at the conference by demanding from the start 10,000 new warplanes and the organization of aircraft production to reach an annual capacity of 20,000 planes within a year. Arnold went away from his first presidential conference – which became almost his last, by a trick of Roosevelt's prejudice against him – confidently encouraged to trench the deep foundations for a structure that should shape metal and train men to make the first balanced modern air force in the world.

Two days later, on 30 September 1938, Chamberlain signed the appeasement pact at Munich. He was widely regarded, though not among the chuckling German General Staff, as having saved the world from war, admittedly at the expense of Czecho-Slovakia. He had persuaded Hitler to sign another piece of paper, unconnected with the Sudetenland, and it was this paper that he waved at the hysterical crowds beyond the newsreel cameras in London, declaring he brought "Peace with honour. I believe it is peace for our time." The Staff of the Royal Air Force certainly believed that, whether the peace was to be permanent or not, they had been saved from an immediate conflict that would have annihilated them as swiftly as the Polish Air Force was later to be destroyed. Only the German High Command thought differently. Eight and a half years later, at the Nuremberg trials, Field Marshal Keitel was asked by the Czech prosecutor: "Would the Reich have attacked Czecho-Slovakia in 1938 if the Western Powers had stood by Prague?" The answer came from a weak man, and must be judged accordingly. But Hitler's Chief of Staff said unhesitatingly: "Certainly not. We were not strong enough militarily. The object of Munich was to get Russia out of Europe, to gain time, and to complete the German armaments."[1]

Gain time. In 1938 that was the desperate objective of every future belligerent leader, from Hitler to Roosevelt. And every power devoured the respite with frenzied concentration, turning national effort into destructive potential at an unprecedented conversion ratio; all except France, which with busy muscle and lethargic brain poured concrete into the Maginot Line and not a single new injection into the aircraft industry. *Gain time*. Yet no war, and only rarely a battle, is fought when both military commanders consider they are ready. What is the ultimate compulsion of time? Does man grab time in the gambler's uncertain hope of acquiring in the interim more forces than his enemy? Does Death comply, and wait on time in the surety of a heavier harvest? How efficient should slaughter be? How many died between 1939 and 1945 as bonus casualties, because arms of destruction unready at Munich had time to be coaxed to perfection? Or how many more might have died in a war of 1938, from the impact of blunt weapons clumsily used in an indecisive strategy which could never rise far beyond counting the numbers of enemy dead? The Second World War gave us terror bombing, and shrunken bodies fused to the asphalt in Dresden as well as the smoke from the Belsen crematoria;

1. International Military Tribunal, *Trial of the Major War Criminals*, Nuremberg, 1947.

F

but the First World War had contributed half a million casualties machine-gunned knee-high in mud in one action at Passchendaele, and 174 British cemeteries on the Ypres Salient alone.

Generals are often philosophical men. They tend to speculate on these historical ifs; but not at the moment of action. When a general gains time he uses it, and postpones for later consideration the inquiry into whose lives he has saved or doomed. General Arnold, with three years in which to prepare for war according to the highly accurate estimates of his planners, had to work fast to spend adequately the almost unlimited funds he was now to tap, and built an air force almost from scratch.

Who was Arnold? He was probably the most cheerful example of a deprived personality in military history. At the beginning of his career he was one of the only two qualified pilots in the United States Army, yet he never saw combat in the First World War. He bitterly regretted that, but did not allow it greatly to change his personality. The cliché "inferiority complex" is too often taken to imply an attitude of revenge on life. Many successful men have not been soured by disabilities of birth or career. Bastards have become prime ministers and disappointed fighters have developed as great marshals, and it is arguable that they have done so by converting their disadvantage from a thorn in the flesh to a spur for the flank. In trivial moments Arnold occasionally exhibited both his pride and his diffidence at being what he called "a rookie in the big league"[1] whether as an airman among the top brass of senior services at home or as an American negotiating with glamorous paladins abroad : "When I went to England, as Chief of the Air Corps, I had two stars, but I found myself doing business with Air Chief Marshals, Field Marshals and Fleet Admirals – men who had five stars and whose chests were bedecked with medals from one side to the other. I had two medals on my chest and two stars on my shoulders." But Arnold's steady reaction was to intensify his professionalism, to devote his career to the integrity of the Air Corps, to its most precise and effective expansion, and to the development and operation of a calculated, characteristic global strategy. He was an air force man through and through, from the seat of his pants where he learned to fly to

1. H. H. Arnold, *Global Mission*, Harper, New York, 1949.

the cortex of his brain with which he waged war.

Arnold was born in 1886 in Montgomery County, Pennsylvania, the son of a doctor and grandson of a nail maker who had fought at Gettysburg. After four years at West Point he was commissioned in the infantry and in 1911 transferred to aeronautical duty with the Signal Corps. By 1918 he was Assistant Chief of the Air Service. When peace came he took a local command, and then, after useful planning experience at the Army Industrial College, joined the Staff in Washington. In the running controversy over air power compared with land and sea power – always a delicate subject in the United States, where the Army controlled the Air Corps[1] – Arnold let his air sympathies show too clearly and was exiled to another local command. Following a Command and General Staff School course he took over a technical depot and then an operational base at March Field, California, from which he later commanded the First Wing of the GHQ Air Force. In January 1936 he returned to Washington as Assistant Chief of the Air Corps, and his base was in Washington for the rest of his career.

It can be said of Arnold more accurately than of any other marshal that his air force was his own creation and his own weapon. When he came to lead it in 1936 it was tiny but by no means ineffective : a lively and vigorous cub.

The Air Corps of the United States Army was between the wars a small force considerably hampered by inter-service rivalry, yet a body which maintained a separate and integral spirit and kept a clear idea of the direction in which it wanted to develop towards the exploitation of air power. In 1918 it was the fourth ranking air force in the world and by 1938 it had dropped to seventh. In the twenties and thirties it was always a subordinate organization, and there seems little doubt that its command structure stifled its development as a strategic force. Yet it began to increase in stature at a most favourable time, when the revolution in aircraft design was sweeping all machines designed before 1933 swiftly into limbo. Arnold himself declared, "We could not have had any real air power much sooner than we got it,"[2] arguing that the four-engined bomber was the nucleus of the new strength.

1. The name was changed from Air Service on 2 July 1926.
2. Arnold, *Global Mission*.

In 1935 the tactical units of the air arm were concentrated in a striking force, the GHQ Air Force, not at first responsible to the Chief of the Air Corps but directly to a member of the General Staff, Brigadier General Frank M. Andrews. But the Air Corps Staff, who were still responsible for procurement, believed that the combat strength of the air arm depended on the heavy bomber, and that the GHQ Air Force should have it. An elaborate deception had to be conducted against the War Department, which could veto new designs, and often did. The official purpose of the proposed new bomber was for long declared to be defensive coastal reconnaissance and the reinforcement of bases in Hawaii, Panama and Alaska.

The experimental four-engined Boeing B-17 proved so promising at its evaluation in 1935 that a tentative order of 65 machines was suggested for 1936, to replace 185 twin-engined aircraft already envisaged. But in a totally unpardonable accident attributed to the negligence of maintenance engineers and pilots the bomber crashed on take-off at its official inspection flight. Although a crash analysis completely vindicated the aircraft's design, the initial order was cut from 65 to 13. These aircraft, the first of the Flying Fortresses, were the sole heavy bomber strength of the Air Corps when war broke out in Europe. The vast difference in production facilities *for future models* imposed by an 80 per cent reduction on the pioneer order had an appreciable effect on the bomber strength of the West during the first years of the war. On 13 May 1938 the Chief of Staff and the Chief of Naval Operations had a verbal agreement restricting the Army Air Corps to flights within 100 miles of the coastline. The Deputy Chief of Staff told the Assistant Secretary of War that no research on four-engined bombers was necessary and that the Chief of the Air Corps had been informed that the experimentation and development for the fiscal years 1939–40 would be restricted to that class of aviation designed for the close-in support of ground troops and for the production of the relevant types of aircraft such as medium and light bombers, pursuit and other light aircraft. "Our national policy contemplates preparation for defence not aggression."

The Army Air Corps did in fact pay considerable attention to air-ground collaboration in support of infantry and armour – more than the Royal Air Force had practised in peace-time, in spite of the opportunities offered by reluctant subjects in the sandy areas of the Empire. One American staff officer confessed that Göring had been a useful model – and, indeed, the support operations of the Luftwaffe in its first nine months of warfare are a classic staff-college study. Yet the American air leaders could not concede that ground-support was their only task. With the utmost tact and discretion in the face of reactionary Army superiors, the Air Corps managed to retain – and even to teach in its Tactical School – the principle that "the special mission of the air arm should be to attack the whole of the 'enemy national structure'."[1] This was a theory of air power, closely guarded within the brotherhood of the Corps, which had a strong affinity to the conception of air power held by the Staff of the Royal Air Force. In Trenchard's words : "The role of the Air Force is not to defeat the enemy's armed forces but to attack direct the centres of production, transportation and communication from which the enemy war effort is maintained."[2]

The man who was responsible for the continued acceptance of this doctrine in the United States Army Air Corps was a friend of H. H. Arnold's with whom the Air Corps had regretfully been obliged to part as a serving officer : General William E. Mitchell.

Before the First World War Billy Mitchell had been known as a brilliant captain serving on the General Staff at the age of thirty-two, which was then considered young in the United States Army. He went out to France as a major in the Air Service and within months was a brigadier general and Chief of Air Service Army Group with an outstanding reputation among the Allies for the cunning and forceful deployment of aircraft. In September 1918 he supported the American infantry advance on the Meuse-Argonne with the first real blitz air assault in military history. With a force of 1,500 aircraft – by no means all American-flown and none American-designed – he sent in waves, 500 at a time, to reduce the enemy salient at Saint-Mihiel. Only one-third of his force was acting strictly as a ground arm. The rest were used as two air brigades to strike at the enemy's local communications and supply and to

1. Office of Air Force History, United States Air Force: Wesley F. Craven and James L. Cate (editors), *The Army Air Forces in World War II*, Washington, 1948.
2. Memorandum on The War Object of an Air Force, 2 May, 1928.

make independent attacks on the V of the salient or where the enemy was concentrating to counterattack. Trenchard called the operation "the most terrific exhibition I have ever seen". Mitchell had already conferred with Trenchard and shared his theories of air power and the ultimate supremacy of independent strategic air bombardment.

Mitchell came home, remaining in the Service, and began to propound his striking propositions for the conduct of air operations. His tactical suggestions were superb, though naturally they were studied only by professional airmen. It was his strategic theory that commanded more general attention. He declared that war had been revolutionized by the advent of "air power which can go straight to the vital centres and entirely neutralize or destroy them". The vital centres consisted of "cities where the people live, areas where their food and supplies are produced and the transport lines that carry these supplies from place to place". He maintained that "it is now realized that the hostile main army in the field is a false objective and the real objectives are the vital centres. . . . Armies themselves can be disregarded by air power if a rapid strike is made against the opposing centres."

This is almost a direct echo of Trenchard's secret discourse to the British Air Staff in 1923 : Why attack the civil population from the air instead of bombarding the enemy Army? "Because we were able to do this while the Army were not, and so go straight to the source of supply and stop it. The Army policy was to defeat the enemy Army – ours to defeat the enemy nation. The Army only defeated the enemy Army because they could not get at the enemy nation."[1]

Mitchell had a far harder task than any propagandist in Britain to persuade America of the importance of air power, simply because the United States had not experienced bombing, did not greatly fear it, and was unconvinced of its accuracy. Aerial bombing of Britain in the First World War had bequeathed a deep psychological legacy – and no mean casualties, considering the armament available. On one morning in 1917 fourteen German bombers killed 162 Londoners and injured 432, a deadlier score than many a mission in the Second World War. It was on the basis of this experience that the British

1. See page 47.

provided 750,000 beds for anticipated air-raid casualties on the outbreak of the Second World War. The Americans did not detail one reserve bed for the victims of aerial bombing.[1]

Strategic air bombardment as an independent task for a separate air force was the subject of an American inter-service squabble which seems so childish and unrealistic to the detached observer that one wonders how the protagonists could ever have been allowed to run their country's affairs. Mitchell said he would prove the demise of sea power by destroying a variety of obsolete warships after the First World War, and he systematically sank them, admittedly without flak opposition, but ending with the "unsinkable" German battleship *Ostfriesland* with four separate skins of steel and intricate watertight bulkheads. Yet a Navy politician had publicly said that he would stand bareheaded on the bridge of any battleship during any bombardment by any of Mitchell's aircraft. This type of contemptuous technical bickering over the power of life and death went on through the thirties and into the war, in Britain was well as in the United States.

General Mitchell publicly attacked, while a serving officer, the "incompetency, criminal negligence and almost treasonable administration of the national defence by the War and Navy Departments". He was deservedly court-martialled, and retired from any major personal influence on public policy, although his ideas remained cherished by some of the Air Corps. The court martial was made into a far more significant political trial of the proponents of aviation as a positive strategic power in war-time, and, as one of these protagonists, Major H. H. Arnold was marked as a troublemaker and removed from Washington. His only form of revenge was a keener application to his profession. When he came back, as Assistant Chief of the Air Corps, the air force men within the Army had learned more finesse – and had already ordered the four-engined bomber.

Arnold was always known as "Hap", a nickname which

1. Without long-range bombers it was thought that the Luftwaffe could never reach the American continent. But Werner Baumbach, General of the Bombers, was involved in schemes to bomb the Panama Canal and New York, ditching the aircraft afterwards in the Atlantic where submarines were to take off the crews. Werner Baumbach, *Broken Swastika*, Hale, London 1960.

General Ismay, Churchill's representative on the Chiefs of Staff committee, called "a natural", declaring "he was always cheerful and smiling." Arnold himself asserted that he was of a fiery character and would become "impatient, intolerant, and would rant around, fully intending to tear the War and Navy Departments to pieces". There were occasions, particularly amidst the chagrin following Pearl Harbor, when subordinate generals could confirm this. But of all the Allied leaders he was the least cranky. His friendly understanding with the solitary Portal, a man who would never even take lunch in company if he could avoid it,[1] was of the greatest benefit to the air effort of the West. The one serious difference between the two concerned the allocation of heavy bombers and their precise use in the Allied bombing offensive. It was not a small divergence. From many points of view it was the most vital decision of the war. Yet Arnold, although faintly embarrassed by Portal's longer war experience, yielded hardly a pace.

Arnold's strength was that he had a comparatively one-track mind, but a many-sided personality. He applied his mental intransigence to the construction of his force and its operation according to a determined strategy. He used his management of men to get his ideas accepted. He was an air force man, a specialist who had never had the broader and perhaps more flexible approach of the ideal chief of staff. But he never wanted to be an overall chief of staff in the sense in which the United States Army operated. (Marshall became Army Chief of Staff on 1 September 1939; Arnold, as Chief of the Air Corps, was made a Deputy Chief of Staff on 30 October 1940.) Arnold made it his job to be sure that the Chief of Staff, and the President, too, had all the arguments for the air force point of view. He made no effort to get through to his first Secretary of War, Woodring, who was an isolationist, but concentrated first on General Marshall. "When George Marshall first took over in 1937," Arnold later admitted, "he needed plenty of indoctrination about the air facts of life." But Arnold certainly drove his points home. "The difference in George [compared with Woodring], who presently was to become one of the most potent forces behind the development of a real American air

1. Marshal of the Royal Air Force Sir John Slessor, *The Central Blue*, London, 1956.

power, was his ability to digest what he saw and make it part of as strong a body of military genius as I have ever known."[1]

Arnold was not an original strategist. What he did catch from Marshall was a renewed insistence on the old strategical principle of concentrating all available force at the decisive point. The Air Corps had a very complete and sound strategy, and had worked out its principles of offence while it was still theoretically confined to defensive principles. But to carry out strategy the Air Corps needed force. Arnold's first task was to make possible a gargantuan aircraft production.

He was a superb fixer. His favourite description of any negotiation was that he was "doing business" with someone. He did business with the aircraft manufacturers when he had very little to offer them and the major product was goodwill. He cultivated technicians and research specialists, flattering them, perhaps, that a technical service still had a lot of know-how to learn. He collected meteorologists and optical experts. Above all he saw from the beginning the necessity for creating a balanced force, securing simultaneously machines, men and the geographical *space* to handle the huge forces he envisaged. He declared outright at his first meeting with Roosevelt on 28 September 1938: "The strength of an Air Force cannot be measured in terms of airplanes only. Other things are essential – productive capacity of airplanes, of pilots, of mechanics, and bases from which to operate. A sound training programme is essential to provide replacements."[2] And his replacement schedule was conservatively pessimistic. He worked to the assumption that he must provide for the loss of a quarter of his bomber force during every month of action. His fleets were calculated to "turn over" three times a year.

His straightforward statement at the presidential conference was the only personal contact he was to have with Roosevelt for over nine months. He had never caught the fancy of the President. The Chief of the Air Corps, General Oscar Westover, had been killed in a flying accident on 21 September 1938. Though Arnold was the Acting Chief, he was not confirmed in his appointment until the 29th, and was still officially "floating" on the 28th. The reason for the delay was a report

1. Arnold, *Global Mission*.
2. Arnold, *Global Mission*.

given to Roosevelt that Arnold was an incorrigible drunkard who had publicly disgraced the Service while in his cups at Honolulu. The facts were that he had never served in Honolulu and had not drunk spirits for the last eighteen years. The appointment was finally sanctioned on the insistence of Harry Hopkins. It was Hopkins, too, who persuaded the President to appoint General Marshall as Army Chief of Staff. Marshall believed that Roosevelt lacked complete confidence in him even then, until after Pearl Harbor. Shortly after Arnold's appointment the air chief gave clumsy and politically damaging evidence before a hostile congressional committee. He was openly threatened by Roosevelt with dismissal and exile to a Pacific command. He was barred from White House conferences, and kept in touch with decisions of high policy only through Hopkins and Marshall. Only after the war in Europe had started was he deemed to have worked his passage by his zealous supervision of the expanding air force, and he was invited to dinner at the White House. Roosevelt was making cocktails when he entered, and his first words were, as Arnold reported : "Good evening, Hap. How about my mixing you an Old Fashioned?" With perhaps more feeling than in the usual polite rejoinder Arnold answered : "Thanks, Mr President. I haven't had one for about twenty years, but I assure you I will enjoy this one with you, tremendously."[1]

By now Arnold's friendly intimacy with the American aircraft manufacturers was beginning to show results. He had gone away from the White House in September 1938 to give immediate instructions for a private national conference of the leaders in the industry. He had no money : the President could not recommend this all-out expansion to Congress until January 1939, when he asked for an Air Corps allocation of $300 million. Arnold asked the manufacturers to tool up for the orders he promised them and to borrow money until the State could hand it out. The factories were already comfortably expanding on the proceeds of payment for new sites and tools made to them by the British and French Governments. Arnold asked them to prepare now the plant, tools, power and facilities for training skilled workers in anticipation of the feverish race that lay ahead. He asked for the end of competitive bidding in favour of

1. Arnold, *Global Mission.*

an 8 per cent or 10 per cent profit on costs. He cut red tape in the awarding of contracts and set projects moving along before the formal documents were signed. Without intense goodwill, youthful adaptability in the industry and – it must be emphasized – the unstinted funds which the nation was now diverting towards its starveling air force, this massive rearmament could never have been accomplished at the pace it achieved. Construction was not simple. The American aircraft were untried in war, but Arnold had observers in England and France as soon as European hostilities began. Modifications in design, armament and armour were being introduced to the blueprints from February 1940. And this was the pattern of production. In the six years 1940–45 it resulted in a grand total of 229,230 planes as the output of the American aircraft industry.[1]

How were these planes to be used in battle? What sort of war was envisaged? The strategy planned for the coming war decided the balance of the air force to be built. At the time of Pearl Harbor the actual firstline strength of the United States Army Air Forces (the official title as from 20 June 1941) was as follows:[2]

	Groups	Aircraft per group
Heavy bombardment aircraft	14	35
Medium bombardment aircraft	9	57
Light bombardment aircraft	5	57
Pursuit aircraft	26	80
Transport aircraft	6	35
Observation aircraft	10	55

This made a total of nearly two fighters to every bomber – actually 2,080 fighters to 1,288 bombers. But within two months after Pearl Harbor the Army Air Forces had already decided on the following firstline strength to be achieved in less than two years, by December 1943:

Heavy bombardment aircraft, for 14 groups now 66 groups

Medium bombardment aircraft	9	18
Light bombardment aircraft	5	30

1. Actual acceptances were 158,880 aircraft.
2. Craven and Cate, *Army Air Forces in World War II*.

Pursuit aircraft	26	58
Transport aircraft	6	24
Observation aircraft	10	28

Under the advanced scheme (which was not the last) the longer time taken to produce large aircraft was showing results. The number of bombers exceeded the number of fighters, and the number of frontline heavy bombers alone exceeded the fighters available two years previously. (It should be remembered that reserves were to be 300 per cent of the frontline.) The United States Army Air Forces were planned with their primary strength lying in strategic bombing. That conversion of strategy from the concept of defence to a policy of decisive attack occurred – if any single watershed in history can be isolated – in the railroad car of President Roosevelt at noon on 12 September 1938.

The concept of strategic bombing was only a *theory*, advanced between the wars by Trenchard, Mitchell and the Italian General Douhet. It had never been tried in practice. The air operations of the thirties in China and Spain, and later in Poland and France, were a magnificent demonstration of the *old* technique of effective support for ground forces, rather than anything new. Yet the principle of strategic bombing was accepted by the American Air Staff as the fundamental exercise of air power. And the principle implied full dependence on bombing which should be *accurately applied to precise targets in daylight*. Such a policy was dependent in its turn on bomber crews trained to keep tight formation at all altitudes, to bomb with accuracy and shoot against attacking fighter aircraft with accuracy, and to work within each aircraft, squadron and group as drilled and fully integrated crews. The great distinction between the bomber policy of the United States Army Air Forces and the Royal Air Force by the time the war came to America was that the British had abandoned precision. They had started the war with the aim of precise daylight bombing, and had been forced by the strength of the enemy opposition into imprecise area bombing at night with the avowed intention of striking at the morale of the civilian population in the main industrial areas.

In spite of Billy Mitchell's insistence on the vulnerability of an enemy's "vital centres" and his doctrine of hitting civilian morale, the United States Army Air Forces had edged away from any policy of attacking civilians as the means of destroying the enemy's will to resist. The Air Planners precisely stated that in the coming war against Germany it was not intended to practise area bombing against civilian centres *until* German morale began to crack. The primary aim was the breakdown of the industrial and economic structure of Germany, and the essential for this was "the selection of a system of objectives vital to continued German war effort, and to the means of livelihood of the German people, and tenaciously concentrating all bombing towards the destruction of these objectives".[1]

How was the execution of this aim to fare under the actual stress of war? The strong influence of the Royal Air Force was directed against it because, in the light of their experience, precision bombing was impracticable at that period by reason of the weakness of their bomber force on the long haul into Germany against fighter and flak attack – hazards which American aircraft, too, must face; in addition they emphasized, as a makeweight, the valid effect of the weakening of enemy morale through area bombing – a feature which they indisputably exaggerated in the light of later findings. But their intense propaganda had a certain effect, even upon Arnold. He visited England in April 1941 to ascertain from Portal the maximum practical aid which the Air Corps could offer the British. He was lionized far beyond his expectations and recorded his uninhibited gratification at being accepted into "the major league". The significant effect on the "visiting fireman" was the hardening of his belief in strategic air power, and the beginning of faith in an attack on civilian morale. He confessed :

My discussions with Portal, Churchill and the others left me with the impression that by air alone we might bring Germany so completely to her knees that it might be unnecessary for the ground forces to make a landing. Certainly, destruction by air power could make a landing of ground forces possible. The Navy could insure the existence of England, but air power and air power alone could carry the war home to Central Germany, break down her morale, and take away from her the things essential to combat.[2]

1. Craven and Cate, *Army Air Forces in World War II.*
2. Arnold, *Global Mission.*

This conclusion has the distinct ring of Churchill's actual words: "The Navy can lose us the war, but only the Air Force can win it. . . . The Fighters are our salvation, but the Bombers alone provide the means of victory." Since Churchill originally uttered them six months previously, he was himself beginning to waver from complete faith in the air forces, and was soon to say so bluntly. But Arnold, the American, was the great source of the bombing aircraft which the Royal Air Force needed – against other bidders, and principally Arnold's own air force – to be allocated from American manufacture. For Arnold, faith in air power had to be demonstrated as absolute.

CHAPTER NINE

ARNOLD IN CONFERENCE

I conceive that a part of my business, and perhaps not the most easy part, is to prevent discussions and disputes between the officers who may happen to serve under my command.

THE DUKE OF WELLINGTON

On the night of 7 September 1940, in the first terror bombing of London, the American correspondent Drew Middleton was dining in London, "very tired and shaken", with Colonel Carl A. Spaatz of the United States Army Air Corps. They were sitting amid the Edwardian brass-and-plush of Rules in Maiden Lane. After the short twilight lull the roar of the night bombing became intrusive and the waiter observed that Jerry was at it again.

"By God," said Spaatz, "that's good, that's fine. The British are winning. They've forced them to bomb at night. I tell you the Germans don't know how to go about it. And look at this bunch here. Do they look worried or scared? We're both a damned sight scareder than they are. The Germans won't beat them that way."[1]

Spaatz went back to his hotel and reported in this strain to General Arnold in Washington, for in 1940 that was Spaatz's job in London. And Arnold cogitated very keenly and intently on the central theme of Spaatz's message: "The British are winning. They've forced the Germans to bomb at night."

If night bombing was a sign of weakness, the British had some explanations to make. Arnold knew that in the first six days of September Royal Air Force Bomber Command had claimed to have made precision attacks on named factories producing motors, oil, aluminium, electric power, aircraft, aircraft engines, gas, armaments and steel in Berlin, Munich,

1. Drew Middleton, *The Sky Suspended*, Secker & Warburg, London, 1960.

Nordenham, Bitterfeld, Kassel, Hanover, Cologne, Magdeburg, Stettin, Bremen, Kiel, Regensburg, Frankfurt, Dortmund, Ludwigshafen, Leipzig, Stuttgart, Emden, Mannheim, Turin, Genoa, Alessandria and Sestro San Giovanni. Precision attacks, made at night. If this, in Spaatz's view, was failure, the United States air arm would need to train to produce something much more conclusively successful. But how did the British, who were demanding bombers by the thousand from the United States, explain the "precision" of their attack? Arnold foresaw that, during any future trip to England, many cards must be laid on the table.

Major-General Henry H. Arnold set off for England in April 1941 and, as a neutral observer in a belligerent country, left his uniform behind. He also left his dinner jacket in Washington for, as he admitted, "I hardly knew what to expect. I could not see why I should be received by any of the top-ranking British officers and had little hope of meeting any of them. At that time in the United States I was definitely in the 'minor league'." To Arnold's astonishment and unconcealed delight he found that engagements had been sought with him by the Chief of the Imperial General Staff, the First Sea Lord, the Chief of the Air Staff, Lord Beaverbrook (the Minister of Production), the Prime Minister of Australia, the Commanders in Chief of Bomber and Fighter Commands, the Foreign Secretary, the Air Minister, and the Head of the Department of Scientific and Industrial Research. Finally, he was informed, he was invited to spend a long week-end with the Prime Minister and summoned for an hour's audience with the King. In a cumulation of confusion he managed to borrow a dinner jacket for the visit to Churchill, but slightly bungled the protocol at Buckingham Palace. Modestly deciding after three-quarters of an hour that he had taken up enough of the Monarch's time, he got up and said "Sir, I know you are a very busy man and have a lot to do, so I will leave." He found his way somewhat unsurely through the long picture-hung corridors turbulent with the draught from the bomb-blasted windows. In the ante-room he found a shocked British major-general. "My *God*, Arnold! *You* don't leave the *King*! Not ever! The King always leaves *you*!"[1]

The self-effacing Arnold had some justification for not expect-

1. Arnold, *Global Mission.*

ing the V.I.P. treatment. It was twenty-three years since he had last been in England, arriving during the closing weeks of the First World War only to go into hospital with pneumonia, then break his convalescence to dart eagerly to France in a vain hope of flying in a war machine over the front line before the armistice. Since then he had known Britain as never more war-like than a Noel Coward musical, the home of pacifism and appeasement and the phoney war. It was but ten months since Dunkirk and seven since the Battle of Britain. Though unwavering in his own sympathies, he came from an officer corps whose mixed emotions had not matched Britain's gathered resolution. In the words of Robert E. Sherwood, "In the Army there was a tendency among officers of both ground and air forces to admire Germany for her achievements in building up these arms [the German Army and Air Force]. This led in some extreme cases to the hope that Germany would conquer England, thereby providing historic demonstration of the superiority of land and air power over sea power."[1]

Arnold had noted that, as if the senior British officers were aware of these cool sympathies, they were reserved even when they came to "do business' with America in the final feverish haste to swell their stocks of aircraft. For long they declined to impart any military intelligence on aircraft performance, or a necessary modification whose advantage they had gleaned from the war in Spain, but "withheld such information as they had from us as carefully as did the future enemies". Gradually the British had thawed. The United States eventually insisted that military aircraft could be bought only if the British traded in their latest combat airplane data. The acquisition of this first-hand information determined the equipment of United States Air Corps machines, before the test of battle, with the armour-plating, the heavier-calibre guns and the tail armament that the British had found, through costly experience, that they must have. The bargain saved many American lives.

Gradually the Americans thawed, too, and the warm personalities of their liaison officers were their country's greatest asset. Air Corps officers like Major-Generals Spaatz and Kenney, who had been observers in Britain since the shooting war began, were given every aid in absorbing and transmitting the lessons

1. Sherwood, *The White House Papers of Harry L. Hopkins.*

of action in the air, and the Service friendships they formed were a powerful source of strength for the future. The situation was not uniform all down the line. Some officers in London worked not only badly with the British but badly within the United States Army orbit. Major-General James E. Chaney, the first Commanding General United States Army Forces in the British Isles, was a man who had worked well in liaison with the British since the Battle of Britain. Yet among his staff some officers were so pro-Army and anti-Air Corps in their attitude that they threatened to sabotage the incipient Eighth Air Force effort. When Brigadier-General Ira C. Eaker took over as bomber commander in Britain in February 1942 he found some staff officers "unalterably opposed to an Army Air Force in Britain". One senior officer had the rule of sending back to an Air Corps staff officer "all his staff work which mentions Army Air Forces, requiring them to be re-written to eliminate the word *Air*".[1]

This internecine rivalry was to come. At the moment it was Easter 1941 and the Chief of the Army Air Corps found nothing but cooperation from his own Mission and a succession of red carpets from the British. Perhaps Arnold should not have been so astonished. It did not need any deep cynicism to interpret the British welcome. The nation was desperately short of munitions of war and eager to earn practical good will. Roosevelt, declaring that Britain was the front line of America and her defence "vital to the defence of the United States", had carried through the Lend-Lease Act. In general the British were profoundly grateful, although there were some, like Air Marshal Arthur Harris, who observed that, the aid having been deferred until Britain's fluid resources had been exhausted under the old Cash-and-Carry Act, "Lease-Lend – 'the most unselfish act in history' – coincided with the expenditure of our last dollar."

Arnold had flown over, mostly for England's sake but, like a good businessman, partly for his own. He wanted to get to know Portal and, as he told the Englishman at their first meeting in the private suite in the Dorchester Hotel permanently maintained by the Chief of the Air Staff, "to find a practical way in which the United States Army Air Corps could be of maximum aid to the British". Britain wanted aircraft, and

1. Craven and Cate, *The Army Air Forces in World War II*.

Arnold, the supreme fixer, had become the virtual dictator of the allocation of American aircraft. The contestants intriguing desperately and – all being fair in war – cunningly to get the goods included not only the Royal Air Force and Arnold's own Air Corps, but the United States Navy, and also the Royal Navy, which was putting in a strong claim for powerful reconnaissance and bombing machines for the Coastal Command of the Royal Air Force which it controlled. With the Chinese and the Russians moving towards the tail of the queue, Arnold could echo Churchill, cuffing his clamant Service ministers to keep the peace with the remark, "Too many little pigs, and not enough teats on the old sow". But for Arnold there was a certain gratification in being courted.

Arnold could hold out to Portal the prospect not only of aircraft but of the essentials of air power – what he had already described to Roosevelt as the productive capacity for pilots and aircrew and the space in which to operate. Among his first offers to the Royal Air Force were the use of one-third of the American training establishments and facilities, an open door to the Air Corps Navigation School in Miami, and the relief of Britain's hard-pressed flying personnel by using American pilots and crews to ferry all American aircraft being delivered to Britain across the Atlantic.

For his part Arnold wanted an extension of the intimacy, so that he should have a commanding insight into British technical and strategic thinking. He knew that it would be more detailed, direct and instant than the filtered pap he could get in Washington from diplomatists and attachés. In this aim he was astoundingly successful. Beaverbrook gave him eight aircraft – British day and night fighters and medium bombers – to take home and test. He sent Arnold unhesitatingly to any factory, test airfield and research establishment he wanted to see. For the first time the United States was to have full information on the aircraft modifications, armour, armament, radio and radar used in the Royal Air Force. A highly appreciative Arnold never afterwards faltered in his admiration for Beaverbrook, "a most capable, far-seeing man, with tremendous executive powers". Given *carte blanche* for discussions at Bomber Command, Arnold came away with valuable information on the mass-production of bombs and incendiaries and with reinforced determination to go all out for reliance on heavy bombers himself, a course to which he had still to persuade his General Staff. He was shown Whittle's pioneer jet aircraft and resolved to get those specifications back to the United States. At Fighter Command he got essential data on the required maximum performance for machines at various heights, knowledge urgently necessitating modifications to his own aircraft which he was able to pass on to his home manufacturers. In view of the somewhat feline post-war rivalry between the Air Forces of the West over who did what and when, it is interesting that Arnold freely acknowledged not only the areas where the British were ahead – be it bomb design, jet propulsion or atomic energy – but also that the advantage had been unquestioningly passed across for American use.

All this technical know-how was along Arnold's own line, and to be expected in any generous exchange between the executive heads of sister Services. What Arnold did not expect was his easy welcome into circles discussing high strategy and foreign policy, "all kinds of things I probably had no business to be talking about, but subjects which they were obviously eager to discuss and have some kind of answer to". Field Marshal Sir John Dill, then Chief of the Imperial General Staff, talked to him of threats and counter-measures on every potential front in Europe. Admiral Sir Dudley Pound, First Sea Lord, was frank about his problems from the Atlantic to Singapore. The two-day discussions with Churchill embraced the strategic future from Iraq to Norway, North Africa and the Azores. This was at a time when there had never been any meeting face to face between the two "former naval persons" directing the policies of the major Atlantic powers. When Arnold finally reported to Roosevelt on the results of his mission he declared : "I gained the impression this was the first time the President, as well as his cabinet members, including the Secretary of State, the Secretary of War, and the Secretary of the Navy, had received a complete report on military dispositions and conditions in Europe, from the point of view of the British High Command."[1]

On one of the evenings with Churchill the after-dinner conversation dissolved into a duologue between Portal and the

1. Arnold, *Global Mission*.

Prime Minister. This was not yet the time when Churchill's faith in air bombardment was strongly bleeding away, but the Chief of the Air Staff had to endure some routine knocks. Arnold declared: "Portal handled himself brilliantly, and was able to hold his own in the conversation with the Prime Minister, in spite of the many quips the Prime Minister made, either seriously, or in a joking way, about the Air Force." In this respect Portal was tougher than Dill, who shortly retired from the head of the Army Staff, it has been said because of Churchill's baiting.[1]

Relationship with subordinates is always an important aspect of leadership. Hitler's literally maniac rages had the result that men of talent and stout heart, like Rommel, were grossly insulted and with increasing frequency murdered; men of intermediate courage, like Göring, genuinely feared him and learned how to deceive him; and craven generals, particularly Keitel and von Brauchitsch, were singled out by Hitler as his only tolerable intimate subordinates and were appointed as nominal Chiefs of the High Command or the Army transmitting out Hitler's martial decisions. Churchill, with a far lesser degree of megalomania, generally discharged his static pugnacity by bullying and only occasionally raving against his immediate intimates, like a basically well brought up spoilt child who keeps his tantrums for nurse and family.[2] Roosevelt had deep wells of stored animosity whose pressure was partially eased

1. Brigadier-General Sir Leslie Hollis, later Commandant General Royal Marines, then assistant secretary to the War Cabinet and the Chiefs of Staff Committee, wrote: "Dill was a man of extreme sensitivity ... quite unable to stand up to Churchill's jibes about the Army and the alleged unwillingness of the generals to fight." (Leasor and Hollis, *War at the Top*, Joseph, London, 1959.) Dill remained in the United States at the end of the Washington Conference, January 1942, as Churchill's personal military representative with the President. He died in November 1944 after three invaluable years of work with General Marshall. He was buried in Arlington War Cemetery – the only Englishman ever to receive this honour.

2. In the intimacy of war-time travel the following dialogue was overheard in the aircraft in which Churchill was flying home after the Casablanca Conference. Sawyers, Churchill's manservant, to Churchill as he attempts to tuck him into bed: "You're sitting on your hot water bottle. That isn't at all a good idea." Churchill: "That isn't an idea, it's a coincidence." The charming exchange could have taken place in a nursery at Blenheim sixty years earlier.

by dictating scurrilous speeches against his enemies – and tearing them up once he had got them off his tongue.

Among the marshals, Arnold and Dowding had the controlled irascibility to be expected of determined commanders. Göring, a distorted and less intellectual Churchill, had not the mental resources for skilled torture – his personal escutcheon shows a mailed arm wielding a bludgeon. His reaction came in violent personal abuse far more venomous than Churchill's, and he had not the intuition to limit his blows to well armoured cronies. His victims ranged from fighter pilots like Galland – in outbursts which had their inevitable ricochet on to the morale of a fighting corps – to commanders like General Ernst Udet, his director of aircraft research and production, and General Hans Jeschonnek, his Chief of Staff, both of whom committed suicide after enduring his fury. Göring also suggested suicide to Field Marshal Erhard Milch, who preceded Jeschonnek in his post and succeeded Udet in his; but Milch preferred to be dismissed and live. It is a remarkable distinction between dictatorships and democracies that, taking Germany alone, scores of high-ranking officers killed themselves in formal disgrace while, on the Allies' side, the practice was observed only by commanders of a few naval vessels. Dill, Pound, and indeed Arnold did *work* themselves to death.

The imperturbable Portal characteristically released tension by performing solitary card tricks – by temperament he was a fishing man. He had to face critics far cruder, if less powerful, than Churchill. General Hollis delineated him as a "calm character with a brain like a rapier. I never saw him ruffled, even under vicious and uninformed attacks on the Air Force. He would sit surveying the critic coldly from beneath his heavy-lidded eyes, never raising his voice or losing his temper, but replying to rhetoric with facts. A great man, Portal, who enjoyed the complete confidence of the U.S. Air Chiefs."

There were times when Portal retained more dignity than Churchill, who knew the use of emotional blackmail. At one of the first Chiefs of Staff meetings presided over by Dill's successor as C.I.G.S., General Sir Alan Brooke (later Field Marshal Lord Alanbrooke), Portal and Churchill were involved in an exchange which wholly depressed Brooke. Portal had been trying to reason with Churchill to stop him making a definite promise to Stalin to transfer ten Royal Air Force squadrons from Libya to the Russian front. The time was after midnight, an hour chosen by Churchill, when he was often at his best and others not necessarily so. Portal's intervention, Brooke recorded in his diary,[1] "produced the most awful outburst of temper. We were told that we did nothing but obstruct his intentions, we had no ideas of our own, and, whenever he produced ideas, we produced nothing but objections, etc., etc. . . . Finally he looked at his papers for some five minutes, then slammed them together, closed the meeting and walked out of the room (without saying Good Night) – It was pathetic and entirely unnecessary." But it was also an ingenious method of sublimely not accepting professional advice. For the next day (by the calendar the same day, but after sleep) Churchill wrote a directive to Anthony Eden, the Foreign Secretary, who was preparing to go by warship to Russia. In this he said that the battle in Libya would prevent him sending two British divisions to fight in the defence of the Caucasus. "The best form which our aid can take (apart from supplies) is the placing of a strong component of the Air Force, say ten squadrons, on the southern flank of the Russian armies. . . . These squadrons will be withdrawn from the Libyan battle at the earliest moment when success has been gained. . . . The High Command in the Middle East has been ordered to make plans for this movement." Portal might never have spoken.

The Libyan victory took another year to clinch. The squadrons did not go to Russia. Two days after Churchill's directive, as Eden was sailing out of Scapa Flow, the Japanese fell on Pearl Harbor. There were a host of new dispositions to be made. The incident has been narrated, not only for the light it sheds on characters, but because Churchill's passionately emotional attitude to the Russian struggle, and the promise he had privately either made, or implied, to help Stalin rapidly by direct forces or a second front, had an important bearing on his reaction to the use in Europe of Arnold's American Air Force, as will be recounted in the following pages.

Another striking influence on the final use of the Eighth Air Force was cast by Arnold's personal experience of modern bomb-

1. Sir Arthur Bryant, *The Alanbrooke Diaries, The Turn of the Tide*, Collins, London, 1957.

ing in April 1941. The outbreak of the war between Germany and Russia in June 1941 was preceded by the grand climax to Göring's attempted subjugation of Britain by indiscriminate night bombardment. Arnold's first stay in London (his experience of England in 1918 had been restricted to a hospital area in Southampton) coincided with the two heaviest bombing raids on the capital ever to be made.

The Battle of Britain was converted into the battle for Britain by a strategic bombing offensive against the production, supply and administration centres of Great Britain and against the morale of the civilians in these areas. The main weight of this attack, apart from the V-weapon assault of flying bombs and rockets in the last year of the war, fell between 7 September 1940 and 16 May 1941. Starting with the night attack of 7 September, London endured the longest continuous aerial bombardment in history: for 67 nights until 13 November (though the Luftwaffe claimed to have put no bomber over London on 3 November) a total of 11,117 bombing sorties were flown over London, 13,651 tons of high explosive were dropped, and 12,586 canisters of incendiaries, according to German statistics.[1] On the day after London's successive nights under major attack the Luftwaffe made its spectacular first bombardment of Coventry, then came back to London for the next three nights and for 16 more major raids before the so-called Blitz petered out. In the intervals they devoted their main attention to (chronologically) Coventry, Southampton, Birmingham, Bristol and Avonmouth, Liverpool and Birkenhead, Portsmouth, Sheffield, Manchester, Cardiff, Plymouth and Devonport, Derby, Swansea, Glasgow and Clydeside, Hull, Tyneside, Belfast, Barrow-in-Furness and Nottingham. By far the most heavily bombed areas outside London were Merseyside, Birmingham, Clydeside, Bristol, Plymouth and Hull. Before the German bombers went to Russia they killed 43,381 civilians in Britain and maimed 50,856. The great majority of the casualties were in London. The attack on the capital was conducted with increasing intensity. On the first 67 nights the average assault was 163 bombers dropping 201 tons of high explosive and 182 canisters of incendiaries. For the last nineteen nights the average raid was by 243 bombers dropping 294 tons of high explosive

1. Collier, *The Defence of the United Kingdom*, Appendix XXVI.

and 1,273 canisters of incendiaries. The nightly discharge of high explosive had risen by 50 per cent, and that of incendiaries by 700 per cent. The last raid of all in this series occurred on 10 May 1941. Three thousand people were killed or maimed; St Paul's Cathedral was ringed by fire and the House of Commons Chamber destroyed; over 2,000 fires were started and the main railway stations were put out of action for weeks. This was described by Churchill as "the most destructive attack of the whole night Blitz". By the mischance that an abnormally high number of water mains were punctured and there was an abnormally low tide in the Thames this was so. But, for the actual effort and energy expended, the two heavy raids carried out on London on 16 and 19 April during Arnold's visit were never excelled. On the later night 712 bombers dropped 1,026 tons of high explosive, of which over 500 tons were the more destructive large bombs, and 4,252 canisters of incendiaries. This is comparable with the bomb-load discharged a year later by the Thousand Bombers over Cologne (when, of 1,046 starters 898 bombers reached their target and dropped 540 tons of high explosive and 915 tons of incendiaries).[1]

General Arnold was not particularly impressed by the bombing of London. It is true that he did not have to endure it physically. He was out of town on both nights of the heavy raids, being occupied one night at Cambridge and another at Bomber Command headquarters. He did experience a minor raid which the Luftwaffe hardly bothered to enter in the operations log. From the roof of the Dorchester Hotel he watched the searchlights and the burning buildings, marked the guns in Hyde Park opposite, and heard the high sirens signal All Clear. "It was a big thrill," he admitted. "But it was not – according to my mind – in any way a display of Air Power." He had the same reaction when he came back into a London which was being cleaned up after the heavy raid, when Selfridge's store was still burning and 4,000 injured were being evacuated into the countryside. "The thought occurred to me : this wreckage has been caused by not more than 500 German bombers. In the United States we are thinking in terms of not less than 500,

---

1. Figures of German and British operations come from German and British sources respectively. The British calculation of the German raid of 19 April was that 350 bombers were over London.

and perhaps more than a thousand bombers. Suppose London had been hit by 800 or 1,000 bombers last night. The greater part of London might have been wiped out. Air power means employment of airplanes in numbers large enough to ensure complete destruction."

The actual number of bombers sent over London had been, as has been said, 712 of which the British thought 350 had arrived, and Arnold was in error about the potential of "complete destruction". But the significant thought coupled with the fresh reasoning about the power of bombing necessary to achieve strategic domination was that the United States air chiefs were harbouring serious doubts about the efficacy of any precision bombing at all as handled by the Royal Air Force. From the first night of Arnold's visit he had talked to bomber pilots and had been assured that the strength of German anti-aircraft fire and the persistence of their day-fighter attacks made it impracticable to attempt any precision bombing because of the constant evasive action that bombers were forced to take in daylight. He was told that bombers needed a twenty-second straight run approaching the target if they were to use *any* bombsight properly and that this could never be achieved except at extreme altitude. He thought he recognized a British as well as an American campaign decrying the American principle of daylight bombing, and he made a note in his diary at the time, phrased with what seems genuine humility :

"Either I am an optimist or just plain dumb, but I think the British still have much to learn about bombing. But who am I to question the experiences of the R.A.F. in two years of bombing in real war? We must make a study of the whole matter of day and night bombing as soon as I get back. The British are not using the Sperry sight that we sent over."[1] A reason for this omission which he did not mention was that the stabilized automatic bombsight needed a clear view of the target for a considerable distance, and this was not possible at night.

And yet, like Portal, Arnold was unable to prevent the fires of optimism, or faith, from burning through. The memory of Mitchell and the offensive tradition of the Air Corps seemed as powerful in Arnold as the inheritance and tradition of Trenchard in the British Air Staff. Arnold's logic modified but did not shake

1. Arnold, *Global Mission.*

his loyalty to an earlier philosophy. "My discussions with Portal, Churchill and the others left me with the impression that by air alone we might bring Germany so completely to her knees that it might be unnecessary for the ground forces to make a landing. ... Air power and air power alone could carry the war home to Central Germany, break down her morale, and take away from her the things essential to combat." This was the secret thinking of the man who was planning to build 47,000 bombers a year, and had to make that decision before it could be tested by one shot fired in anger. The air war of 1941 was being waged not by computing systems but by marshals, and men, with ideals disturbing reason. It is a fact of life and death that applied then and applies now to any future war. What computers cannot allow for is the strength of preconceptions in the process of evolving plans.

When Arnold came back to Washington from London, seven months before Pearl Harbor, he found that in his absence the War Plans Division of the American General Staff had worked out the basis of a strategy for the coming war which did *not* rely on "air power and air power alone", yet gave the air arm a leading role in the struggle and, moreover, assigned to the bombers an independent function in a strategic offensive. The long years of Air Corps indoctrination had at last produced staff officers who had overcome the essentially defensive Army thinking and echoed something of the Mitchell line.

The United States went into the Second World War *mentally* better prepared than any other nation which has ever moved into an ideologically defensive war. The military professionals were thinking positively. Though careful to order heavier armour for the future, they had already girded up their loins : which is only a knightly expression of the more homely view that Uncle Sam's boxing pants were not only not down, but drawn extremely tight around his jockstrap. This can be said in spite of the cross-purposes evident among many citizens and some officers, and notwithstanding America's tactical unpreparedness for the first Japanese assault. From the time of the Battle of Britain the strategic planners had recognized that it was possible that the United States would be involved in a war in which only the land mass of the Americas would be standing out against a Europe, Asia, Africa and Australasia dominated by Germany,

Russia, Japan and Italy. Arrangements had to be made, therefore, for the waging of an entirely solitary war. But, if only
Great Britain could stay in the fight after the fall of France, the
United States would already have effected the military equivalent of an invasion of Europe far more valuable, costly and
bloody than the eventual D-Day and the subsequent fanning out
in Normandy. It was no rhetoric of Roosevelt's that Britain was
America's first line of defence. And it was not a trifling flutter
of opinion, but a dangerous weakening of the conception of
American strategic defence, when Joseph P. Kennedy, U.S.
Ambassador in London, and William C. Bullitt, U.S.
Ambassador in Paris opposed American aid to Britain when
she was at her weakest after Dunkirk. They urged Roosevelt
in 1940 that Britain was about to capitulate and, instead of
fighting to the last airman in France, "the British might be con-
serving their Air Force and Fleet so as to use them as bargaining
points in negotiations with Hitler." Fortunately Franklin
Roosevelt and Cordell Hull resisted this view.

Consequently, from the beginning of 1941 the Service staffs
of the United States and Great Britain were increasingly col-
laborating. Their concern was not to make a mere appreciation
of the possible events of the immediate future. An inspired or
lucky guess about the coming military clash, on the pattern of
what Harris signed in 1936, was no longer enough. Now they
had to make plans, real plans, in what could no longer be
trifled with as a war game. By 27 March 1941 the Americans
and the British were broadly agreed on a common military
policy with which to defeat Germany and her Allies if the case
arose that the United States should be driven into war.

The success of such a planned strategy depended on the
accuracy with which the staff officers forecast the probable
course of the war. The officers were remarkably accurate. They
assumed that, if war came, the United States would be ranged
not only against Germany but against Japan and Italy. So the
battlefront would be world-wide. Therefore certain bastions
would need to be maintained in the Far East, in India and the
Near East, whatever the initial losses might be because of a
surprise attack. But the essence of final success lay not in the
limbs but in the heart. It depended on the maintenance intact
of the sources of industrial manufacture and productive and

fighting manpower. Even Australia might be sacrificed in a crisis, but the enormous potential of the United States homeland and the British Isles must be preserved.

Then the planners, working in the dark spring of 1941, made their most important decision. Whoever got into the fight on the other side, the main enemy must be considered to be Germany, the main effort must be made against Germany, and "the Atlantic and European area is considered to be the decisive theatre."[1] Such a conclusion might be comparatively easy to draw as a theory amid the calm of American non-belligerency; it was far harder to keep in the actual circumstances of the outbreak of war, with the crippling and humiliating attack on Pearl Harbor and the subsequent swift advance of Japanese forces across a third of the world. The resolve to keep this initial plan did falter when the arbitrament came, but the Service leaders finally stood by it.

By March the means by which the main effect would be concentrated against Germany had been agreed. Anyone who opposed the Axis would be supported : this was the decision that prompted speedy aid to Russia. The strongest economic pressure would be exerted against Germany by a blockade and other means. There would be a "sustained air offensive against German Military Power" wherever it was operative, and the war would be swung towards a final build-up of armed might for the penetration and subjugation of Germany by land forces. The role of the air services was to be vital. It would be defensive with regard to overseas bases and the defeat of an Atlantic blockade by Germany; it would support the offensive by preparing the way for an invasion; and, after the fastest possible establishment of air superiority over the enemy, particularly through the long-range striking force of the potential Allies, it would operate an independent offensive by the direction of "U.S. Army air bombardment forces . . . in collaboration with the Royal Air Force, primarily against German Military Power at its source". The offensive air striking force was to operate from English bases.

This basic strategy had to be developed in detail. The

1. Joint plan ABC–1, submitted 27 March 1941, quoted by W. F. Craven and J. L. Cate, *The Army Air Forces in World War II*, Office of Air Force History, U.S.A.F., 1948.

United States General Staff had already worked out five war plans to suit possible permutations of a struggle in which America would be involved. The fifth, known as RAINBOW No. 5, best fitted the conception of a strategic defence against Japan and a dominating offensive in the decisive theatre of the Atlantic and European area. During the time that Arnold was in England this war plan was perfected in detail. The first emphasis was to be given to the naval defence of the Atlantic and the bombing of Germany from England. Within a month of the approval of the details the situation had changed radically through the German declaration of war on Russia. Russia, the country against whom British and American volunteers had been grouping to fight in Finland little more than a year ago, was now an Ally. Or was she? Under other leadership this might have thrown Great Britain, then with the Commonwealth the only power fighting Germany, into some irresolution. Churchill did not hesitate. As he put it to his private secretary, who asked if the new war did not complicate the issues of freedom, "Not at all. I have only one purpose, the destruction of Hitler, and my life is much simplified thereby. If Hitler invaded Hell I would at least make a favourable reference to the Devil in the House of Commons."[1]

The British Chiefs of Staff saw the German attack on Russia as undeniably a tremendous weakening of the concentration of German might. They were grateful for the relaxation of pressure – the winter bombing had inflicted greater losses on Britain than had Dunkirk. But they had no urge to take the weight off Russia by fighting Germany anywhere – not even, for one important period, in the Western Desert. The Army preferred to build up Singapore against the Japanese rather than fight hard in North Africa, where a war with Germany was already in being. The Chiefs of Staff opposed outright the suggestion, first made by Stalin to Churchill as early as 18 July 1941, that a second front should be established against Hitler in Northern France and (in Stalin's words) "in the North – the Arctic".[2]

1. Account of Mr Colville, quoted by Winston Churchill, *The Grand Alliance*.
2. Message from Stalin to Churchill 18 July 1941, quoted in Churchill, *The Grand Alliance*. Stalin asked for no troops or artillery (except a division of Norwegian volunteers) for the Arctic Front, but wanted British naval and air operations.

They were not at first convinced that a second front *at any time* was a clear necessity. Arnold, during his stay in England, had been converted to the same optimism : "by air alone we might bring Germany so completely to her knees that it might be unnecessary for the ground forces to make a landing." This important train of thought was in effect a desertion of the war plans agreed between Britain and America in the spring, that there should be a final build-up of force leading to the land conquest of Germany. When Arnold came back into the orbit of the dominant strategic thinking of his Chief of Staff, General George Marshall, the principle of the trident of power through land, sea and air forces was re-established. But the British, who had aided Arnold in his heresy, had not been purged. And now, on 4 August 1941, the British were advancing in full strength on the Americans for the Atlantic Conference to be held in warships anchored off Argentia in Placentia Bay, Newfoundland.

The Atlantic Charter was a political document drafted by Churchill, but instigated by Roosevelt, with two main objects. It was to impress the world that the non-belligerent United States had joined in conference with the war-torn United Kingdom in serious concern for the state of the world *after* the war, which the democracies would win : Japan please note. It was also a finely calculated move to strengthen the determination of the citizens of the United States towards acceptance of the coming war by detailing high principles, less for the conduct of the war than for the basis of a peace which should follow it. The Charter put ideals into the British-American alliance. But the other business conducted at Argentia put teeth into it. While the President and the Prime Minister conferred in their first personal exploration of each other's mind, the Chiefs of Staff got down to warlike details.

All conference is, to some extent, conflict.

Arnold, who was only slowly conquering a feeling of inferiority towards the British, believed that they had won the battle of will hands down. They had arrived in a phalanx, not only of determined Service chiefs familiar with the tactics of close support but deploying the inestimable fire-power of their military-minded political leader. The Americans had as yet no common Service front, and Roosevelt was not the convincing master of strategy that Churchill appeared to be. Churchill made a keynote speech to all the military leaders on the first night of the conference at dinner aboard the U.S.S. *Augusta*. He emphasized that this was a mechanized, mobile war, "not," as Arnold paraphrased him, "a war of 1917–18 where dough-boys in the mud and trenches fought it out to a conclusion". This play on the futile slaughter of millions in a static land-war was one of the recurring debating points of the British, and it always tended to lead towards insistence on the role of bomb-ing aircraft in lessening – could the implication be "eliminating"? – the sacrifice entailed in an invasion. In the same speech Churchill clearly called for American bombers "to bring home to the Germans the horrors of war, just as the Germans had brought it home to the British". These parallel demands, for highest priority for the bomber offensive and for bringing home the horrors of war to the Germans, were to cause the American strategists much trouble.

Portal did not come to the Atlantic Conference. Churchill left him behind, as he phrased it, "to mind the shop", and brought his deputy, Air Chief Marshal Sir Wilfrid Freeman. Arnold himself had attended only at the insistence of Harry Hopkins, since there was as yet no direct air representative on the American General Staff. But when two American admirals and two generals besides Arnold put their conclusions on air strategy to the conference, Freeman was not only confused but comparatively ineffective. He remarked to Arnold, whose "air-mindedness" he recognized, "When Portal comes over, I am going to insist that he sees just two people; one is the President of the United States, and the other is you."[1]

The flattering remark was made at the end of a meeting at which the British Chiefs of Staff had put in a strategical review previously prepared in England and, indeed, already signed by Portal. This appreciation could not be answered immediately by the divided Americans and they took it away from the conference to study without distraction in Washington. The British stated that Germany was too strong to attack frontally without a preliminary undermining of the foundations of the war machine and of national morale, an objective which they proposed to achieve by blockade, subversive activities and a

1. Arnold, *Global Mission*.

gigantic intensification of the bombardment from the air. "It is impossible to over-emphasize the importance of the bomber offensive as part of our offensive strategy." By these means alone, the Chiefs of Staff stated, German ability and will to resist might well be overcome. But, in case blockade and bombing were not enough, an invasion by mechanized forces should be prepared. The American contribution was hoped to be a decisive share in the bombing effort and the participation of American armoured forces in the final invasion.

This was the document that the American Chiefs took home to study. Once removed from the pressure of British advocacy they saw clear ground for objecting to two of its principal features : the reliance on bombing power to the point of neglecting a strong ground invasion force, and the insistence on making German civilian morale a target of the bombers.

Apart from considerations of high strategy, the British emphasis on an all-out bombing assault, and the underlying assumption that only the United States could provide sufficient bombers in time, brought particular difficulties to Arnold as effective controller of aircraft allocation. Throughout 1941 he had been forced to conduct a fatiguing rearguard action against the United States Navy, which resisted every move favouring the swinging of national production priority to the manufacture of heavy bombers rather than naval craft. Eventually the President ruled that the big bomber programme should go through, and the guerrilla warfare eased off inside the Aircraft Board. But as soon as one source of tension was overcome another took its place. The British efforts to secure heavy bombers from the United States had become insistent. At the Atlantic meeting Air Chief Marshal Freeman, the Vice Chief of the Air Staff, had set the Royal Air Force target at an air combat strength of 10,000 aircraft of which 4,000 heavy bombers were needed immediately. At this time the planned production of the United States industry would produce little more than 4,000 heavy bombers during the current year, and if even a substantial proportion were handed over to Britain the calculated expansion of the Army Air Corps would be irretrievably crippled.

In any case, Arnold was deeply dissatisfied with the use made by the Royal Air Force of the four-engined aircraft he had

G

already given them. They seemed to like the B-24 Liberators, though in Arnold's view they took too long to convert them to their own specifications and tended to use them as Coastal Command defensive machines rather than as true offensive bombers. But a first force of twenty B-17C bombers – an early and very lightly armed edition of the Flying Fortress – had been, in Arnold's view, grossly wasted on the British : they had not used them in strong formation, took them up too high in order to bomb; and after twenty-two sorties they had lost eight aircraft, dropped only two bombs on assigned targets, and had shot down no enemy fighters. It could not be expected that Arnold should appreciate as early as the British, who were using the aircraft in action, that the defensive armament was poor, there were many mechanical failures, and the machine-guns froze at the altitudes for which the Fortress was designed. The Americans, in fact, never went into action in the B-17C. It was a failure, and only thirty-eight machines were built.

Air Marshal Harris was now in Washington leading a mission to expedite the delivery of aircraft and other munitions. For the sake of Anglo-American relations it was as well that Arnold did not invite him to share his counsels. Arnold was extremely worried whether it was worth while giving the Royal Air Force any heavy bombers at all. He thought that, if war came, he could use the machines to better advantage himself. In addition to this problem he was assailed during the last six months of 1941 by a nagging indecision : he had got the go-ahead from the President for priority heavy bomber production, and he had set the programme in train; but had he already made a mistake? Should he be spending all that money, mortgaging years of future time, condemning many thousand aircrew to death in battle, when it might be possible to win a war in another way? There was still time to switch if he could be convinced. Should he rely for his aerial bombardment on radio-controlled pilotless aircraft : flying bombs?

In 1917 the Americans had produced a pilotless aircraft capable of carrying a bomb-load of 300 pounds for 40 miles and delivering it – under the best conditions – within a hundred yards of its set target. By 1941 the range had been put up to 200 miles, the bomb-load to 2,000 pounds, and electronic refinements had increased the delicacy of its control. Five hundred of these controllable bombs could be produced for the price of one heavy bomber, and a fleet of 500 would carry sixty times as much explosive as one medium bomber. Everything depended on the extension of range that could be squeezed out of the project in the interval available for research before war actually broke out.

The time was too short. When war came the range had not been stepped up to reach Germany from the English coast. In December 1941 the project was finally reviewed, and shelved. Arnold could concentrate on bombers – and war.

The 7 December dawned over the Pacific. In Pearl Harbor alone five battleships were sunk or written off, and 96 Army aeroplanes lost, together with half the naval aircraft, in a maritime extension of the Göring type of blitzkrieg. Churchill immediately declared war on Japan – actually getting his declaration in before Congress – and announced to Roosevelt that he was travelling to meet him. The British party reached Washington on 22 December. Portal, with the other Chiefs of Staff, accompanied Churchill. Harris had been in Washington for seven months. Arnold, Portal and Harris met on 23 December. Portal's immediate interest was in the American Air Staff's plans for the use of their heavy bombers. Were they to be sent in large numbers against Japan? He said outright that he could use a large number of American bombers, since he now had more trained bomber crews than he could put into aircraft.

The Washington Conference decided, with what in the circumstances was extraordinary restraint and moral fortitude on the part of the Americans, that the strategic plan agreed in peace should be adhered to in war. The attack was to be carried against Germany first and the Japanese should, if possible, be held. The only positions which should be defended in the Pacific were those that would "safeguard vital interests and deny Japan access to needed raw materials". Even after its theoretical acceptance the principle of the plan was not to go through without a struggle. All the British staff officers have borne witness to the tough intransigence of Admiral Ernest King, the American Naval Chief, and to his conception of the fight against Japan as his private war. Roosevelt himself badgered his Air Staff for at least one demonstration against Japan, to give the Japanese a taste of "the real meaning of war". It was an echo

of Churchill and it was by implication and in its actual operation
an endorsement of bombing aimed against civilian morale : the
Doolittle carrier-borne raid on Tokyo was finally accomplished
in April 1942. But there were many other insistent and well-
founded tactical demands for air matériel. The constant calls
for more aircraft made on Arnold by subordinate air generals
in the Pacific theatres could not be continually refused, and
seriously drained the pool of factory production. However, a
more serious diversion was to come.

On the first day of the Washington Conference, 23 December
1941, Roosevelt declared that he and Churchill had agreed
that heavy bombardment operations would be begun from
English bases as soon as possible. Arnold persevered with his
view that bombing was more important than invasion, and
stated that he could probably get his first group of 35 frontline
bombers in England by the following March. He later said that
it was his aim to have 800 heavy bombers in England by the
end of 1942. The air war was seen as the only hostile action of
any weight that the Allies could take against Germany in the
near future. It was intended to have its effect on the morale
of the Americans rather than the Germans. It was an official
rebuttal of the Navy view that Japan should be fought first,
and it was planned to be presented as an indication that, once
Uncle Sam was fighting, the offensive ceased to be phoney.
This was not to be. The United States Army Air Forces did
not play any significant part in the war in the West in 1942.
One reason was the extraordinary diversions of aircraft necessary
even to "hold" the Japanese. Another was the imposition of a
twelve-month moratorium on the main clause in the contract
of the pre-war plan. The master plan was diffused, and the
air arm dissipated.

The original plan had insisted on a gathering of forces for a
land invasion of Europe after a bombing offensive. Churchill,
however, arrived at the Washington Conference with a tightly
argued recommendation for the occupation of North Africa.
This supported Roosevelt's wish to engage the enemy there.
"The war in the West in 1942" Churchill had written in a
paper composed during his voyage and handed to Roosevelt
immediately he arrived, "comprises, as its main offensive effort,
the occupation and control by Great Britain and the United

States of the whole of the North and West African possessions of France, and the further control by Britain of the whole North African shore from Tunis to Egypt, thus giving, if the naval situation allows, free passage through the Mediterranean to the Levant and the Suez Canal."

This was a departure from the original strategic plan, and the Americans recognized, again with chagrin, that the British Service chiefs were already familiar with it and corporately favoured it. Arnold spoke out very stoutly against it, putting forward the classic strategic line for which Marshall had so far been the chief protagonist. Arnold said :

I think the way to win the war is to hit Germany where it hurts the most, where she is strongest – right across the Channel from England, using the shortest and most direct road to Berlin. We will have the air power to destroy her factories, communications, facilities, concentrations of supplies, and to defeat her Air Force. We can also isolate, by bombing, any part of the coastline in the area we desire to use for landing troops. We will be able to secure command of the air and remove that threat from the troops making the landings.[1]

This was no more than a restatement of the attitude which Portal had expressed from the beginning of his tenure of power.

The British and the United States Navy turned their full, authoritative broadside on this argument. In particular Churchill spoke of "a Channel full of the bodies of British soldiers". It was the first of a series of references by the British to the heavy casualties they had endured in the First World War and even during the Battle of France. They seemed haunted by the horror of the frailty of massed men against explosive metal. They conveyed imputations which it was difficult for the Americans to counter with courtesy. For the truth was, and it was well understood, that any massive invasion of Europe in 1942 would depend on the trained infantry and assault troops of the British and Canadians rather than the United States Army, which could not be ready in the force required. Arnold continued to press vigorously through the spring for a strategy of concentrated effort on the shortest route to the heart of Germany. But the North African landings were to become an

1. Arnold, *Global Mission.*

established plan, with all the subsequent costly strategic thrusts against one of the hardest underbellies in the world.[1]

War is a struggle of wills, not only between enemies but between allies : marshals strive to impose their desires on brother marshals. The Americans were to become tougher as the war progressed, but at Washington they were turned away from their resolve. This was conceded as much by a spirit of gentlemanliness as of realism in their acceptance of the arguments put, with the greatest assurance, by British marshals who played the cards of their suffering and endurance as well as their military experience. Roosevelt, for his part, was over-ridingly conscious of the effect of immediate operations on the willpower (which is the morale) of the Americans, of the conquered or threatened peoples who were tentatively forming the United Nations, and also of the Russians, who had to be kept in the war. As Roosevelt saw the situation, *something* dramatically offensive had to be seen to be done soon. An invasion must be mounted. If it could not be in Europe it must be in North Africa, for which plausible arguments were being advanced. According to Arnold, "he forcibly stated that, if possible, we

---

1. If animal analogies are to be insisted on, the land-masses with the clearest soft underbellies are Australia and the sub-continent of North America. Europe is, by contrast, a turtle on its back, open to the spear-thrust through the plains of northern France, Holland and Germany – and there were no Atlantic Wall fortifications in 1942. Churchill's analogy to Stalin, when he told him in August 1942 that there would be no second front in Europe that year, was of a crocodile. He told him : "If we could end the year in possession of North Africa we could threaten the belly of Hitler's Europe." As he afterwards described the scene, "to illustrate my point I had meanwhile drawn a picture of a crocodile, and explained to Stalin with the help of this picture how it was our intention to attack the soft belly of the crocodile as we attacked his hard snout." The *we* who were to attack the snout has generally been interpreted as the British and Americans, who finally invaded northern Europe in June 1944. But Churchill was talking to Stalin, who was already facing the "hard snout" of the Germans in Continental Europe. It would be surprising if Churchill had drawn a crocodile with its back turned against Russia in Stalin's presence : but it is not impossible. If Churchill's crocodile was facing Russia, then the Russians were the *we* who were attacking the hard snout, but the implication here would be a minimization of Anglo-American effort. Whoever was dealing with the snout or being contemptuously flailed by the tail, it was not an altogether happy symbol.

must get operations of some kind started in the European Theatre, or in North Africa, right away, as early as it could be done. He even went so far to say that such a move in 1942 by Britain and the United States might be called an 'operation of desperation'." In the meantime he had reached a firm agreement with Churchill that an operation of even greater desperation would be undertaken in extreme circumstances. "In the event of things going very badly for the Russians this summer [1942] a sacrifice landing would be carried out in France to assist them."

It was a line of thought very far removed from the strategic principle of the application of Air Power.

CHAPTER TEN

ARNOLD AGAINST ENGLAND

> If I am in a scrape, as appears to be the general be-
> lief in England, although certainly not my own, I'll
> get out of it.
>
> THE DUKE OF WELLINGTON

The original "operation of desperation" took nearly a year to
bring off. The Allied landings in North Africa were made in
November 1942. During this year Arnold hardened into the
maturity that made him, under Marshall, the greatest administrative war leader of America. He was toughened in the fires of
the back rooms of war. The man who was over-conscious that
he had never seen combat demonstrated a courage and resolve
that achieved more than a local victory. Paradoxically, though
his strategic enemy in the West was the declining Göring, he
fought no personal duel with him. Throughout the year of
1942 the great moral struggle of the air war was maintained
between, on the one side, Lieutenant-General Henry H. Arnold,
Commanding General United States Army Air Force, and, on
the other, Air Chief Marshal Sir Charles Portal, Chief of Staff
Royal Air Force. Portal had powerful allies, particularly
Churchill and Harris. Harris eventually became a firm personal
friend of Arnold, but the American mainly fought on his own.

Portal and Arnold respected each other. On Arnold's side
there was undisputed admiration for Portal's "remarkably agile
and logical mind". Perhaps it was this very agility that saved
the situation for the Allies. Arnold had a simple gospel of air
warfare and he developed a bulldozing determination to carry
it through. If his beliefs had been entirely wrong, nothing
could have saved the Allies. Portal thought they were wrong
with respect to 1942 and 1943. But he never thought they were
diametrically wrong in the context of the whole war. And because Portal stood for victory – not, since Churchill's notable
"lecture" to him, victory through the Royal Air Force or victory

through air power, but victory unqualified – he saw that if anyone was to adjust it should be he. He integrated with Arnold, and did not openly betray the immense distress that the melting of his own will cost him. But in the fire there was welded the interdependent strength of the Royal Air Force and the Eighth Air Force which carried through the final strategic bombing offensive.

At the Washington Conference Arnold concluded an agreement with Portal that the Royal Air Force should receive during 1942 a total of some 10,000 aircraft. The allocation during January, February and March was to be up to 82 heavy bombers, 224 medium bombers, 494 light bombers, 747 pursuit (fighter) aircraft and 203 transports, after which the pace was to be roughly doubled. But on 1 April 1942 the American General Staff, in conference with the President, took a decision that was to stop all future supplies to Britain of heavy and medium bombers. Portal was to realize that in 1942 alone he would be short of 500 heavy bombers and 1,500 medium bombers on which he dearly depended.

The decision was a logical extension of the advocacy for a speedy cross-channel invasion which Arnold had voiced at the Washington Conference. The General Staff had worked up the plan for such an operation to take place in the fall of 1942 or the spring of 1943, and on 1 April the President passed it. It provided for "an all-out offensive from England, directed towards the heart of Germany, preceded by a maximum air offensive and ending with the ground troops invading France and meeting the German army where it was strongest". The President's approval meant that Arnold could go ahead immediately with building up the United States Army Air Forces in Britain as fast as units could complete their training, aiming at maximum strength by April 1943. The direct outcome of this was that American supplies of aircraft to both Britain and Russia should be cut. Arnold was directed to go to Britain and acquaint Portal of the important decision.

General George Marshall and Harry Hopkins had flown to Britain soon after the presidential staff conference and had – as they believed – succeeded in persuading the British to accept a Normandy landing in the summer of 1943, though they conceded that an earlier North Africa landing was still to be made.

Arnold flew over on 23 May 1942 and, after a night train journey south from Prestwick, had an early-morning conference with Portal before adjourning to meet Churchill.

The decision to deprive the British of medium and heavy bombers in order that Americans, flying from England, should have them was taken hard. But in this sphere Arnold was paying the piper and had to be conceded the right to call the tune. Arnold declared that not only had he the force of young men who "could fly the United States planes better than the young-sters of any other country" but that it was also a matter of morale at home. The people of the United States wanted to see their men fighting. "They wanted a United States Air Force now; they wanted action in Europe."[1]

It was over this *action in Europe* that the real fight was waged, though at first in guarded terms. Arnold did not then know, because Churchill did not tell Roosevelt until June, that the decision had virtually already been made that the priority operation for 1942 was to be the North African landings. This meant that, in the British thinking, an emergency descent on the coast of northern France in 1942 was impossible. Its actual effect was far graver than this : it finally made it impossible for an invasion of France to be launched even in 1943; D-Day was over two years away. Sensing something of the likelihood of this, Arnold had always personally opposed the North African adventure. What was clear in the minds of the British leaders, facing Arnold in May 1942, was that the putative American bombing offensive against Germany was not only unlikely – for most of the aircraft would be switched to Africa – but also, to their thinking, comparatively valueless. Churchill had written out of his planning any decisive intervention by the United States Air Forces against Germany in 1942, and would rather have had the available planes flown by the more experienced British crews. In pursuit of this end, Arnold was given a re-markable run-around during his visit to London. The object was to blow the trumpet for British bomber operations.

He was invited to Bomber Command headquarters. There Air Marshal Arthur Harris, who had taken over the command on returning from Washington in February, took him to what

1. Arnold, *Global Mission.*

he privately called his "conversion room".[1]

Arnold was showed photographs of the recent incendiary attack on Rostock, the Baltic port raided on the four consecutive nights of 23–6 April in a combination of indiscriminate area bombing to burn the town and precision bombing against the Heinkel factory at Marienehe. It had been one of the operations which Harris called his "commercial travellers' samples which I could show to the War Cabinet". Arnold was impressed: "I could see that R.A.F. Bomber Command was doing a magnificent job. Their operations gave us something to shoot at." A few days later, at the end of his brief stay, Arnold went down to the Prime Minister's country retreat at Chequers for his final indoctrination. On the British side Churchill was supported by his military aide General Ismay, with Air Chief Marshal Portal and Air Marshal Harris. Also present were the American Ambassador to Britain John G. Winant, Roosevelt's personal envoy W. Averell Harriman, the head of United States Naval Aviation Admiral John H. Towers, Brigadier-General Ira C. Eaker commanding the United States Eighth Air Force, with General Arnold.

It was the night of 30 May 1942. For four days an armada of 1,000 bomber aircraft had been standing by for what was intended to be the most sensational stroke of the war. One-third of the crews had never been on bombing operations before, for 367 aircraft had been drafted in from operational training units. They had fretted in the uneasy lull before a great battle, their mood aggravated on this occasion by unfavourable weather.

1. Harris said in his *Bomber Offensive*, "I did my best to convince the people who mattered." He described his reception of Field Marshal Smuts of South Africa in 1942 in the house he occupied as Commander in Chief: "After dinner ... I steered him into what we called the 'conversion room' next door and got his nose into one of the stereopticons which showed the damage we had already done to Germany.... At first he had not been remarkably keen on listening to my exposition of bombing theory, but by the time he had seen two or three of the photographs he was fumbling for a focus, pulling up his chair, and obviously sitting down to absorb things....Beyond a few ejaculations he made no comment, but when he had finished, he walked back into the drawing-room, turned to me, and said: 'It is extraordinary, it's fantastic, it is something entirely new, something which I never even suspected; it's tremendous.' ... I knew I was assured of his support in military affairs if I should require it."

Even while Arnold had been examining the photographs in Harris's conversion room they had been braced to take off for an assault on Hamburg, only to have their briefing cancelled at the last moment. For three days more they waited. Shortly after noon on 30 May Harris issued the executive order "Thousand Plan Cologne", and nothing short of a disastrous new weather forecast could stop the raid. As Harris ate dinner with the party at Chequers the bombers were heaving into the air from English bases. At thirty-eight minutes past midnight the first of 1,455 tons of bombs were loosed on Cologne and at ten past three the last of 600 acres devastated in the city received its destructive blast. Of the 1,046 bombers which had set out forty did not come back, and 116 more were damaged, twelve beyond repair.

The full reports of the Thousand Bomber Raid could not be known until later. But the demonstration of the might of Bomber Command was clear, not only to the group of American leaders at Chequers but to American public opinion at home. The concentrated attack on Cologne inflicted more damage on the city than all the previous raids had effected during the war. It was magnificent propaganda for the Royal Air Force brand of bomber offensive and for its continuation with as many fresh aircraft as possible, built by the Americans and manned by the British, undiluted by green American fliers. That night of all nights was a poor occasion for Arnold to continue his argument with Churchill urging speedy bombing operations from England to be conducted by United States crews. Churchill told Arnold with the confidence of authority: "Your programme apparently will provide an aerial striking force equal to, or in some cases larger than, that provided and planned by us. Perhaps your programme is too ambitious. You are trying to do within a few months what we have been unable to accomplish in two or more years."[1] Nevertheless, on the next day, in a two-hour session in the garden at Chequers, Churchill gave in on the allocation of bombers. Arnold had won the first round. There was a far harder struggle to come.

Arnold flew to Washington. With him on the crossing was Vice-Admiral Lord Louis Mountbatten. He had recently been nominated Chief of Combined Operations, holding the honorary

1. Arnold, *Global Mission*.

ranks of Lieutenant-General and Air Marshal, and was a full member of the Chiefs of Staff Committee when combined operations were discussed. Mountbatten was travelling to the United States to inform the American Chiefs of Staff that the early invasion of northern France, which had been previously agreed, presented difficulties. The Americans believed, right or wrongly, that Mountbatten was willing but his seniors were not. At the confrontation in the White House Roosevelt begged Mountbatten to remind Churchill of their agreement on a "sacrifice landing" in France if the Russians were in extreme straits that summer. Mountbatten did this, and also told Churchill on his return, as he reported to Roosevelt, "that you had asked for an assurance that we would be ready to follow up a crack in the German morale by landing in France this autumn and that I had given you an assurance that such an operation was being planned and was at present held at two months' notice".[1]

Roosevelt was taking the British propaganda about the moral effect of air bombardment seemingly more seriously than anyone else, for the only instrument potentially capable of "forcing a crack in the German morale" that summer was Bomber Command. But in June Churchill came to Washington and authoritatively discouraged the 1942 landing; and in July, after Marshall and Hopkins had vainly argued with Churchill and his Chiefs of Staff in London, the project of an early second front in Europe was abandoned; Stalin was not informed for a month.

Within the American General Staff there was a strong undercurrent of feeling that if the planned invasion of Europe was superseded the major American effort should be switched to the war against Japan. Roosevelt discouraged this reaction and the remnants of the original strategy were in some measure retained. But the postponement – even if it were temporary – of concentration on the grand strategy hit Arnold. He had planned to have 3,640 combat aircraft in Britain by April 1943. In July 1942 he had to agree to a Combined Chiefs of Staff decision to send fifteen groups from this aggregate to spearhead local offensives which had been swiftly planned for the Pacific. That diverted about one-third of the force he had

1. Letter, Mountbatten to Roosevelt, June 1942, Sherwood, *The White House Papers of Harry L. Hopkins.*

intended to send to England. Many of the rest would go to the North African operation, which was effectively to sap his bomber force. In July also the British had proposed that as some substitution for the aborted French invasion the bomber offensive against Germany should be intensified. The Thousand Bomber raids (of which only the first was solidly successful) were now being hawked around as Harris's travelling salesman's samples to the Americans at the very time when events had made it impossible for the Americans to participate in the direct offensive in any force. Everything that Churchill had told Arnold on the night of the big raid was coming true : "Perhaps your programme is too ambitious. You are trying to do within a few months what we have been unable to accomplish in two or more years." But if personalities were to be indicted, the man who had forced Arnold into the position where his programme was demonstrated as too ambitious was Churchill.

And now the British launched another raid on Arnold's aircraft resources. He was still getting a few bombers over to England. Eaker was busying himself in giving the crews advanced training. The Royal Air Force looked on with an attention which was both patronizing and envious. They knew all about Flying Fortresses. They had proved that they were no good for day bombing and carried too light a load for the most effective saturation night bombing. The Americans ought to face up to one of three choices : they should send the Forts on shipping patrols as the British had done; or they should hand the aircraft over to an air force that at least knew how to use bombers, ineffective though the machines might be; or, best of all, they should cut down the concentration on manufacture of Fortresses and Liberators, and switch over their profuse production machinery to building for the Royal Air Force the Lancaster, the really worthwhile efficient bomber that would win the war. This was no irresponsible campaign of persuasion. As Arnold admitted, "it was all very friendly, but it was diabolically persistent. We had a tough time in Washington, and so did 'Tooey' Spaatz, Ira Eaker, George Kenney, and all the other Air Force commanders, and we knew it."[1]

The British were fundamentally opposed to an early invasion of Europe. In compensation they were in favour of an in-

1. Arnold, *Global Mission*.

tensification of the area bombing of Germany by night. The Americans preferred invasion preceded by the accurate bombing of strategic German targets by day. The core of the struggle between Portal and Arnold was the knowledge that the American intervention was putting back into the forum of debates the two entrenched British judgements on aerial bombing: that in its general pattern it could not be precise, and that enemy morale was not only a legitimate but a vulnerable target for the night bombers.

On the night of the first Thousand Bomber raid Arnold declared, "as an airman who had preached bombardment for many years", that "I was as thrilled as the Prime Minister himself." But he reflected on the irony that "of all the moments in history when I might have tried to sell Mr Churchill and his R.A.F. advisers on the future of American precision bombardment by daylight, I had picked the night when they were selling their own kind of bombardment to the world."

The strategic bombardment of Germany, which had been conducted on a small scale since 1940, had been the expression by "air-minded" men of an abiding strategical faith. It had been accepted by other military leaders on the general staffs, but viewed with far less fanaticism, as an expedient. For many it was an expression of weakness, a *faute de mieux*, tolerated and even welcomed as a practical and morale-building aggressiveness while the military manpower and matériel of the adversaries were of such greatly differing proportions; but a policy to be abandoned for "the real thing" when the armies were more matched.

In Britain, however, which had been engaged the longest, the principle of strategic bombing had gradually gained a deeper approval from military thinkers who had not started as markedly "air-minded" men, but who had been won over by the convenience of the operation. Throughout their history the British had always relied on small professional armies. They had greatly preferred wars where even the armies they did pay to go into battle could be made up of hired mercenaries or Continental allies. The British had used a proficient navy with great skill to keep war from their shores, and perhaps had grown blasé in their insularity. This complacency was broken under the shock of the slaughter of a generation of Britons in the First World

War. The violence of the awakening had not been forgotten by the ruling class of 1939, who saw themselves with a certain clarity as only the diminished survivors of a breed whose loveliest and best, the subalterns of Flanders, had led the way to death. These, the living, had recognized with the chill of a *déjà vu* the German successes up to the time of Dunkirk as a fresh reminder of the hazards intrinsic in the deployment of massed men in land warfare. The emergence of the Royal Air Force as a possible equivalent of Nelson's Navy seemed not only a natural, but a highly welcome and practical event. Churchill approvingly declared to the House of Commons, in the speech in which he paid tribute to "The Few" that this war, "a conflict of strategy, of organization, of technical apparatus, science, mechanics, and morale", was entirely different in character from the last, when "millions of men fought by hurling enormous masses of steel at one another." He went on : "There seems to be every reason to believe that this new kind of war is well suited to the genius and resources of the British nation and Empire, and that once we get properly equipped and started a war of this kind will be more favourable to us than the mass slaughters of the Somme and Passchendaele."[1]

The entry of Russia into the war only emphasized, in the minds of some leaders, the resemblance of the "new" war to the classic wars waged by the Royal Navy and the remote armies of subsidised allies. The Royal Air Force was the modern bombardment and blockading arm, and the cannon-fodder were foreigners. An American colonel quoted the British Air Minister, Sir Archibald Sinclair, as saying early in 1942 "our mightiest weapons are the Russian Army and the R.A.F."[2]

Sinclair was whistling hard to keep up, not his own courage, but the faith of influential British public opinion and the War Cabinet in the potential of bombers as an absolute strategic force. For the fact was that in the three winter months before the appointment of Air Marshal Arthur Harris to be Commander in Chief Bomber Command there had been extremely little strategic bombing. When, in the previous autumn, Portal lost

1. Churchill in House of Commons, 20 August 1940.
2. Informal Report by U.S. Air Attaché Lt. Col. G. De F. Larner, 28 April 1942, quoted by Craven and Cate, *The Army Air Forces in World War II.*

his struggle with Churchill for a tenfold increase of Bomber Command to a force of 4,000 bombers, some dramatically successful coup was necessary to restore the Prime Minister's faith in the bombing arm. Instead, the low morale of crews and the lack of instruments for securing navigational accuracy on winter nights produced results which were ludicrous in their impact and tragic in their losses. On one night in October, when Bomber Command had only two targets in Germany, its aircraft bombed twenty-seven separate cities. On a night in November, 133 aircraft attacked Boulogne, Ostend and Cologne without loss, but 267 other bombers, sent to Berlin, Mannheim and the Ruhr, incurred losses of 37, a destruction rate of some 14 per cent. Churchill immediately ordered a drastic diminution of effort which in practice resulted in an end to the bombing of Germany, save Kiel, and a lighter concentration on the French Atlantic ports, the shifting habitats of the German capital ships.

By February 1942 the British air protagonists were ready to conduct a full-scale ideological struggle in support of their convictions. Their spokesmen included Sinclair, whose audience was Parliament, the Defence Committee and the War Cabinet; and Portal, working on the Chiefs of Staff Committee and the Combined Chiefs of Staff. Their main objects were to get a renewal of the bombing effort made acceptable, to insist on their trusted pattern of night area bombing directed against industrial targets, and to get as many American bombers into Britain as possible, preferably for operation by British crews. The principals at whom their propaganda was directed were the experts, particularly in naval circles, who influenced Churchill, Churchill himself, Roosevelt and his advisers, and the key man, Arnold.

Arnold was himself waging an individual struggle with two important aims : to get numerous bombers to Britain in order to start his own strategic bombing of Germany; and to gain acceptance of the Air Corps' own conception of strategic bombing by precision attack in daylight. To get the bombers to Britain was a matter of departmental skill in balancing competing claims within his own Joint Chiefs of Staff committee. To gain acceptance of their operation in precision daylight attacks he had to convince not only the British but an important section of American opinion, particularly the Navy. American strategic thought had been influenced in general by the reviving success of British night area bombing in 1942, and in detail by the specific doubts voiced by American naval chiefs on how precise Arnold's precision bombing really was.

Portal and Sinclair were therefore allies of Arnold in the effort to obtain acceptance of strategic bombing as a powerful offensive and to get American bombers into Britain. They were opponents of Arnold on the daylight precision issue; but if they or anyone else pressed too hard for universal night area bombing they would also damage Arnold's efforts in America to get United States heavy bombers into Britain.

In February 1942 a new British radar navigation aid, *Gee*, allowing bombers to locate with much greater accuracy a target within 400 miles of base, had been produced in sufficient numbers for it to be handed over to Bomber Command. Its life was expected to be short. Effective German counter-measures, it was anticipated, would be developed in less than six months. It was necessary to use *Gee* rapidly to its fullest extent. At the same time the wasteful funnelling of bombers to the French coast was eased with the escape of their constant targets, the *Scharnhorst* and *Gneisenau*, from Brest to Germany. On 14 February the British strategic bomber offensive was resumed with a directive stating absolutely bluntly that the primary targets of the bomber raids should be the four in-dustrial areas round Essen, Duisberg, Dusseldorf and Cologne, and "the primary object of your operations should now be focused on the morale of the enemy civil population and, in particular, of the industrial workers."[1] Portal personally under-lined the fact that the objective was morale and not industry with a note: "I suppose it is clear that the aiming points are to be built-up areas, *not*, for instance, the dockyards or aircraft factories ... This must be made quite clear if it is not already understood."[2] These orders were awaiting Harris when he took over Bomber Command on 22 February, and it is clear that his claim that he did not originate this policy is justified.

1. Bomber Command Directive, 14 February 1942.
2. Minute, Portal to Bottomley (Deputy Chief of the Air Staff), 15 February 1942, quoted Webster and Frankland, *The Strategic Air Offensive Against Germany, 1939–1945.*

Three days after Harris's appointment, however, the Commander in Chief scented the first strong expression of political opposition to strategic bombing. After a critical Vote of Confidence debate in the House of Commons, Churchill had been constrained to take into the War Cabinet Sir Stafford Cripps, who then commanded great prestige in the country, though Beaverbrook described the public's regard as a "fleeting passion. It is already on the wane." On 25 February Cripps, as Leader of the House of Commons, referred in a debate on the war situation to "the question of the policy as to the continued use of heavy bombers and the bombing of Germany. A number of honourable members have questioned whether, in the existing circumstances, the continued devotion of a considerable part of our effort to the building up of this bombing force is the best use that we can make of our resources." Cripps reminded the House that the policy was begun *before* the Russian armies were engaging the Germans. He assured Parliament that "the original policy has come under review" by the Government "and the moment they arrive at a decision that the circumstances warrant a change, a change in policy will be made." Next day the Royal Air Force Delegation in Washington reported that Cripps might have played into the hands of those Americans who favoured maximum United States effort against Japan; he had given valuable ammunition to the leaders of the movement – far more influential than in Britain – opposing the conception of long-range bombing in its entirety; and the immediate effect might be a reduction in the American manufacture of heavy bombers. "Unless authoritative affirmation of our belief in Bomber offensive is supplied immediately, the effect both on strategical and production planning here may well be irremediable."[1]

It was in these circumstances that the fiery Harris began his career at Bomber Command. The doubters both at home and in the United States might well stifle the efforts he planned. There was need enough for his "conversion room" and the world-wide moral effect, as well as the local physical impact, of the demonstration of the Thousand Bomber raids. As he summed it up :

The result of using an adequate bomber force against Germany

1. Letter, R.A.F. Delegation Washington to Air Ministry, 26 February 1942, quoted by Webster and Frankland, *The Strategic Air Offensive Against Germany, 1939–1945.*

would be there for the world to see, and I should be able to press for the aircraft, crews and equipment we needed with far more effect than by putting forward theoretical arguments, however convincing, in favour of hitting the enemy where it would hurt him most. Such a demonstration was, in fact, the only argument I could see which was at all likely to prevent our squadrons from being snatched away and our effort diverted to subsidiary targets.[1]

After the first Thousand Bomber raid – as a consequence of which he got a rapid knighthood – Sir Arthur Harris knew that he had made an enormous impact on Arnold, whom he had in his orbit, and on American public opinion. He also believed that he had successfully begun the reconversion of Churchill : "No one understood better than he the vast strategic consequences of this single operation, which proved that a serious bombing offensive against Germany itself was a real possibility." He had established direct personal relations with the Prime Minister (indeed, the two met every week) and he capitalized on Churchill's resurgent enthusiasm by presenting a personal minute on how to win the war. It began like a Papal encyclical : "Victory, speedy and complete, awaits the side which first employs air power as it should be employed." He played on Churchill's known sensitivity by castigating the conception of a continental land campaign which "would lead to the slaughter of the flower of the country's youth in the mud of Flanders and France" and he declared unequivocally : "It is imperative, if we hope to win the war, to abandon the disastrous policy of military intervention in the land campaigns of Europe, and to concentrate our air power against the enemy's weakest spots."[2]

Churchill was not so convinced as Harris thought. Nevertheless, he shrewdly retained the forceful commander's interest by asking him to prepare a Note on the Role and Work of Bomber Command, which Harris completed on 28 June. In the main this was a closely argued defensive apologia for the work of Bomber Command, a force constituting only eleven per cent of Britain's air strength. But it concluded with an eloquent brassy coda :

What shouts of victory would arise if a Commando wrecked the entire Renault factory in a night, with a loss of seven men ! What

1. Harris, *Bomber Offensive*.
2. Personal minute, Harris to Churchill, 17 June 1942.

credible assumptions of an early end to the war would follow upon the destruction of a third of Cologne in an hour and a half by some swift moving mechanized force which, with but 200 casualties, withdrew and was ready to repeat the operation 24 hours later! What acclaim would greet the virtual destruction of Rostock and the Heinkel main and subsidiary factories by a Naval bombardment! All this, and far more, has been achieved by Bomber Command; yet there are many who still avert their gaze, pass by on the other side, and question whether the 30 squadrons of night bombers make any worthwhile contribution to the war.

Churchill thought highly of this paper. But, in the pessimism of 1942, he could not see the bombers achieving independent power, and relegated them to secondary importance in the war. In a Review of the War Position on 21 July he wrote:

> We must observe with sorrow and alarm the woeful shrinkage of our plans for Bomber expansion. The needs of the Navy and of the Middle East and India, a short-fall of our British production programme, the natural wish of the Americans to fly their own bombers against the enemy, and the inevitable delay in these machines coming into action, all these falling exclusively upon Bomber Command have prevented so far the fruition of our hopes for this summer and autumn. We must regard the bomber offensive against Germany at least as a feature in breaking her war-will second only to the largest military operations which can be conducted on the Continent until the war-will is broken. Renewed, intense efforts should be made by the Allies to develop during the winter and onwards ever-growing, ever more accurate and ever more far-ranging Bomber attacks on Germany.[1]

The ideological assault of the airmen went on. Next month a veteran came back into the fight. Lord Trenchard, whom Churchill called "my friend, whom I had known and often worked with over a quarter of a century", sent a vigorous personal memorandum to Churchill and others.

> *Time is short and we are at the parting of the ways.* . . . For the country to get mixed up this year or next in land warfare on the continent of Europe is to play Germany's game – it is to revert to 1914–18. . . . Our strength and advantage over Germany is in the air – the British and American Air Force. . . . As the enemy con-

---

1. A Review of the War Position, 21 July 1942. Churchill, *The Hinge of Fate,* Cassell, London, 1950.

quered Poland and France by the "tank blitz", so we can smash the German machine by the "bomber blitz" . . .[1]

Churchill circulated Trenchard's paper and Harris's earlier note to the Cabinet, commenting that they "serve as a considerable answer to those who attack the usefulness of our bombing policy". In the case of Harris's note he did more : he sent it to Roosevelt in mid-September as "an impressive contribution to thought on the subject". He coupled with it a plea for the swift build-up of the American bomber force in Britain :

I am sure we should be missing a great opportunity if we did not concentrate every available Fortress and long-range escort fighter as quickly as possible for the attack on our primary enemy. . . . A few hundred Fortresses this Autumn and Winter, while substantial German air forces are still held in Russia, may well be worth many more in a year's time.[2]

From the point of view of Arnold, who had much to suffer in the battle of ideas between British and American air interests, this was the most positive rapprochement of the year. It supported him in his advocacy of strategic bombing by American aircraft from Britain, and did not foster the United States Navy Department's insistence on a more vigorous war in the Pacific by raising any controversy over the delicate precision issue. Arnold had endured heavy fire. His status in America had been damaged by early British criticisms of the undeveloped Fortresses given to the Royal Air Force, and by the consequent pressure to turn American production over to aircraft designed for bombing according to the British pattern. Harris himself realized that the campaign was giving excessive aid to the general propaganda in Britain against the entire heavy bomber offensive and wrote a personal letter to Arnold deprecating the British belittlement of Bomber Command's record. "We can defeat the enemy," he said, "if we are not defeated by our friends." Arnold realized that the Air Corps had made a mistake in 1940 by discouraging the P.51 Mustang, which the British had ordered at that time, and which could be converted to a long-range escort fighter. It was now seen to be necessary for

1. Trenchard to Churchill, 29 August 1942. Churchill, *The Hinge of Fate*.
2. Churchill to Roosevelt, 16 September 1942.

Fortress operations. Arnold was making every effort to push Mustangs through the production line. What still remained to be settled once and for all was the argument over daylight precision attacks as against night area bombing. In spite of Churchill's tactful reticence in his letter to Roosevelt, the controversy was still keen in British Air Staff circles.

The *theory* of precision attacks by daylight had always been correct. The Royal Air Force had held it at the beginning of the war, and had abandoned it only because their bombers, like the Germans, were beaten out of the sky in daylight. Afterwards they made a virtue of the necessity of area bombing, especially by their insistence on its valuable effect against morale. The United States Air Forces had clung to the ideal of precision for reasons which perhaps originated in a backwoods pride in marksmanship but were reinforced by the development of mutual support from formation flying and by the possession of the Norden bombsight, which was very accurate in the best conditions. Having shaped their bomber policy in this way they could afford to be more objective about the effect of indiscriminate bombing on civilian morale. They had no vested interest, as the British Government had, in insisting that civilian morale was the easiest target to hit by strategic bombing, and the first to crumble. The American Chiefs of Staff had rebutted the emphasis on morale bombing in the paper submitted by the British Chiefs at Argentia, and in their own target priorities had listed precision attacks on the German electricity grid, transportation network and oil industry before attacking the urban areas. They declared that there should be no resort to area bombing of civilian concentrations until German morale began to crack. Yet, in the first bombing offensive to be undertaken after they had joined as Allies, the Americans found that the British had promoted to top priority area bombing by night against "the morale of the enemy civil population and, in particular, of the industrial workers". This was contrary to every fundamental principle that Arnold had tried to instil into the United States Air Forces since he assumed command.

But by the autumn of 1942 Arnold had done *nothing* practical to prove his own theories. He had lost hundreds of heavy bombers and fighters by diversion to the impending North African invasion. The few aircraft operating in England were sent out only by the dozen, with Spitfire protection, and not yet against the formidable defences of the German homeland.

It was now Arnold's turn to sweat along by faith alone. For the autumn period was critical for production. If Arnold was wrong about the efficacy of precision daylight bombing by strong forces which he did not yet have, *and if Arnold would admit he was wrong,* there was still time to switch production and training to the night bomber: which meant to the Lancaster, for neither the Fortress nor the Liberator were efficient night bombers. A strong campaign now developed in England to convince the Americans that this was the solution.

At first the discussion was confined to the British Air Staff. Portal's view was that the Fortresses would be comparatively defenceless over Germany when beyond the range of Allied fighter cover, and would be so harried by continual fighter attack that they would resort to general area bombing; the Americans should begin to train for night bombing and their industry should convert to the construction of Lancasters. This opinion was contested by his Assistant Chief of Staff (Policy), Air Vice Marshal John C. Slessor, who had had long liaison experience in Washington. But Portal's view was accepted by Churchill. It was developed, however, by the Prime Minister with a ruthless logic that gave Portal a chill of sudden alarm. For Churchill not only told Harry Hopkins, Roosevelt's confidant, that the British had little trust in the performance of the Fortress beyond the range of fighter protection, and urged the necessity for development of an American night bomber; privately to the British Chiefs of Staff he depreciated the American bomber effort in a much more derisory fashion, and said "We must try to persuade them to divert these energies (a) to sea work, beginning with helping *Torch*[1] (including bombing the Biscay ports), and (b) to night work."[2]

Here in diamond clarity was the conclusion which the Air Staff had been moving towards, and when it confronted them it repelled them. It entailed the complete absence of American forces from the strategic bombing offensive for at least eighteen months. And this would really mean the end of the British

1. The North African invasion.
2. Churchill to Chiefs of Staff, 22 October 1942, quoted by Webster and Frankland, *The Strategic Air Offensive Against Germany, 1939–1945.*

bombing offensive, which had already been placing psychological reliance on the tardily approaching American contribution. The future of the Royal Air Force Bomber Command depended in practice on the welcome given to the United States Eighth Bomber Command, and in extending to them the liberty to operate by the principles in which they believed.

Swiftly the Air Minister, Sir Archibald Sinclair, refreshed his memory of the pro-American arguments explained by Air Vice Marshal Slessor. On the day after Churchill's electrifying summary of the controversy Sinclair addressed a minute to his Prime Minister as the potential saviour of both Bomber Commands. Arnold had found an unexpected ally. "American opinion," said Sinclair, "is divided; some want to concentrate on the Pacific; others against Germany; some want an Air Force which would be mainly ancillary to the Army ... others want to build up a big bomber force to attack the centre of German power. It is in your power to crystallize American opinion and to unite it behind those schools of thought which want to attack Germany and want to do it by building up an overwhelming force of bombers in this country." And then came the solemn warning: "You will throw these forces into confusion and impotency if you set yourself against their cherished policy of daylight penetration."[1]

In the face of the prospect of the withdrawal of the American strategic bomber force, Portal also exposed his authoritative conclusions, formerly so damaging to the standing of American daylight precision bombing, to some reconsideration. He declared to Churchill that, though the Americans must expect great losses in unescorted daylight raids, if they were prepared to lose as many Fortresses by day as the British were now losing night bombers, and assuming that for each Fortress shot down three German fighters were destroyed, "the German fighter force would within a few months be so weakened as to leave the whole country open to day bombing and air superiority on all land fronts in the hands of the United Nations."[2]

This was exactly the sort of statistical argument which

1. Minute, Sinclair to Churchill, 23 October 1942, quoted by Webster and Frankland, *The Strategic Air Offensive Against Germany, 1939–1945.*
2. Minute, Portal to Churchill, 7 November 1942, quoted by Webster and Frankland, *The Strategic Air Offensive Against Germany, 1939–1945.*

Portal knew Churchill distrusted, and it is a measure of the airman's dire need that he used it. He tried to assess the probability of American success, and found it not high, but not negligible. "If success could only amount to a tour de force having no real military value, I should be entirely with you in trying to ride the Americans off the attempt altogether. Actually, however, success would have tremendous consequences."

Portal's minute to Churchill on this subject, on 7 November 1942, had interrupted his drafting of air operations for 1943–4 – in which, incidentally, he and the other Chiefs of Staff were relying on the United States for two-thirds of the final bombing force. He addressed himself once more to these plans, and to the methods of gaining American agreement for them. But, in the Prime Minister's mind, the subject of American precision bombing by day was not settled, and because of that the strategic bombing pattern for the next two years was not even adumbrated.

Churchill had not accepted Portal's professional opinion, nor Sinclair's fervent advocacy. He believed, as he told the Chiefs of Staff, "the United States Air Force have not shown themselves possessed of any machines capable of bombing Germany either by night or by day." If he could not rely on the Americans he could not underwrite a major bombing offensive. Moreover, he was greatly incited *not* to sink into a bombing offensive the high proportion of available production, manpower, supply and transport which would be necessary for any strategic plan of first priority. For Churchill had a stronger favourite : the second front in Europe in 1943 on which he had made a personal commitment to Stalin in August. It was a strategic priority which was all the more galling to the British Chiefs of Staff by reason of the fact they had had no part in giving the assurance, which was strongly against their inclinations; and, indeed, Sir Alan Brooke directly rejected it. But this opposition, as in the matter of Portal's ten Libyan squadrons, did not erase the commitment from Churchill's mind.

The climax to all this confusion came at the Casablanca Conference in January 1943.

General Arnold knew that the outcome of the conference would either make or break him. He was aware of Portal's weighty criticism of American potential; he knew that Churchill had expressed the British view to Hopkins, and that both the President and the Secretary of War had deep doubts about the practicability of daylight bombing; he did not know that Portal had partially retreated and – perhaps mercifully – he believed that Churchill thought comparatively kindly of the American bombing force. But, once at Casablanca, Arnold was warned by Hopkins and Harriman that Churchill was about to be very stern.

At the conference Churchill suggested outright that the heavy bombers of the Eighth Air Force should join Bomber Command in its night campaign. Arnold had had an hour's informal conversation with Churchill on the subject, but for the official defence of the Eighth Air Force he called in Brigadier General Ira C. Eaker, Commanding General Eighth Bomber Command. Eaker was a good choice for the task. By no means a doctrinaire, he had come over to England with an open mind on bombing policy and with sincere respect for British experience. He had declared himself ready to use his force "both day and night" as soon as a satisfactory exhaust flame dampener could be produced for his Fortresses and his crews could be given night training. But his force was never equipped or trained for night work.

Eaker told Churchill that the American rate of loss in day operations in Europe had been lower than that experienced by the Royal Air Force at night. The day bombers could not only find, sight and hit small important targets, but bomb five times as accurately – or with a force a fifth of the size of the night raiders. Day bombing and night bombing were not mutually exclusive methods of war, but complementary: they used airfields, air space and communications networks most economically, kept the enemy under twenty-four hour pressure, and could mark targets for each other by fires and smoke. Day bombing was the surest method of bringing into action enemy fighters who would not face challenging fighter sweeps. The Eighth Air Force had been grievously weakened in aircraft and key personnel by the demands for the North African invasion, but he would be ready within a fortnight to set 100 bombers and 100 fighters by day against the German homeland.

Churchill bore witness that Eaker "pleaded his cause with

skill and tenacity" against the Englishman's "formidable point". It was Eaker alone who persuaded the Prime Minister to make an astonishing surrender. "Considering how much had been staked on this venture by the United States and all they felt about it, I decided to back Eaker and his theme, and I turned completely round and withdrew all my opposition to the daylight bombing by the Fortresses."[1] Roosevelt and Marshall immediately followed Churchill's lead, and this was itself something of a volte-face, for they had been influenced by American and British criticism. The delighted Arnold had the strong impression that Churchill capitulated somewhat gratefully, having been "harassed by some of his people about our daylight bombing programme and had to put up a fight on the subject".[2] This is not true. Churchill declared throughout the war that if the Americans had bombed by night from the start the struggle would have been over faster. But he was conscious of the influence he had had on Roosevelt: "General Eaker afterwards said on several occasions that I saved the Fortress bombers from abandonment by the United States at the moment when they were about to come into their own. If this is true I saved them by leaving off opposing them."[3]

Amongst the British, when Father said "Turn" they all turned. Henceforward there was no official criticism of American bombing methods. It was a levitating relief to Arnold, at the end of a bad year of war. "We had won a major victory, for we would bomb in accordance with American principles, using the methods for which our planes were designed."

The one necessary thing now was to produce results.

1. Churchill, *The Hinge of Fate*.
2. Arnold, *Global Mission*.
3. Churchill, *The Hinge of Fate*.

CHAPTER ELEVEN

THE BLOODING

You will have heard of our battle of the 18th. Never
did I see such a pounding match. Both were what the
boxers call gluttons.

THE DUKE OF WELLINGTON

The selection of any "decisive battle of the world" is an
arbitrary and controversial judgement. Yet the 17–18 August
1943 may justifiably be included as one of the most significant
days in the history of aerial warfare before the exploitation of
nuclear fission. For two Air Marshals, Göring and Arnold, it
sparked off a retarded reaction which brought both men to the
nadir of their careers, though Arnold fought and rose from his
confusion. For a third Marshal, Harris, the bomber battle fought
that night was, even though over-optimistically appreciated and
negligently denied a follow-up, probably his most brilliant
tactical victory; strategically it was shown to be a major operation inestimably easing the preparations for a smooth invasion of
Europe; and a shining demonstration of the military precept
that a timely strike against the enemy is equivalent to erecting
a steel shield over one's bases.

The Allied targets were Schweinfurt, Regensburg and
Peenemünde. The actions of this day resulted in an outstanding
victory for the German day-fighters; chaotic humiliation for the
German night-fighters, who were brilliantly outwitted by the
British; significant defeat for the United States VIII Bomber
Command; a bloody success for the Bomber Command of the
Royal Air Force; and a vital delay in the projected long-range
bombardment of the armed camp of southern Britain by
German rockets and jet-bombs. The assailants, both British and
American, were to fare worse in the days ahead. But this was
the blooding of the rival emergent heavy bomber forces who
finally joined to wage the combined bomber offensive.

The cost of this experience was high. In the twenty-four

hours following the dawn of Tuesday, 17 August 1943 the British and American strategic bombing forces lost 100 heavy bombers destroyed, with 170 damaged, of which over twenty had to be written off as irreparable. Hundreds of frontline Allied airmen died : erased in the total disintegration of mid-air explosion, or hurled hideously to earth where some fell naked like deposed gods, or rocking limply in the aircraft which their comrades brought uncertainly home. "Home" was not Savannah or Adelaide or one of the far places in three continents where their pledged women waited, but Norfolk, Northamptonshire, Huntingdonshire and Leicestershire, the plains and shires of central east England which had become bomber country.

At Trafton Underwood, Molesworth, Alconbury and Chelveston the American bombardment crews waited in their aircraft for engine-starting through a wet and stormy dawn while fiercer weather further east in Norfolk delayed the co-ordinated take-off. Finally the massed-start was abandoned. The Third Division, target Regensburg, went ahead. It took off from the inland shires, lifting and circling over Podington and Thurleigh and Polebrook, with its tall church spire, seven centuries old with a one-hand clock. The Fortresses climbed, formed, picked up their squadron pattern, merged squadrons into groups and groups into the deeply stacked combat wings of over 70 aircraft. As the wings took up the formation of a fleet they were marked from the ground by bomber aircrews of the Royal Air Force, already primed through the Command grapevine to anticipate a "maximum effort" operation that night.

The appointed Master Bomber, Group Captain John H. Searby, indeed knew already that the operation which he had rehearsed with Pathfinder crews on a desolate stretch of the British coastline was to culminate that night. Soon the British crews were driving to the dispersal bays to take up every Lancaster, Halifax and Stirling engaged for the battle on a low-altitude air test of all instruments, guns and mechanisms, from altimeter to bomb doors. The radio operators made their short transmissions to check equipment : aircraft to signals head-quarters, *QRM? How are you receiving me?* It was all care-fully monitored by Germans listening out in France. The volume of transmission traffic was gauged and reported from the French coast to Paris, from Paris to night-fighter headquarters at Zeist in Holland, where General Kammhuber's Chief of Staff knew that he could expect at least 500 British bombers that night in addition to the day invaders which were already sparking on other radar screens.

The German fighter force was on its mettle. Though its morale was being heavily battered by Hitler and Göring it had many devoted operational leaders who still kept the ranks closed, confident and effective. The fighter was superior to the bomber, as it had been during the Battle of Britain and was to remain – squadron for squadron in the air – throughout the war. The bomber did not "always get through". General Arnold in Washington and General Spaatz commanding the Eighth Air Force from London did not yet believe this. They held an entrenched faith in the self-defending qualities of the Fortress formation bristling with half-inch machine guns. They believed, in Spaatz's words, "that our current type bombers can penetrate existing German defences to the limit of their radius of operation without excessive losses". General Eaker, leading VIII Bomber Command, did not, after a year of battle, agree. Even at the end of the seventh month of actual operations he had concluded that the German fighter force – in its actual strength and its potential strength as a result of successful aircraft production – could block the strategic bomber offensive in its main task : to paralyse German power to the extent that an invasion could be attempted. In the so-called "Eaker Plan", the plan for a combined bomber offensive issued on 12 April 1943, he declared "if the growth of the German fighter strength is not arrested quickly, it may become literally impossible to carry out the destruction planned." This view had at least convinced the Combined Chiefs of Staff to the point where their declaration of immediate Allied bombing policy put the offensive against the German fighter force, both in the air and in the factories where it was being shaped, as "an *intermediate* objective second to none in priority". The American bombing missions of 17 August 1943 were directed to this end. Their target objectives were the complex of Messerschmitt fighter construction factories at Regensburg, and the anti-friction bearing (ball-bearing) works at Schweinfurt which supplied German industry with half its needs. The additional purpose, as in all the American daylight

H

raids, was to challenge German fighter squadrons to battle and to shoot them down in the air.

Belief in the adequate self-defence of the Fortress formations had not, however, degenerated into dogma, particularly after fierce fighter onslaughts at the end of July 1943 which had reduced the strength of VIII Bomber Command to 275 aircraft. Repairs, replacements, and a fortnight's bad weather (which had turned the Command's thoughts seriously once more towards the proposition of bombing Germany mainly from North Africa instead of England), had brought the complement up to the point where 376 B-17s were scheduled for the twin attack on Regensburg and Schweinfurt. For this, the deepest American penetration of German territory to date, the Fortresses were to be given the fullest fighter cover possible. Eighteen squadrons of Thunderbolts from VIII Fighter Command and sixteen squadrons of Royal Air Force Spitfires were to escort the Fortresses to the limit of the fighters' range – roughly as far as the German frontier. Having refuelled, they were to meet the bombers on their return. In addition, B-26 Marauders of VIII Air Support Command and Typhoons of the Royal Air Force were to bomb French and Dutch airfields to keep German fighters busy in these areas.

The pilots of 300 reserved German fighters and destroyers were not at all interested in these diversionary activities. They had been assembled over Frankfurt, just outside the range of the Thunderbolt and Spitfire escorts, to engage the advancing bombers. The German aircraft were mainly Messerschmitt Me 109Gs, single-engined and equipped with three 20mm cannon and two machine-guns There were also Focke-Wulf FW 190s, single-engined, well-armed and fast – though their performance fell off at 21,000 feet, the usual Fortress height; and a group of twin-engined Messerschmitt Me 110 Destroyers with rockets among their armament.

The last Thunderbolts, the few which had been equipped with belly-tanks to increase their range, peeled off from their defensive stations and turned north-west to refuel and cover the second wave of Fortresses. The bomber fleet kept on its course. The German squadrons climbed and fanned to varying heights and quarters. Their pilots had lost the initial compulsive awe of the tough, destructive Fortress formations and had learned to press home concerted, resolute attacks aimed wherever possible at one combat wing at a time.

A single Messerschmitt Destroyer positioned itself alongside the boxed bombers, a mile to starboard and out of range, to report the course and development of the battle to ground control. Then the fight was on. Squadrons of fighters attacked successively from all directions in sections of two or four aircraft. First they closed from ahead, hustling in a frontal assault and breaking off in half-rolls. Entire squadrons roared upwards in javelin formation to conduct a belly attack against which the bomber pilots could take only clumsy evasive action. As the fighters fell away others came down in vertical dives firing at the top turrets. The rocket firers came on in the more conventional rear attack, launching their missiles from 1,000 yards and coming in with machine-guns and cannon. The scope and co-ordination of the attacks gave time for the fighters to land, refuel and rearm. Then they engaged again as the course of the continuous battle swept 300 miles into Germany, and was taken up again in a running fire when the second force of Fortresses was abandoned by its escorts over the Western frontier. Grimly the Fortress pilots tried to cling to their formation but the rocket attacks broke some up. Then cannon succeeded rockets and machine-guns supplemented cannon as the fighters, three to one against a detached bomber, harried it to the death. Within the bombers, shuddering with the recoil of their guns, the stink of gunpowder and the sweat of desperate, blaspheming men mingled in a single bitter aroma. The free air was curiously littered with the debris of earth-made things and mortal men. A complete main exit door detached from a broken bomber became a missile endangering the lives of other crews. Men fell earthwards, through the stacked combat wings, revolving, knees to head, like acrobats with the sweet confidence of a trampoline beneath them. A burning Fortress veered helplessly to starboard and the second pilot crawled out of his flame-free window, held on with one hand four miles above the ground, reached back for his parachute and incredibly buckled it on, and then let go, to be dashed to death by his slipstream against the horizontal stabiliser. Messerschmitts and Fortresses were blazing in the air. A pilot estimated there were sixty billowing parachutes visible at one time. And always there were the men for whom parachutes were useless : the crews blown apart when entire Fortresses exploded leaving nothing substantial in the air except four burning fuel tanks; the bodies which clumped hopelessly down as the dead and the dying plunged to their graves.

The litter of metal and flesh extended from Aachen to Schweinfurt and Regensburg, and continued over the Alps as the 3rd Bombardment Division set a return course for North Africa on an experimental shuttle that was never repeated. The savaged bomber forces had pressed through to their target. Eighty direct high-explosive hits were made on two main bearing plants at Schweinfurt. Albert Speer, the German Minister of Munitions, believed that if the Americans came again soon in any force German ball-bearing production was doomed. But the German Fighter Command had put in some powerful persuasion against a follow-up attack. They had destroyed 60 bombers and their carefully trained crews at a cost of 25 fighters.

As the lamed formations of the 1st Bombardment Division VIII Bomber Command, anxiously counted by their ground staff, filtered in to East Anglia through the afternoon and gusty evening of the long August day, the crews of Royal Air Force Bomber Command were enduring the familiar tightening of emotional tension as they prepared to succeed the Americans in the skies. At the squadron briefings during the afternoon, when the brown paper was peeled off the target maps to disclose their objective as Peenemünde, none of the aircrews was told the truth about the function of that little Baltic peninsula on the Bay of Pomerania. The main force airmen were instructed that they were to carry out precision bombing, from the unusually low altitude of 8,000 feet, on a triple target : the quarters of scientists, an experimental research station, and large factory workshops. The station was declared to be producing a vital new radar system which would revolutionize German night-fighter defence and jeopardize Bomber Command. The crews were also told that if they did not put the station out of action they would be sent back night after night until their mission was completed. The introduction of this ill-chosen incentive was an indiscretion that miscarried, and was eventually to preserve Peenemünde from entire obliteration.

The bomber crews accepted their target justification and got down to the practical exposition of tactics by officers detailing the anticipated flak and night-fighter defence, the route, target indicator and marker bomb colours for the night,[1] signal procedure and gunnery drill.

At Wyton, a Pathfinder Force station, Group Captain Searby commanding 83 (Pathfinder) Squadron, carefully outlined the marker-bombing control which he would direct over the target. This was the first big occasion on which the Master Bomber technique of verbally instructing the bomb-aimers during the actual raid was applied, though Searby had practised it ten days earlier with 14 aircraft over Turin.

An extremely perceptive airman at Wyton might have wondered that the Pathfinder briefing was attended not only by the Force's commanding officer, Air Vice Marshal Donald C. T. Bennett, but by an apparent civilian. He might have recognized him as the disabled Lieutenant-Colonel Duncan Sandys, son-in-law of the Prime Minister and a Joint Parliamentary Secretary to the Minister of Supply. He could not have known that Mr Sandys was the coordinating investigator of all intelligence on German long-range rocket development, that Mr Sandys's information was that German rocket attacks on Britain would be begun in August or September 1943, that the Home Secretary estimated the casualty rate at 100,000 Londoners killed every month, and that Sir Arthur Harris had been ordered six weeks previously to wipe out Peenemünde, the prime source of these rockets, at the earliest opportunity.

At nine o'clock, half an hour before sunset according to the manipulated time observed by the British during the war, eight Mosquitoes of 139 Pathfinder Squadron were airborne from Upwood, heading into the rolling darkness and a full moon rising. After an hour they were over Denmark. They switched on their detectable radio equipment. They curved towards Peenemünde, prompting a full air-raid warning there, then turned hard south and raced towards Berlin. Soon after eleven they were releasing an entirely disproportionate number of 64 pathfinder flares over the capital, and dropping the occasional blockbuster whose impact went unregarded against the roar of the full anti-aircraft barrage of the most heavily defended city in Germany. Forming in intricate order behind the Mosquitoes

1. The colours were changed frequently to prevent German simulation on decoy sites.

as they set out, but not following them to Berlin, was a heavy bomber stream which in its various sections was to stretch for 200 miles. It was led by a solitary Lancaster, the aircraft of the Master Bomber, who was flying very low over the North Sea to Denmark, escaping radar detection. Behind him came some thirty Lancasters, the Pathfinder Blind Markers, Visual Markers and Backers Up of the first target-indicating force. Well bunched and flying low at four miles a minute there followed 227 Stirlings, Halifaxes and Lancasters, the first wave main bombing force intended for the principal target : the research scientists. Within this force there were other Pathfinder aircraft, Backers Up who were to re-indicate the target if the bombing went awry. A smaller group of Pathfinders scheduled to indicate the second target led the next main force wave, an integrated fleet of 113 black Lancasters carrying four tons of bombs apiece. The third wave, sweeping along in the remorseless stream four minutes behind its own Pathfinders, included even more Lancasters, 126 of the famed No. 5 Group, with 54 Halifaxes. Upon the 4,000 men in this total force, briefed with a complexity of orders which would have been technically infeasible in the recent hit-or-miss days of the Command, depended the course of the next year of war.

From Utrecht to Stettin the German night-fighter force was waiting to pounce. Since four in the afternoon, when German monitors recorded and decoded – having cracked the cipher – a Bomber Command "lay off" signal to coastal defence stations at Cromer warning them not to fire on the stream, Luftwaffe Fighter Command had anticipated a raid to the north of Germany rather than on the Ruhr or Italy. They had planned accordingly. Two hundred fighters were in readiness. It was the largest night defence force the Germans had yet assembled. Taking its place in the order of battle for the first time was the 30th (Wild Boar) Fighter Division, 55 free-lance single-engine fighters manned by volunteer pilots of exceptional skill. They were to operate independently of General Kammhuber's Twelfth Air Corps of night fighters.

The Wild Boar Division, in its fast Focke Wulf FW 190s, coordinating directly with Colonel-General Hubert Weise, Commander in Chief of the Reich Home Defence, was airborne from its bases in the Bonn area and heading for Berlin even before the Mosquitoes had arrived there. The much more tightly controlled twin-engine Messerschmitt Destroyers of the Twelfth Air Corps were dependent on the ground-to-air instructions of their controller, who was reacting to the imprecise echoes of the bomber stream at low altitude over the North Sea, and at first directed the night defence to Bremen, then to Wilhelmshaven, and then to Kiel. But suddenly the overall control of the Twelfth Air Corps died. The information which should have been fed into General Kammhuber's operations room through Arnhem from his fighter command units and observation posts was checked abruptly by an unaccountable signals fault. The frenzied test-inspection of all line junctions and vulnerable points failed to reveal the cause of the fault, and Arnhem was out of contact with Germany for the whole of this, Kammhuber's most eagerly awaited, battle. This was particularly relished by the two British agents who worked in the Arnhem-Deelen operations room, and continued to work there after what they regarded as the glorious fiasco of 17 August.

Kammhuber's controller, deprived of the minute-by-minute intelligence he needed, could only be briefed through indirect and delayed auxiliary channels. The tight direction of the 148 Messerschmitts in the sky faltered, then faded. In Metz, 200 miles south of Arnhem, where the Fourth Fighter Division was listening out critically on the conduct of the battle, General Junck quickly realized that the night fighter general was impotent. He telephoned Göring, who was in contact with the Luftwaffe Operations Headquarters though not physically present. Göring told Junck that the Wild Boars were already racing to Berlin and ordered him to take over, from his bunker beneath Metz in France, the fighter defence of Berlin. It was an improvisation. Junck's staff did not have the full information, equipment or experience to direct a night-fighter battle using an empirical technique of ground-to-air communication that was only three weeks old, having been hastily improvised to meet British radio counter-measures during the fatal Battle of Hamburg. Half an hour after the Mosquitoes arrived over Berlin, and ninety minutes after the first night fighters had scrambled to intercept the intruders, Junck signalled the Berlin flak to keep their fire below 18,000 feet in order to give the Wild Boar Division free play at its own ceiling. Almost immedi-

ately, the transmitter tuning being completed, Junck annexed
the German night fighter radio frequency and broadcast the
order : "All night fighters to Berlin."

This signal was monitored by British radio operators at Kings-
down, at the top of the white cliffs between Dover and Walmer.
It was relayed to Bomber Command Headquarters at High
Wycombe, where it was received with the greatest satisfaction.
The broadcast had been put out at 11.35, when the first wave
of British bombers was half an hour from Peenemünde. And
Berlin was exactly where Bomber Command wanted the Ger-
man fighters to be.

Air Chief Marshal Sir Arthur Harris had recently been sending eight Mosquitoes over Berlin on every night possible. Always
they had taken the northern route, coming in from the Baltic
over Peenemünde. The result was that the rocket scientists and
flying-bomb testers in Peenemünde had endured a succession
of air-raid warnings, and some were beginning to disregard the
gravity of the alarm. At the same time the Berlin defence had
been kept moderately active, and keenly expectant. General
Weise could recognize a nuisance raid, but had to guess which
guard he was being persuaded to lower. On 17 August, when
the first firm report of a strong raiding force had come from
Danish coastguard stations and Mosquitoes were already whin-
ing towards Berlin, he could be forgiven a certain irresolution.
Single bluff on Harris's part would be to feint at Berlin and
hit another target. Double bluff would be to send his bombers
storming in to Berlin after the Mosquitoes had gone through
the motions of their nightly nuisance raid : and double bluff
was indicated that night, since the Mosquitoes had released
flares enough for a major raid. Treble bluff would rely on
Weise eventually discounting the double bluff, but holding on
to his fighters too tight and too late. Complicating Weise's decision were two further considerations. First, it was a bright
moonlit night, giving perfect conditions for night fighters and
making it operationally a very risky mission for the enemy to
send out massive bomber forces on deep penetration : *unless*
they needed moonlight to identify a hitherto virgin target. No
moonlight was necessary for the general area saturation bombing of Bremen, Wilhelmshaven or Kiel. The characteristic pat-
terns of their land shapes interlocked with water showed like

a silhouette map on the radar screens of the marker bombers and the ports could be hit through ten-tenths cloud. Berlin was easy to locate but an intensely difficult area in which to pinpoint precision objectives. Moonlight might help. But, against that factor, the city's flak and searchlight defences were notoriously strong and the certainty of night-fighter activity in the most favourable conditions made it a very dangerous target to attack in this phase of the moon.

And here Weise had to take into account his second additional consideration.

Perhaps the British had decided on terror bombing whatever the cost. It was only a fortnight since the end of the Nine Days of Hamburg, the greatest slaughter yet wrought in the history of aerial bombing. The full details of the casualties were not yet known.[1] But on one night of unprecedented concentration, 27 July, 722 aircraft had dropped 2,000 tons of bombs in 43 minutes – nearly half a ton of high explosive and over 200 incendiaries dropped every second – and the resultant whirling fire storm had sucked the life out of the great majority of those, rumoured to be 100,000,[2] who had died in Hamburg.

Was Berlin earmarked for the Hamburg treatment? Speer had already told Hitler that a continuation of attacks on the Hamburg scale might bring about a rapid end of the war. General Weise had a heavy responsibility for the safety of the capital. There was much justification for the summons to all night fighters: "To Berlin."

At three minutes to midnight a German night-fighter group based on Copenhagen, which was not in the first defence network, was put into the air to rendezvous at Falster radio beacon, 100 miles to the north of Peenemünde, and catch the British bombers on their return from Berlin. At that precise moment the Master Bomber was orbiting over Peenemünde itself, disquieted to observe that a smokescreen had been started which was obliterating the northern lines of the target. One hundred and twenty

1. The cellars were too hot and the burial parties undermanned. Three months later 100 bodies a day were being taken from the shelters. Most had died from carbon monoxide asphyxiation caused by the fire-tornado.

2. After the war deaths in the Battle of Hamburg were agreed at 43,000.

miles further south there was utter confusion over Berlin. The Mosquitoes had not yet withdrawn, but the radar echoes of Kammhuber's approaching Destroyers gave an indication which was read as a large bomber force approaching Berlin. Soon these aircraft could be physically heard. Hundreds of anti-aircraft guns shot into the sky. The Wild Boar pilots, skilled navigators and daring fliers, but with little experience of night fighting, assumed from the flak activity that the enemy were present in force and resolutely attacked any machine larger than their own : a lapse in aircraft recognition which bore hardly on the unfortunate crews of the twin-engined, twin-ruddered Messerschmitt Destroyers. Only one Mosquito was shot down, by a Focke Wulf, that night. Meanwhile the flak predictors trained the guns on aircraft which were almost inevitably friendly. Field Marshal Milch, then in charge of aircraft production, saw from his shelter entrance his own fighters being attacked by the Berlin guns although identification signals were being desperately flashed. Milch telephoned Göring to try to get the guns silenced. Göring, though willing, could not obtain sanction for the order either from Hitler's Headquarters or from the office of Colonel-General Hans Jeschonnek, Chief of the Air Staff – an interesting sidelight on the limited authority of the Reich Marshal. Jeschonnek, 370 miles east of Berlin at the Luftwaffe operational headquarters at Goldap in East Prussia, still believed that Berlin was under heavy attack. In any case he was disinclined to cancel an order from the Führer-headquarters. He was smarting wretchedly from the effect of an unnerving tirade against the Luftwaffe which he had had to endure from Hitler that day, in the customary absence of Göring. But, even as he was brooding on the indignities he had suffered, a scared aide asked him if he would take the telephone. Göring, almost in a state of apoplexy, had put in a personal call to his Chief of Staff.

Amid the galloping confusion over Berlin, the harassed German fliers suddenly glimpsed, far to the north, the intense illumination of white parachute flares going down on the Baltic coast. The British Pathfinder Force was orientating itself over Peenemünde before dropping the target indicators. Some pilots called the Berlin ground controller by radio, asking permission to fly north to the apparent target. This officer ordered the aircraft to remain over Berlin. He was working on his own, unable to discuss the situation with the sabotaged Kammhuber and unaware of the target potential of Peenemünde, which had been on a top secret classification since 1936. Most of the pilots continued to circle above Berlin until their fuel ran low. Even at this stage they could have landed and refuelled, replaced the ammunition they had shot at their friends, and received the orders to go north which did come tardily through. But 100 of the fighters, not having been allotted a landing field, chose to come down, almost simultaneously, at Brandenburg-Briest. Thirty of them crashed on landing in a series of concertina pile-ups, and the airfield was so littered with wrecks that no aircraft could take off again.

A few experienced pilots disobeyed the orders of the Berlin controller and headed for the flares in the north. There was action enough awaiting them. At five minutes past midnight the Master Bomber had reconnoitred the target and established radio contact with his Pathfinder marker aircraft. The first crews swept in from the north, scanning their radar screens for the picture of the land below. But the majority of these mis-read the image, mis-identified the approach to the target, and made a two-mile error in dropping the crimson spot fires intended to mark the beginning of the main force's bombing run. Group Captain Searby had exactly five minutes to retrieve control of the operation and correct the blind marking. The actual target of the first wave, the living quarters of the scientists, had been accurately identified by one Visual Marker of 156 Pathfinder Squadron who marked it with a yellow target indicator. Searby himself flew low to reinforce this yellow with another, and called on two waiting Visual Markers to drop more yellows. The four yellows were then emphasized by three greens dropped by his Backers Up. The 227 bombers of the main force first wave were now thundering up. Searby broadcast to them to concentrate on the correct greens. This was the first time that most of the bomber crews had had their missiles "talked down" by the Master Bomber. Their immediate impression was not of the value of the constant encouraging running commentary but of the sheer lift in their morale achieved at the moment of their greatest strain by an English voice, cool and friendly, coming in loud and clear over the static.

In the next ten minutes 450 tons of bombs went down on the scientists' housing estate, killing or burying alive in the soft sand some scores of research workers including two irreplaceable experts. Unfortunately about seventy of the bomb-aimers would not be talked out of bombing the wrong indicators, and a heavy attack was made on a slave-labourers' compound two miles south of the target. Among the 600 who died there was a band of deported Luxembourgers who had been getting some of the secrets of the German rockets through to British secret agents. This source of intelligence was wiped out.

The first wave withdrew, having suffered only two losses from flak, though if they dallied they might yet be caught by the destroyers from Copenhagen speeding to the Falster beacon. Independent elements of the German fighter force were also spurting north from Berlin. The markers for the British second bombing wave were already making their runs. Both they and their first Backers Up overshot, so that they marked the target already punished by the first wave. The Master Bomber got the later Backers Up to put their greens correctly on the second target, the pilot rocket factory to the north of the scientists' quarters, and instructed the advancing Lancasters to bomb the northern green markers. The Lancasters bombed, but hit the first-wave target as often as the second. At the rate of 14 aircraft a minute they bombed, curved back to the shore and headed north. They were only just in time. Thirty night fighters from Berlin had reached Peenemünde.

The critical importance of the diversion of 200 night fighters to Berlin instead of Peenemünde can be seen from the precise timetable of the final stages of the raid. The third wave marking started at 39 minutes past midnight (0239 GMT). Five German fighters were over Peenemünde at 35 minutes past midnight. They had found and reached the height of the bombers within nine minutes and began to kill : one destroyer shot down five bombers in a quarter of an hour.[1] The third wave marking was bad and was not corrected by the Master Bomber for the first three minutes of main force bombing, until a Path-

1. But many of the German fighters never saw a Lancaster although they were over the bomb bursts. They were searching at from 18,000 feet, a typical Bomber Command altitude, but for the precision attack many of the British bombed at under 8,000 feet.

finder Backer Up pinpointed the rocket development works and laboratories. Then only some of the Halifaxes and Lancasters bombed it. But by now the bombers were preoccupied with intensive fighter attack. Eighteen aircraft in the last wave are known to have been shot down over Peenemünde and eleven more did not get home. Most of the latter were caught from Falster beacon, where the waiting Messerschmitt Me 110s from Copenhagen had found their discipline and the weather conditions so favourable that they had pushed home two rare and murderous formation attacks in the bright moonlight.

The night's total losses to Bomber Command were 40 heavy bombers destroyed on the main raid and one Mosquito shot down over Berlin. The minimum delay, as estimated with hindsight, effected on German V-weapon warfare was from six to eight weeks. If this halt had not been imposed the Germans would have advanced the bombardment of southern England by rocket to July 1944 and by jet bomb to April 1944 : five weeks before D-Day. At the time, Bomber Command overestimated the results of its attack. On 19 August, thirty hours after the last bomber had come home, the Chiefs of Staff declined an American offer for VIII Bomber Command to finish the job in daylight. Major General Walter Dornberger, having learned from captured British aircrew that they had been told that they would be sent back repeatedly until they had knocked out the research station completely, decided to simulate a knock-out immediately – and worked under a camouflage canopy of bomb debris until he was ready to disperse his production throughout Germany. Bomber Command did not touch Peenemünde for nine months; by that time its importance as a V-weapon production centre had vanished.

Before the first reconnaissance Mosquito had flown over Peenemünde at ten in the morning of Wednesday, 18 August, Harris's attack on the research station had claimed its most distinguished victim. Colonel-General Hans Jeschonnek lay dead on the floor of his room in Luftwaffe operational headquarters with a bullet in his head and a note by his side reading : "I cannot work with Göring any more. Long live the Führer."

The last phase of Jeschonnek's breakdown had begun with the German defeat at Stalingrad in the previous winter. Göring, already being harried by Hitler, loudly blamed Jeschonnek for the Luftwaffe's failure to bring Paulus any sort of air lift. Later came the German defeat in Tunis and the invasion of Sicily. Göring bitterly berated his Chief of Staff when Jeschonnek transferred squadrons to Italy to meet the pulsing emergency. Kesselring was in Jeschonnek's office when he had taken a telephone call from Göring in which Kesselring overheard such a stream of abuse that he immediately volunteered to act as Jeschonnek's witness in a court of honour. Jeschonnek refused with the words "It's always like that with the man and it always will be." Then, after further humiliation of the Luftwaffe in Russia, Jeschonnek, a young but beaten man, asked Hitler to take over personal command of the Luftwaffe from Göring. Milch had made this same request to Hitler even earlier, after the Stalingrad defeat, but it had not come to Göring's ears. This time the informants were keener. Göring was acquainted with the details by 17 August.

On that day of violent air action Jeschonnek suffered two personal reverses. The chaos of the night deception over Berlin was the sort of bad luck that can hit any commander and normally should not be the excuse to unseat him from power. But Jeschonnek was at fault in the basic theory by which he accepted the daylight operations as a German defeat. He overestimated the American bomb damage at Schweinfurt and Regensburg (as everyone tended to at first). But he failed to see the daylight air battle as a German victory simply because, like Hitler and most of the Luftwaffe leaders, he was not a fighter man. The British, who are perhaps sharper to detect a victory in an apparent defeat, justifiably celebrated the winning of the Battle of Britain even though their land got badly bombed in the process of winning it. They could see the strategy, the skeletal struggle for air power behind the confusion of the daily mêlées and they could perceive that they had snatched the mastery of their own air space. But now the same struggle was on in Germany, and in the daylight battles – part of whose object was to destroy the German fighter force – the home defence was again confirming its domination. The Luftwaffe was winning the air battle and Jeschonnek could not even discern it.

On 17 August, therefore, Jeschonnek had suffered a crushing blow to his esteem, endured an unrelated attack from Hitler

on other Luftwaffe deficiencies, and by midnight had some indication of a bad blunder over Berlin. Then came the personal
call from Göring. Jeschonnek's support for the Führer-order,
which rejected Göring's request to silence the anti-aircraft guns,
would have provided fuel enough for a major conflagration
without other incitement. There is evidence that Göring
widened the issue into a furious discussion of Jeschonnek's suggestion that Hitler should take over the Luftwaffe. "I shall have
you indicted for insubordination . . . unless you find a way out
of the situation which you have created." Through the long
night hours Jeschonnek made no final decision. In the morning
he heard the full story of the defence chaos over Berlin and the
low moonlight attack on Peenemünde which, properly intercepted, might have cost the British 200 bombers. He was due
to meet Hitler at the daily war conference. He chose instead to
die, but to leave a dead finger pointing at Göring's control of
the Luftwaffe.

Göring was sliding, and Hamburg, Schweinfurt and Peenemünde were interlinked with his fall. Göring was a "bomber
man" like most of the Luftwaffe strategists. The function of an
air force was to attack. As an intelligent man Göring, in his
theorizing moments, stripped air force attack down to its naked
essentials: from attacking as the army's extended artillery
through to attacking the substance and sources of the enemy's
air power, and on to attacking as an integrated strategic arm
with an independent purpose. But, although the independent
strategic use of the Luftwaffe was clearly a function which
would have given its Commander in Chief the greatest prestige,
Göring did not consistently press this emphasis. The reason
for his reluctance is difficult to accept from a professional military man. To champion an independent strategy in the air
meant to cross the will of Hitler, whose thinking always put
the air arm in an auxiliary role. Göring began his political
career with a genuine admiration for Hitler, an esteem which
perceptibly developed into veneration, awe, and, at the end,
fear: particularly fear of his wrath. Göring's other relevant
characteristic was a lazy mind, a refusal to make a hard decision between strenuously-backed alternatives. This increasing
moral cowardice showed itself in many crises – technical, as in
deciding the balance of the Luftwaffe, or moral, as concerning

Hitler's order to shoot fifty recaptured Royal Air Force prisoners of war at Stalag Luft III, a camp at Sagan. In these agonizing moments Göring again and again *tried not to know* the full scope of the issue, in order that he should not have to give a difficult ruling.

It was the fault of Göring that the apportionment of emphasis on the different functions of his air force remained vague, though it is true that he shared this lack of precision with most of the other Luftwaffe leaders. What is much more clearly Göring's failure is that he did not, as a Commander in Chief and Air Minister could be expected to do, give some credence to his own young generals with immediate war experience. They maintained that unless the air force defended *itself* in Germany the nucleus of German power could be obliterated, with no energy generated for attack outside the Reich. It was a recurrence of the recognition of the strategical necessity of defence which had occurred in the Battle of Britain.

Hitler could never see this. Göring did see it dimly, was temporarily converted, but could not maintain the view against Hitler. Hitler responded to the ominous assault on Hamburg with uncontrolled rage, but his only positive words were "Attack! Attack! You can only smash terror with counter-terror." It was the reaction to Hamburg which prompted Hitler to give immediate and extraordinary priority to the A-4 project (the V-2 rocket) then being perfected at Peenemünde. A fortnight later Peenemünde was bombed on the day of the substantial blow against Schweinfurt. Göring could see that at least a key centre like Peenemünde must be protected, until its products could be used for Hitler's "attack". At a Luftwaffe High Command conference leading air force generals including Milch, Galland, Korten (who had been appointed to succeed Jeschonnek) and even Peltz, the General of the Bombers, who would lose prestige by any change of emphasis, reasoned with Göring to give at least a temporary priority to fighter production and fighter pilot training. Göring gave ground, and then in a generously great turn of heart came forward to meet his generals and lead a constructive discussion based on a rare unity of purpose. Göring himself summed up the conclusions of the conference. He said that the time had come for the Luftwaffe, after its highly successful offensive period, to concentrate on air defence against attacks from England. What had to be preserved above all was the potential of the German war industry. Given this protection by the Luftwaffe, war industry would in turn revitalize the Luftwaffe and give it the means to spring back to the attack with the counter-blows against the enemy which were already being prepared. Göring concluded with a moving call – for the man's personality was such that he could still move men, even military men. He said he knew he was asking of his air generals and the men they commanded more than he had ever asked before. But he knew that his Luftwaffe – and here the generals saw, behind all the vainglory, that this in truth was his created Luftwaffe – would not shake off the new responsibilities he was putting upon it.

Göring strode out of the room to see Hitler immediately and get his consent to the shift of policy. In the emotion of their dynamic harmony the air generals waited confidently for Göring's return, with incredible trust in Hitler's reasonableness.

The Marshal came in. He was white, strained and speechless. He passed straight through the conference room. After an interval Peltz and Galland, the Generals of the Bombers and Fighters respectively, were called in to him. They witnessed not only the personal breakdown of a man, a marshal. It was the most astonishing evidence of the strange power of Hitler, which has not always been given its due recognition, to inspire successively affection, respect, devotion – and then sheer terror of his anger and acquiescent acceptance of his instructions when given in the spate of passion. It is one of the oldest and most effective forms of brainwashing. Galland has described the scene:

We were met with a shattering picture: Göring had completely broken down. With his head buried in his arms on the table, he moaned some indistinguishable words. We stood there for some time in embarrassment until at last he pulled himself together and said we were witnessing his deepest moments of despair. The Führer had lost faith in him. All the suggestions from which he had expected a radical change in the situation of the war in the air had been rejected; the Führer had announced that the Luftwaffe had disappointed him too often, and a changeover from offensive to defensive against the West was out of the question. He would give the Luftwaffe a last chance to rehabilitate itself by a resumption of air attacks against England, but this time on a bigger scale. Now, as before, the motto was still – attack. Terror could only be smashed by counter-terror.[1]

And now Göring performed the self-abasement which signalizes and confirms all the most effective conversions.

Göring said that he had realized his mistake. The Führer was always right. All our strength was now to be concentrated on dealing the enemy in the west such mighty retaliation blows from the air that he would not risk a second Hamburg. As a first measure in the execution of his plan the Führer had ordered the creation of a leader of the attacks on England. Göring rose. "Oberst Peltz," he cried, "I herewith appoint you assault-leader against England."

The farcical climax to this episode was that four months later Göring himself was sent by Hitler's personal order to the Western air fleet to supervise bomber retaliation against England in the so-called Baby Blitz. The supervision did not last long, but Hitler's confidence in Göring's subservience was shown to be well founded. In February 1944 Göring was back in Berchtesgaden. Milch and Galland made a last effort to convince him of the continuing importance of the fighter defence of Germany. The issue at the moment was Hitler's decisive and impractical order to convert into a bomber the outstanding jet fighter which Willy Messerschmitt had produced : the Me 262. Milch, working hard against the tide, had effected an astonishing surge in fighter production only to see the majority of his new aircraft cast away in a year of defeat, destroyed or abandoned in the retreats in Russia, Africa and Italy. A favourable decision on the jet might at last swing production priority over to the fighters.

Milch accompanied Göring to an interview with Hitler when the Reich Marshal was to attempt this last persuasion. Hitler merely developed the recurrent fit of anger which the manipulation of the Luftwaffe seemed to induce in him. He roared "I want bombers, bombers, bombers. Your fighters are no damned good, anyway." Hastily and humbly Göring capitulated before his Führer and acquiesced in a positive decision on weapons which was to be a direct cause of defeat. For the jet fighter could have been in action in Spring 1944; its speed

1. Galland, *The First and the Last.*

gave it a 100-m.p.h. edge on the top Allied fighters at a time when the result of the fighter duel was all-important; its fuel was a cheap and relatively unrefined oil – and the lack of high-octane aviation fuel caused by the Allied bombing of oil plants was to be a major factor in Germany's defeat. Ironically this vital interview between Hitler and Göring took place as the reinvigorated American Air Force was sweeping back into Germany with full fighter protection, and while Arnold and Eaker were planning the "Big Week" of air operations which were to initiate the extinction of the German fighter arm as a determining force in the war.

General Arnold had had a bad winter. The August attack on Schweinfurt had been finally assessed as a comparative failure to affect the ball-bearings bottleneck in Germany, and he ordered another raid. On 14 October 1943 a force of 291 Flying Fortresses set out from England for Schweinfurt, and only 93 returned undamaged. Of the rest 60 were shot down and 17 irreparably damaged, giving a total loss rate in machines and men of over 25 per cent. Arnold declared that he could absorb this aircraft wastage (though it equalled his estimated maximum monthly loss) but he knew that his crews could not endure a succession of losses of this nature. They would assail only those areas which were within the range of their fighter protection. The proclaimed policy of reliance on the self-defending Fortress formation was relinquished. It was a temporary concession of defeat. In order to lessen the political and military consequences – for public opinion might surge to support Navy Department pressure to force the main bomber offensive to the Pacific – Arnold declared : "Our attack was the most perfect example in history of accurate distribution of bombs over a target. It was an attack which will not have to be repeated for a very long time, if at all." But he knew when he said it that the expert British appreciation of the damage done at Schweinfurt was the loss of $1\frac{1}{2}$ months' production. Meanwhile Eaker had decided on a tactical retreat. Nothing could be done in daylight to destroy the sources of German aircraft production until a long-range fighter force could escort the bombers.

The necessity for a long-range fighter force had been only indifferently accepted even by the British. Churchill had urged the development of this arm for the Royal Air Force as early as June 1941, but Portal told him that long-range fighters could never hold their own against short-range fighters. In July 1942 the Operational Research Section of Bomber Command declared it improbable that bomber operations with fighter cover could ever constitute a significant sector in a daylight bombing programme against the heart of Germany. Portal reversed his theory on the potential of long-range fighters in the autumn of 1942, but apparently more from a desire to keep VIII Bomber Command – buttressed by a putative fighter support which it did not then enjoy – in Europe rather than the Pacific. Only Churchill was consistent in his encouragement of long-range fighter development. He told Roosevelt on 16 September 1942 : "For keeping up and intensifying the direct pressure on Germany the Fortress and the long-range fighter are indispensable." He urged Harry Hopkins a month later to hustle the production of a long-range Mustang, though he also asked him to develop an effective American night bomber.

The American Air Warfare Plans Division had considered the development of an "escort fighter" in 1941, but, becoming increasingly confident in the defensive power of the Fortress formation, had abandoned it a year later. By 28 May 1943, however, General Eaker, soon to be backed by Mr Robert A. Lovett, the Assistant Secretary of War for Air, was calling from England that the range of his fighters must be increased by fitting extra fuel tanks. These were introduced on the Thunderbolt in four stages, starting with a 75-gallon drop tank and ending with two 150-gallon wing tanks, which increased the range of this machine from 230 miles to 475 miles between June 1943 and February 1944. Meanwhile, by September 1943, the American P-51 Mustang, which had come into service with the Royal Air Force in 1941 but had been virtually ignored by the American Army Air Corps, had been developed into the P-51 B with a Packard/Rolls-Royce Merlin engine giving it a range of from 600 to 700 miles and a speed and manoeuvrability which outclassed any German fighter then in use. But the Mustang had been regarded in America as a fighter-reconnaissance aircraft. Only after the crisis of the second raid on Schweinfurt did Arnold recognize the ideal role of the machine. When he did act he moved with his usual energy.

On 30 October 1943 he ordered that all Mustangs, along with all long-range P-38 Lightnings, should be assigned exclusively as fighters on the European front.

The Mustangs were first used to support VIII Bomber Command on 5 December 1943 in a minor operation over Paris. In the first large-scale action over Germany only one squadron of Mustangs was available to escort a mixed force of 603 Fortresses and Liberators all the way to the target – an aircraft production centre. In a battle bitterly fought by 207 German fighters 60 American bombers were brought down. But this was almost the last considerable victory of Luftwaffe Fighter Command.

The long-range Mustangs were being rushed into service in multiple squadrons every week. Their introduction was the lever by which air superiority over Germany was gained. The Fortresses were once more a free-ranging force after a near-neutralization of four months. The episode had demonstrated an interesting inflexibility of American air strategy reacting with a characteristic flexibility of American aircraft production. Arnold's air force had sunk all its intellectual capital in the theory of precision bombing by daylight. Arnold and his chiefs resisted every effort – and the attempts were tenaciously pressed – to turn his bombers either into a predominantly night force or a force relying on general area bombing.

But Eaker's fierce desire to participate in the war did result in a considerable number of American night raids; moreover, the strangely unforeseen murky weather over Europe did force the Eighth Air Force on many occasions to bomb blindly through cloud; and the keenly pressed German fighter attacks forced many other missions off any pretension to accurate and precise bombing, or pushed formations so completely off course that they could only release their bombs on so-called "targets of opportunity" which were in reality the city centres of un-identified towns.

Arnold's sheer inability to change his bombing policy, as well as his loyalty to his strategic principles, forced him to maintain his stand. He hung on, although for months the Eighth Air Force was largely ineffective. But when the need for support fighters was realized, the admirably adaptable resources of American industry allowed the production of the Mustangs at a speed incapable of being paralleled anywhere else. Arnold stuck it out, and celebrated the re-entry of VIII Bomber Command into serious warfare with the massive offensive of "Big Week".

Big Week, the famous six-day air attack on German aircraft production starting on 20 February 1944, was not the overwhelming success which the propaganda of the time alleged it to be. What was important was the great tactical surge that followed it. In March 1944 the newly confident American fighters went over to the attack. They did not wait for the German fighters to assail the bomber formations. They sought out the homeland aircraft, in the air and on the airfields. Now technically dominant against all but the still rare German jets, the American fighters demonstrated an unquestionable air superiority. The strategic bombing of German aircraft production centres continued, but with extremely poor overall effect on the massive total production. Air superiority over Germany was achieved by the destruction in the air of German fighter pilots and the bombing on the ground of German fuel production. The aircraft industry itself was never directly conquered.

Air Chief Marshal Sir Arthur Harris had never believed that the German aircraft industry, as a separate agency, could be conquered by air bombardment. Constantly he cavilled at all suggestions that attacks on selective targets were the key to success. He dismissed them as impractical "panacea policies" whether the target recommended for immediate and concentrated attack was oil, ball bearings, communications, the aircraft industry or a molybdenum mine at Knaben. In a classic exposition of his attitude he declared to Air Marshal Sir Norman Bottomley, Deputy Chief of the Air Staff, that he had become "cynical with regard to the continual diversions of the bomber effort from its legitimate role in which, as we all know, it has inflicted the most grievous and intolerable damage to Germany. In fact, I am completely convinced, while not denying that the claims of the 'Panacea' mongers are put forward in good faith, that the continual stressing of targets which necessarily remove bombing pressure from the German nation as a whole, to concentrate on objectives such as the above [ball-bearings, transportation, oil] (and, as a further instance, such as

'Crossbow' sites)[1] is in many cases a deliberately engineered A.R.P. manoeuvre initiated by enemy sources."[2]

The "legitimate role" and primary objective of Royal Air Force Bomber Command, as Harris saw it, was "the progressive destruction and dislocation of the German military, industrial and economic system aimed at undermining the morale of the German people to a point where their capacity for armed resistance is fatally weakened". The corollary to this argument was that any diversion from the general area assault would be "to remove bombing pressure from the German nation as a whole" and thus to delay the surrender he believed the bombing offensive could achieve. In effect, Harris had adopted general area bombing as his own panacea.

Resolute in this attitude, Sir Arthur Harris, exercising an extraordinary independence of the Combined as well as the British Chiefs of Staff, pursued his individual policy until spring 1944, when even he, by his actions but not his words, admitted that it had failed. The night fighters were bleeding his force to death. At the end of March 1944 he halted the night bombing offensive, his face saved somewhat by the Allies' full concentration on preparations for the invasion. When the offensive was substantially resumed, the successful invasion of France – which the intermediate operations of Bomber Command had greatly aided – was found to have solved the problem of German air superiority. The early warning areas, the bases, and the German night-fighter force itself, were all mutilated.

From the Allied point of view the outstanding feature of Harris's bombing policy until the preparations for D-Day was that it doggedly ignored as a "panacea" the nomination by the Combined Chiefs of Staff of the German fighter force as "an *intermediate* objective second to none in priority". Long before the formulation of a plan for the Combined Bombing Offensive Harris had been asked to attack Schweinfurt, a key aircraft-component centre. He had answered, on 11 April 1942, "I am keeping an open mind on this target and, given the right conditions, I might decide to burn the town and blast its fac-

1. V-1 weapon launching sites.
2. Letter, Harris to Bottomley, 20 December 1943, quoted by Webster and Frankland, *The Strategic Air Offensive Against Germany, 1939–1945.*

tories."[1] He did not so decide, although extraordinarily patient pressure was put on him by Portal, for twenty-two months. Then he was directly ordered on two occasions to attack Schweinfurt as top priority until the town was destroyed. Four weeks after receiving the last order he complied with it. On that day, 24 February 1944, the revived VIII Bomber Command also attacked Schweinfurt. This was the first identifiable operation of the Combined Bomber Offensive, nearly a year after it had been projected in the Eaker Plan.

When the Casablanca Directive on Allied bombing policy listed early in 1943 the precise strategic bombing aims as German submarine construction yards, the German aircraft industry, transportation, oil plants and other industrial targets, Harris blandly remitted all these specific objectives in "the German military, industrial and economic system" to VIII Bomber Command and reserved to the Royal Air Force the assault on the morale of the German people. On 10 June 1943 the Casablanca Directive was amended to the target policy statement known thereafter by its code word "Pointblank". Harris and Eaker were told :

> The increasing scale of destruction which is being inflicted by our night bomber forces and the development of the day bomber offensive by the Eighth Air Force have forced the enemy to deploy day and night fighters in increasing numbers on the Western Front. Unless this increase in fighter strength is checked we may find our bomber forces unable to fulfil the tasks allotted to them by the Combined Chiefs of Staff.
>
> In these circumstances it has become essential to check the growth and to reduce the strength of the day and night fighter forces which the enemy can concentrate against us in this theatre. To this end the Combined Chiefs of Staff have decided that first priority in the operation of British and American bombers based in the United Kingdom shall be accorded to the attack of German fighter forces and the industry upon which they depend . . .

But in the same directive the intermediate objective of hitting "German Fighter strength" which now stood in priority *above* the primary objectives of German submarine yards and bases,

---

1. Letter, Harris to Air Commodore Baker, Director of Bomber Operations, 11 April 1942, quoted by Webster and Frankland, *The Strategic Air Offensive Against Germany, 1939–1945.*

the remainder of the German aircraft industry, ball-bearings and oil, was assigned to the Eighth Air Force alone. And this re-allocation (as it was) took place within the week of 3–10 June 1943. For in the draft of this directive, which was in Harris's hands on 3 June, all the objectives were assigned to "the bomber forces" both British and American, and "your combined forces" were requested to destroy the German fighter force production and the German fighters in the air and on the ground. One of the two Allied bomber commanders to whom the draft was submitted got all the precise objectives shovelled across to the Americans – and there are no grounds for believing that this commander was Eaker.

The Pointblank directive did not say that the success of *daylight* bombing alone depended on a check in the increase of German fighter strength. The future impact of night bombing was also affected. By the autumn of 1943, at the time of the first attacks on Schweinfurt, it was clear that the American day bombers were momentarily beaten by the German fighters. What was not then so obvious was that the future of British night bombing was also in jeopardy.

Sir Arthur Harris did not then concede this. He had triumphed at Peenemünde, by a narrow margin of minutes, through an admirably successful outwitting of the German night-fighter defence system. It was not admitted that, if German night-fighter strength and tactics improved, the delicate skirmish of wits might be swallowed up in a bloodier battle of force. Bomber Command's survival depended on systems of feinting to avoid contact with fighters, and evasion if contact was impending. *Bomber Command did not set out, as the Americans did, to shoot down fighters.* If the German fighter force became too experienced, or too numerous, for the various deception measures to be successful, Bomber Command's only salvation would lie in evasive tactics. In following these the force might substantially preserve its members, but it would have been driven off effective bombing. The fighters would have won.

If, from Harris's viewpoint, morale bombing failed, and if, from Eaker's stand, air superiority over Germany was not achieved and the fighters won, the objective of Pointblank was lost. The only formal reason for the bombing offensive against Germany in 1943–4 was to clear the way for "Overlord", the invasion of Europe. By the autumn of 1943 the Americans were in eclipse. Was the British effort doomed too?

It was the Deputy British Chief of Air Staff, Air Marshal Sir Norman Bottomley, who was more percipient on this issue than Sir Charles Portal. On 25 September 1943 he warned Portal that "we are not progressing rapidly with measures to overcome the German night fighter defences" and prophesied "we may find that either we are unable to maintain the night offensive against Germany, or that the Germans can sustain the intensity of attack which we can develop."[1]

The Commander in Chief Bomber Command was not then, however, deterred by any such reservations. Area bombing was winning the war. And on 3 November 1943 he minuted Churchill with an impressive list of German towns "virtually destroyed" and called for the intense cooperation of the United States Air Forces in a speedy, joint, decisive attack on Berlin. "It will cost between 400–500 aircraft. It will cost Germany the war." On 7 December 1943 he went further. He wrote to the Air Ministry declaring that, if he could have full production priority for his Lancaster force alone, with no mention of the Eighth and Fifteenth Air Forces, he could win the war in under five months at a cost of 800 aircraft and crews. Allowing a loss of 171 Lancasters a month, and postulating 3,421 sorties a month dropping 13,850 tons a month, "the Lancaster force alone should be sufficient but only just sufficient to produce in Germany by April 1st 1944 a state of devastation in which surrender is inevitable."[2]

This plan was put forward apparently as a theoretical possibility for the future. In fact, it was being practised as an actual campaign even while Harris was writing his long and minutely argued letter. On 18 November 1943 he had begun the night bomber Battle of Berlin. He directed sixteen massive assaults against that city in four months, averaging 570 aircraft on each mission. Over 7,000 of the sorties were flown by Lancasters. In addition 8,000 Lancaster sorties were directed in

1. Minute, Bottomley to Portal, 25 September 1943, quoted by Webster and Frankland, *The Strategic Air Offensive Against Germany, 1939–1945.*

2. Harris to Air Ministry, 7 December 1943, quoted by Webster and Frankland, *The Strategic Air Offensive Against Germany, 1939–1945.*

twenty attacks against thirteen other German cities in the same period.

In all, Harris put out 3,450 Lancaster sorties a month for $4\frac{1}{2}$ months and lost 775 Lancasters, or 172 a month. The figures were uncannily near his forecast of 800 lost, made on 7 December. But the outcome was not as he had prophesied. Though he had reinforced the Lancaster effort with sorties by 5,000 other bombers against the German cities and had thus over-fulfilled his promised devastation, German surrender was not "inevitable".

The whole Olympian operation was a failure. The Battle of Berlin ended in decisive defeat for Bomber Command. The cause of the defeat was the inability of the bombers to overcome the night fighters. On the night of 30 March 1944, the eve of his projected Victory Day, Harris lost over 100 bombers – 94 missing and 12 irreparably damaged – in a raid on Nuremburg which was so successfully frustrated that the inhabitants of that city did not know that they were being attacked.

On 7 April 1944 Harris came the nearest in the capability of this staunch man, incorruptible by anything but pride, to admit his defeat. He informed the Air Ministry that "the strength of German defences would in time reach a point at which night bombing attacks by existing methods and types of heavy bomber would involve percentage casualty rates which could not in the long run be sustained."[1]

That point had, in reality, already been reached. What Schweinfurt was to VIII Bomber Command Nuremburg was to Royal Air Force Bomber Command. The rate of loss had become insupportable.

Harris asked for "night fighter support on a substantial scale". It was the ultimate admission that air superiority over Germany, by night and by day, was now more important for the strategic bombing offensive than any formation or bluff or evasive tactics. The German fighter force, in spite of the appalling blunders of the Luftwaffe leaders, was ascendant.

But for the Allies there were two avenues of hope. The American Air Forces had recovered their potential and were beginning the decisive reduction of the German Fighter Command.

1. Letter, Harris to Air Ministry, 7 April 1944, quoted by Webster and Frankland, *The Strategic Air Offensive Against Germany, 1939–1945.*

And Royal Air Force Bomber Command, in spite of its theoretical allegiance to general area bombing, had evolved, through the development of its Pathfinder Force and other means, the basis of a skill in precision bombing which it as yet did not fully realize it possessed. The comparatively successful assault on Peenemünde was only one example. The way in which the air war was to swing in the next few months – towards the precise bombing of targets in France with the least possible loss to the French population – would deepen and widen this technical skill.

In the spring of 1944, therefore, the situation of the rival air marshals was significant of their ultimate fortune.

Göring was in tenuous control of the Luftwaffe. His lieutenants were, in the face of the strongest difficulties, increasing fighter production even though the bomber assault on their aircraft factories had been renewed. But the production effort was not matched by a parallel surge in the training of fighter aircrew, where Hitler still governed the priorities. The German programme for V-weapons bombardment was gravely retarded, more at that time through technical blockages than Allied air assault. Göring, through his inability to stand up to Hitler, had permitted a criminal neglect of the development of jet fighters, in which Germany led the world. And the entire Luftwaffe defence apparatus was about to be assaulted by an invigorated and re-equipped Allied air arm which was to go all out to kill the fighters.

Arnold had hung on through a most exhausting winter. He had refused to be diverted from his entrenched policy of daylight bombing conducted primarily in Europe and ostensibly aiming at precision targets. On many occasions the weak VIII Bomber Command had been reduced to conducting blind bombing, not always on the cities it had been briefed to attack. The pressure to maintain within the United States the prestige of the Eighth Air Force, and the shock endured at its cruel mauling by German fighters, had led at the time of the second Schweinfurt disaster to a rare fight with Portal. The subject was the alleged inactivity and under-development of the Royal Air Force fighters which might have supported the bombers. The outcome was the realization, as often happens in quarrels between good friends, that Arnold was furious at his own failure : the neglect to nurture the long-range fighters. In a great leap of policy change these long-range fighters had at last been provided. They were not only to cover and protect the Eighth and Fifteenth Air Forces – united from New Year's Day 1944 as the United States Strategic Air Force in Europe – but also to *seek out and destroy* the German fighter arm. From that time, as Galland, German General of the Fighters, admitted, "nowhere were we safe from them. We had to skulk on our own bases."

Portal had not manifested the strongest control over his brilliant but self-governing Bomber Commander. Portal had persistently advocated certain selective bombing and Harris had dismissed the principle as "panacea-mongering". Harris had reached the end of the road of night bomber supremacy, and on the way he had lost 20,000 aircrew in one year.[1] His future activity depended largely now on the reduction of the German fighter force, and that task seemed principally within the compass of the Americans.

But the conduct and direction of the war was changing. A new marshal was gathering the reins of power. For a decisive period he would shape the course of the air war in Europe with virtual sovereignty even over Portal. The hour had struck for the entry of Air Chief Marshal Sir Arthur Tedder.

1. Much has been made of the "lost generation" of the First World War: the infantry subalterns who died in their thousands and deprived France, Germany and Great Britain in particular of a wide band of future leaders of public life. There is a stronger case for national mourning of the 57,143 dead of Royal Air Force Bomber Command in the Second World War (of whom 41,548 have no known grave). These were men already seeded, whose training and character had elevated them in their youth to the foothills of leadership, especially in scientific and technical fields. They meant more to Britain, because of their proportionate number, than the lost aircrews of any other nation.

CHAPTER TWELVE

THE RISE OF MARSHAL TEDDER

Good, very good! Not too much smoke.
[Inspecting a painting of the battle of Waterloo]
                    THE DUKE OF WELLINGTON

Among the Air Marshals, Tedder stylishly, visibly won the
war in the West. He stood on Portal's shoulders, and needed
his firm hands for steadiness, while he directed the élan of
Harris, Spaatz and Leigh-Mallory. But he saw most clearly on
which horizon victory lay. He was a different man from the
other marshals because, in the evolution of air warfare, his
experiences worked on his personality to produce the "mutation
leap" – the qualitative change that resulted when influences
previously operating inharmoniously were fused into an integrated drive. He cut through the controversy over the
superiority or inferiority of the air arm to make sense, for the
moment, of the science of war.

Tedder was a scholar, like "the Big Thinker" Portal – he was
a postgraduate prizewinner in history at Cambridge; like Portal
and unlike Arnold and Dowding, he would have had a civilian
career had the First World War not claimed him. He was
noticed early by Trenchard, and the two men became confi-
dants : at the height of his power Tedder was writing to
"my old protector and friend" about the frustration he was
enduring from Montgomery after the invasion of Europe – a
reminder of the influence Trenchard retained throughout the
war. In the 1930s, after the usual staff college appointments
allotted to picked officers, Tedder had been successively Commander of the Air Armament School, Director of Training at
the Air Ministry, Air Officer Commanding Royal Air Force
Far East, and Director-General of Research and Development
at the Air Ministry. He served at the Air Ministry until November 1940 and, on moving to an active command, submitted to
the Air Minister a scathing report on Lord Beaverbrook's

"chaotic" administration of the Ministry of Aircraft Production, "based on force and fear".[1]

Tedder went to Egypt as Deputy Commander, soon to be Air Officer Commanding in Chief Royal Air Force Middle East. He was a fighting commander in the field, in Egypt and Libya, for two years. During a further year he refined his thinking and practice by strategic command in Tunisia, Sicily and Italy. He became, under Eisenhower, Deputy Supreme Commander of the Allied Expeditionary Force and held the unique position – untitled but well defined, and unparalleled before or since – of head of a supreme allied air command. For the six vital months dominating the invasion of Europe he took over the direction of the air war in that theatre from Portal and Arnold. This marshal's $4\frac{1}{2}$ years of intense activity extended to the very last day of hostilities in Europe. On that day, 8 May 1945, the creator of the Luftwaffe, Reich Marshal Göring, who had been attempting to negotiate surrender but had been dismissed and disowned by Hitler on the day the Führer shot himself, was thankful to be arrested by the Americans he had been trying to contact. On that same day Air Chief Marshal Tedder received the signature of Marshal Stumpff as the highest surviving Luftwaffe chief, along with the signatures of Field Marshal Keitel and Admiral Friedeburg, to the unconditional surrender of the German armed forces tendered in Berlin.

During his years in the Mediterranean Tedder, commanding an air *force*, painfully evolved his direction until he was fighting a classic war of integrated air power. He had to struggle with the British Army, which was obtusely slow to cooperate, and which persistently over-valued the morale-boosting sight of the Royal Air Force overhead rather than the Force's more effective distant strategic action. He was opposed for similar reasons by the Royal Navy, whose commanders could not concede that control of the Mediterranean had passed to the air forces on either side, and who in consequence sought parochial command of all relevant operational aircraft. There were internal problems of precedence and command. He had to absorb initially green American squadrons into his command and operational

1. Marshal of the Royal Air Force Lord Tedder, *With Prejudice*, Cassell, London, 1966.

structure, a process which happily proved the least of his worries. He had to work from unsecured bases whose very existence and continuance he could not control – Malta was on occasion blotted out as an air base as effectively as any overrun advanced landing ground in the desert. And there was the continuing struggle for reinforcements. Yet Tedder emerged wielding an *Allied* Air Force under a unified command as a true independent arm, not subordinate but fully coordinate with the land and sea forces.

The experiences which Tedder brought to Supreme Headquarters Allied Expeditionary Force, and tried to apply to the conquest of Europe, were practical contemporary solutions of well worn military postulates.

He had achieved the *concentration of power*. Within the allied air forces this had come from unified command, which enabled all operations – strategical, tactical and reconnaissance – to be promptly keyed into the shifting pattern of the general advance. But concentration of power among the land, sea and air forces had also been achieved through a far keener, friendlier liaison between service units at all levels. Tedder fostered this by encouraging the setting-up of joint Army/Air headquarters (the Navy was not cooperative in this regard), and by discouraging – even using his full powers of leadership to administer public reprimand – chauvinistic attitudes by his own senior officers.[1] From before the time of El Alamein Tedder had nurtured the rapprochement by a radical re-indoctrination course between army and air force mid-echelon commanders, based on their proved previous deficiencies in tactical coordination. He insisted that the soldiers must *know* their tactical needs

1. Typical is the incident involving Air Vice Marshal "Mary" Coningham, Air Support Commander (Tactical Air Force) in North West Africa, who objected to a highly inaccurate Situation Report by a staff officer of General Patton's II Corps implying absence of air support. Coningham signalled to Patton (1 April 1943): "... It can only be assumed that II Corps personnel concerned are not battle-worthy in terms of present operations. In view of outstandingly efficient and successful work of American Air Command concerned, it is requested that such inaccurate and exaggerated reports should cease." Tedder ordered Coningham to withdraw his signal and make a personal apology to Patton. The irony was that Coningham was defending the reputation of an American Air Command. (Coningham was a New Zealander: "Mary" was an R.A.F. corruption of the original nickname "Maori".)

I

at the height of a battle if the air force was to help them. When Montgomery arrived in the desert he urged this course, and Tedder was able to report to Portal :

Cooperation with the Army has further improved, thanks undoubtedly in some part to the lead given by Montgomery on the subject. It was very refreshing to see in Eighth Army Advanced Headquarters the embryo of a real operations room copied directly from our own mobile operations rooms. As I told the soldiers, it was the first sign I had seen of their being able to collect and sift information of their battle, and consequently the first sign one had seen of their being able to control it. For the past two years they have been saying such a thing was impossible.[1]

It could never be said that relations between the Royal Air Force and the Royal Navy were as good as they were with the Army. After the brilliant and bloody capture of Crete by German airborne forces, when the strong Royal Navy, having entirely destroyed one seaborne invasion force and turned back another, could no longer continue with the sparse air cover it was receiving against bombing which sank nine men-of-war and damaged sixteen others, the general cry amongst the evacuated forces cramming Alexandria was "Where was the R.A.F.?" Again, but more bitterly than at Dunkirk, in sickening recrimination among the beaten troops British airmen were savaged by British sailors and soldiers because they had "failed". Commanders were not immune. Tedder recorded in Cairo : "I was surrounded by a motley of sailors and marines, who chanted a little ditty :

Roll out the *Nelson*, the *Rodney*, the *Hood*,
Since the whole fucking air force is no fucking good !

In command circles the tireless Royal Air Force effort in support of Malta and its convoys, dovetailed as it was with continuous naval action, aroused controversy rather than appreciation among the admirals. But at least a grudging goodwill was earned during the end of the battle for Tunisia, when a virtual air blockade of the Sicilian Narrows deprived the Germans of all extraneous support or means of retreat. It was earned even more decisively by the invasion of Sicily, when the

1. Denis Richards and Hilary St G. Saunders, *Royal Air Force 1939–1945, The Fight Avails*, H.M. Stationery Office, London, 1954.

air operations covered the advance of 2,000 craft without loss at sea.

Concentration of power had been the means by which Tedder gained the other great strategic desideratum, *isolation of the battlefield*, giving freedom and fluidity to the land or sea forces to move in battle as their tactics directed. He achieved this by the previous reduction of the enemy air force to inferiority, and by the long strategic bombardment of communications. When Rommel attacked at Alam El Halfa in the first battle of El Alamein, August 1942, Tedder had an air superiority over the battlefield of two to one, which he used unsparingly. What was more decisive was that during the five-day battle nine supply ships, mainly tankers, were sunk, six by aircraft. Rommel said with rueful precision : "The petrol, which was a necessary condition of the carrying out of our plans, did not arrive." The same combination of method was used in Tunisia and, most notably, for the conquest of Sicily. To reduce enemy air superiority it was necessary to destroy aircraft on the ground, to tempt others into the air by offering or threatening valuable targets, to render airfields and maintenance centres untenable, and to prohibit enemy air reconnaissance as far as possible. By invasion day none of the thirty Sicilian airfields was fully operational, 200 aircraft were destroyed on the ground, and altogether 1,100 were found when the airfields were overrun. Immediate air opposition was insignificant. This last object had been achieved by strategic disorganization of airfields and communications far to the rear, in Italy. In Italy the predominant supply line was the north-to-south railway system. It was bombed. But the sea routes might still be used to supply northern Sicily : therefore Tedder had the ports of Palermo and Milazzo heavily bombed. Moreover, the Germans still excelled at air transport; therefore he sought out their transport airfields. Beyond the ferry fields he made a maximum effort to erase the bomber airfield complex at Foggia. For the rest, he concentrated his first strategic bombing on Naples, on the railway bottlenecks to the south, and the ports and ferry terminals of the Straits of Messina.

Tedder's early attention to Sardinia and Sicily before the German surrender in Tunisia had forced the long-range bombers of Air Fleet Two out of the island airfields and over the Apennines to Foggia, where they were again attacked. But his insistent attention to fighter airfields in Sicily also expelled many squadrons of fighters and fighter-bombers to bases around Naples, which put them out of range of the landing beaches. The final result was that, by further pulverizing Luftwaffe bases and by his own defensive patrols, he virtually vetoed air reconnaissance over North West Africa and Malta and thus prohibited air bombardment of the invasion fleet. In the landings he achieved tactical surprise, which was the reason for the initial weak air opposition.

Tedder's third important achievement was the perfection of *close support* for the land forces. Paradoxically, this could be invisible – strategic, not tactical support, as in the retreat before El Alamein. "On no occasion during this long retreat," wrote Tedder, "did the German Air Force seriously attack our retiring columns, although again and again there were horrifying congestions and blocks involving thousands of vehicles: 'Thank God you didn't let the Huns Stuka us,' said Freyberg to me, 'because we were an appalling target.' "[1]

More frequently it was visible cooperation. This was perfected in Italy, during the hard advance on Rome, into the "cab-rank" system whereby patrolling aircraft could be radioed the map grid reference of a target which they could attack as soon as it was identified.

On one form of developing close support Tedder was worried. This was the intensive bombing of enemy forces only fractionally ahead of his Army's front line – the so-called "Tedder carpet". It was first successfully applied to hasten the last days of the battle for Tunisia, on 6 May 1943, when 242 Group and the Western Desert Air Force flew 2,000 sorties to lay a creeping barrage on an area four miles square, ahead of the First Army. It was of even more vital importance when it was used at the Salerno landing to blast the positions and communications of the powerful German wedge-force sent in to counterattack, which threatened to throw the invading troops into the sea. Tedder thought the "carpet" was an extreme measure which the Army might too easily rely on, feeling that they could telephone for a heavy bomber effort at the slightest setback; next year, in Normandy, he was to confirm this, com-

1. Tedder, *With Prejudice.*

plaining that the Army was "drugged with bombs".

Tedder was the one air marshal who had fought and finished an air war as his sector of a truly combined operation; who had had the intellectual courage to maintain and broaden, against much ill-natured opposition, his principles of strategy and command; and who had emerged without grossly exaggerating the claims of the air arm. He was nominated[1] Deputy Supreme Commander Allied Expeditionary Force, in Churchill's words, "on account of the great part the air will play in this operation". "Tedder," he said, "with his unique experience and close relation as Deputy to the Supreme Commander, ought to be in fact and in form the complete master of all the air operations."

When Tedder came to London in January 1944 he knew that, as Eisenhower's deputy, answerable to the Combined Chiefs of Staff, he had to work under Portal with three air commanders. Air Marshal Sir Trafford Leigh-Mallory had long been appointed Commander in Chief of the Allied Expeditionary Air Force, the tactical air force designed to support the invasion. Leigh-Mallory was attempting, with small success, to persuade the two Allied strategic bomber commanders, Harris and Spaatz, to coordinate their plans firmly with his own in order to direct essential heavy bomber effort to the needs of the projected invasion of Europe. Harris was not an immediately dutiful subordinate to the Chiefs of Staff on matters of bombing policy, and was inclined to pay even less heed to Leigh-Mallory, content to have his representatives "proving" to the fighter specialist that Bomber Command could do little before the invasion but ignite a few large fires. Harris, after a good year's bombing, was in the thick of the Battle of Berlin. Spaatz, for his part, was concerned with an elaborate independent strategic bomber plan to attack German oil production and flush out Luftwaffe fighters, and Spaatz refused to take orders from Leigh-Mallory.

All this Tedder gloomily reported to Portal in February. The obvious solution was to place Tedder, as Eisenhower's deputy, in command superiority to Harris and Spaatz. Eisenhower and the American Chiefs of Staff, and also Churchill, favoured this.

1. He was nominated by Churchill, after Roosevelt had nominated Eisenhower as Supreme Commander.

The British Chiefs of Staff resisted. Only on 14 April, seven weeks before the invasion, was the technical superstructure creating a supreme air command under Tedder recognized officially. From this moment the overall direction of the air war, which had hitherto been exercised by Portal on behalf of the Combined Chiefs of Staff, was in the hands of Tedder. It continued thus until, on Portal's representations in September, command of the strategic bombers was taken from Tedder and remitted now to Portal and Arnold jointly, although exercised through their deputies Bottomley and Spaatz.[1]

Tedder's pre-invasion bombing programme re-enacted his well tried assault on communications. It demanded particularly from the strategic bombers heavy attacks on railway marshalling yards and repair depots. Harris, objecting, said that he could do little for two reasons : first, Bomber Command was incapable of hitting precise objectives in the dark or in the daylight; second, he could not countenance a respite in his ruthless general area bombing of Germany that would give the country's industry or its civilian morale an interval for recovery. These considerations were put to the Air Staff. Portal did not argue on the second point of high policy, and challenged the first, the claim to inaccuracy. He ordered specimen night attacks by Bomber Command on six precision objectives in France. The targets were marshalling yards, within the pattern of Tedder's plan. They were raided and hit with an accuracy that brought great satisfaction to the bomber crews concerned and, on Harris's later confession, astonishment to their Commander in Chief. This sudden proof that Bomber Command, using the skill and techniques it had developed during 1943 – and the more powerful bombs that were becoming available – could be the precise and devastating instrument that Harris had prematurely declared it to be at the beginning of the war,[2]

1. The deputies were wearing entirely dissimilar hats: Air Marshal Sir Norman Bottomley was a staff officer, Deputy Chief of the Air Staff; General Carl Spaatz was Commanding General United States Strategic Air Forces in Europe.

2. As Air Vice Marshal and Deputy Chief of the Air Staff, Harris had written to Air Marshal Sir Richard Peirse, Commander in Chief Bomber Command, on 11 October 1940, praising "the accuracy with which our aircraft hit military objectives as opposed to merely browning the towns". Harris was an artist in colourful, partisan language even when he changed his opinion.

launched the command like a rocket into a new phase of effective power. Bomber Command did, in fact, do more by night than the precision United States Strategic Air Forces did by day to disrupt railway communications in France. And, by carrying out these heavy and accurate raids it sloughed off the last skin of immaturity. It emerged as a reliable daylight force;[1] of the 65,000 tons of bombs it dropped in August 1944 over half were launched in daylight; and in the hardening of its temper it immensely increased its punishing power as a night armada for the last dreadful assault on the German homeland.

Harris was impressed with his command's new potentiality, but he was never convinced of the value of ultimate change in strategy that his developed precision indicated : when he was "independent" again he reverted as far as possible to area bombing. In the meantime Tedder had still to convince Spaatz. Tedder argued strongly that, although Spaatz was right in advocating the continuing war against the Luftwaffe Fighter Command, and that his oil plan enclosed the strategic kernel of the eventual halting of German effort, yet a large proportion of the American heavy bomber activity – far greater than Spaatz was willing to concede – needed to be devoted to the intermediate strategy of neutralizing communications in France before the invasion. Finally, at a conference between Eisenhower, Portal and all the air commanders, called on 25 March 1944, a British expert from the Ministry of Economic Warfare declared that a strategic offensive against German oil could have no effect on military operations for four or five months. Tedder's communications plan was somewhat grudgingly accepted.

There still remained Tedder's most formidable adversary, Winston Churchill. The Prime Minister could not accept the "railway plan". He had an estimate from British sources that the selective bombardment would kill between 20,000 and

1. Contributing factors to Bomber Command's new efficiency were, briefly: the weak opposition, not so much that the Germans had no fighters – they built 25,000 in 1944 – but because the Americans shot many down, and comparatively few ever came up, grounded by the combined strategic bombing offensive against oil; the availability of fighter escort; far more accurate bombing techniques; and the more serious damage done by the Lancaster's 4,000-pound bombs, which the B-17 could not carry.

40,000 French civilians.[1] Churchill's sincere concern for the fate
of the French people was never doubted. But it could not be
ignored – and Eisenhower reminded him – that, in 1943 when the
invasion was not imminent and French reaction to the deaths
of their bombed civilians had less political significance, Churchill
had championed, against the military advice of his Chiefs of
Staff, the concentrated bombing of the French U-boat ports with
the avowed object of devastating the towns. The U-boat pens
were almost indestructible and the object of these prolonged
raids, which greatly diverted the bomber effort, was to make
the ports untenable by the workers.

The argument had little effect. Churchill, as Minister of
Defence, sanctioned the bombing of only three of the 74 proposed railway targets in France and Belgium and remitted consideration of the rest to the War Cabinet. The matter, although
declared by the Chiefs of Staff to be of extreme urgency, was
in abeyance for committee consideration for two months, from
10 March to 11 May, and was finally settled in favour of the
Tedder plan after an appeal to President Roosevelt.

The minimum of time remained for the exercise of what
was Tedder's outstanding contribution to the practice of aerial
warfare : the effective isolation of a battlefield by air power. The
transportation plan for D-Day was a far more thorough proposition than anything tried in Italy. Montgomery had asked for
the placing of a complete stoppage on enemy movement within
a radius of 150 miles from the beach head. This isolation would
be brought about by the blocking of air, rail and road transport. But the target was no longer a comparatively concise area
boxed in by mountain ranges, as in Italy. It was 70,000 square
miles of flat country linked by multiple communications with
the greatest industrial support complex in the world : the Ruhr
basin.

It had been planned as a two-months operation. Five weeks
after its supposed start the ultimate sanction to begin had not
been given. And yet, when the three air arms finally sped into
coordinate action, in the short time then available before D-Day
they found that they had contributed to the most successful

1. Bomber Command's first estimate of the Transportation Plan mentioned between 80,000 and 160,000 French civilian casualties. Ultimately
about 10,000 were killed.

immobilization of an area ever known before the nuclear bomb; a purpose achieved moreover by precision techniques that caused gratifyingly few casualties to French civilians compared, say, with the losses of the population of Naples.

Out of 2,000 nominally available railway engines in the area covered by the plan, 1,500 were put out of service. Eighteen of the 24 bridges over the Seine were destroyed. Thirty-four out of 40 major airfields were destructively bombed. All the main radar stations were put out of action and 45 coastal batteries were blasted. All these operations had to be performed in such a manner that the overall picture gave the Germans no clue to the beachheads chosen for the actual landings. For every priority radar station or coastal battery attacked, two others in likely invasion areas had also to be raided.

On D-Day itself the air force was called in even for deception measures. A weaving squadron of Lancasters was made to move at an effective forward speed of seven knots to simulate on German radar, with dropped tin foil, an invasion convoy advancing on the Pas de Calais. The landing was an unquestioned military success. One thousand heavy bombers dropped 5,000 tons on the coastal batteries before dawn, and medium bombers continued the work by day. The most remarkable feat of all was that the Luftwaffe had been almost swept from the skies. Few reconnaissance aircraft were permitted to record and take home any indication of the active armed camp of southern England. No bomber attacked the embarkation ports. There was no challenge to the invasion. In the era of modern communication the Allied invasion force achieved better tactical surprise than the Spanish Armada. Tedder could hardly have expected to repeat over the English Channel his outstanding achievement in Sicily, but the same success was his. The great fleets of transports, gliders, fighters, bombers, photographic and radio commentators, and deception aircraft swept south, and the best the Luftwaffe could do was to raise 150 bombers in the daylight to blast the beaches. Men had died, and mothers were to mourn, but from the marshals' valid viewpoint it was a soft invasion. Air power had preserved armies.

For one week the Second World War became a soldier's war. Armed men were in furious action, and their targets were armed men. Peasants fled in Normandy and some fell, but they were not gunned down for reasons of politics or lust or reprisal. Then, seven days after D-Day, the first V-1 "flying bombs" crashed down on England. Six obscure Londoners died in Bethnal Green. They were the thin vanguard of 8,938 British civilians who were killed in the last assault on England, and even these were but a traveller's sample of the hosts who were to be extinguished in the final year of the war. The deaths in the V-weapons bombardment of England – and the threat of many, many more – forced the Allied marshals, at the insistence of the statesmen, to divert from the Normandy battlefield and from military or industrial targets 149,783 tons of bombs against the V-sites and plants. But this measure was comparatively ineffective, for the bombardment ended only when the launching sites were overrun by troops.

The end of the V-1 bombardment freed the strategic bombing forces in great measure from their tactical ties. Spaatz applied himself legitimately to his campaign against German synthetic oil production. Harris, with his greatly increased technical advantages favouring safety and accuracy,[1] reverted to the area bombing of German cities. Portal directed Harris to give first priority to the petroleum industry. In the next month Harris dropped 6 per cent of his 61,204 tons bomb load on oil targets and 66 per cent on the general area bombing of towns. Tedder urgently appealed to Portal for some coordination and concentration of the newly liberated air power. He said that the war could be won fast by a sustained attack on communications – which included oil plants – confined to the Ruhr. Portal largely agreed, and the Chiefs of Staff ordered Spaatz and Harris to concentrate on these objectives, with an emphasis on oil. But the Chiefs of Staff had to some extent lost control. Harris replied to Portal's new directive on the day he received it, 1 November 1944, asserting that no one outside Bomber Command knew the tactical and weather difficulties that upset *any* target programme unless it was the general destruction of German cities. He reaffirmed his intention to continue with general

1. The Germans had lost the territory containing their early warning radar points and their advanced fighter airfields. The British installed their target-direction radar and their fighter-cover bases in Europe, much nearer the goal – and had greatly intensified the personal and mechanical skill of their bomb aimers.

area bombing. He said there were only twelve cities left on his list to finish off. He named them. They included Dresden and Chemnitz.

Portal replied, good-temperedly enough, urging Harris to concentrate on oil attacks rather than "prolong the war by several months at least". Harris replied defensively. Portal, maintaining the pressure, referred to Harris's personal plan to keep up his average of $2\frac{1}{2}$ German cities devastated each month. "I have, I must confess, at times wondered whether the magnetism of the remaining German cities has not in the past tended as much to deflect our bombers from their primary objectives as the tactical and weather difficulties which you described so fully."[1] The correspondence continued in an atmosphere of increasing strain. Harris contemptuously derided the economic experts who had recommended the oil plan, and stated that his own Operational Research Station believed 226,000 tons of bombs would be necessary to end the war by this means.[2]

The controversy grew sharper. Portal now questioned in its entirety the efficacy of Harris's area bombing programme. Harris responded with fire. He said outright that he had no faith in selective bombing policies and particularly none in the oil plan. For himself, he said he still had twelve cities to destroy. The list included five cities that were not in the twelve he had scheduled, five weeks earlier, but still mentioned Dresden and Chemnitz. Finally Harris challenged Portal to dismiss him.

It was a bitter moment for the two marshals, of whom the junior was only holding more consistently to the view which the senior had taught him. Outwardly it was not a climax of discipline, but of ideology. Harris did not say he would not obey Portal, only that he was unconvinced. But the latitude which Harris had earned and taken as longstanding Commander in Chief of the bombers meant that he would apply the oil plan only under constant cajoling and pressure.

1. Letter, Portal to Harris, 12 November 1944, quoted by Webster and Frankland, *The Strategic Air Offensive Against Germany, 1939–1945.*

2. This was, in fact, half the bomb tonnage (436,000 tons) which the strategic bombers actually delivered to Germany between the date of Harris's letter and the end of the war, and it was not, therefore, an impossible figure.

If Portal dismissed Harris there would be a blazing scandal – but the Chief of Staff would have the bombing policy, faithfully observed, that he had been urging for months on behalf of the Combined Chiefs of Staff.

If he did not dismiss Harris . . . ? It was 20 January 1945. The war could not endure, whatever the bombing policy, long past May, the Chief of Air Staff rightly estimated. Portal's mind may have been working politically. The Russians had started an advance. Stalin had telegraphed that he was launching it prematurely, at the urgent request of Churchill, in order to help Eisenhower out of a bloody ditch in the snows of the Ardennes. The lives of many additional Russians would be expended because of the acceleration of his offensive, and Churchill had wired Stalin his deep gratitude for "your thrilling message". Churchill and Portal would shortly see Stalin at Yalta. Churchill might want to make a gesture of thanks : a dramatic bombing raid in the east on a rearward German city confronting the Russian advance. Very deep bomber penetration. The highest morale needed in Bomber Command. Anyway, it was not the time to sack Harris. For Portal himself had not entirely abandoned faith in the efficacy of a specific operation of general area bombing aimed at the destruction of civilian morale. Among the Combined Chiefs of Staff Portal was the custodian and propagator of the plan "Thunderclap", the proposal to end the war by a sudden catastrophic aerial bombing of a German city.

On 20 January 1945 Marshal of the Royal Air Force Sir Charles Portal wrote to Air Chief Marshal Harris asking him to continue in command of a force which had done so much towards defeating the enemy and had brought such credit and renown both to Harris and the Royal Air Force. "We must wait until after the end of the war before we can be certain who was right." On 22 January the Director of Bomber Operations was suggesting to the Deputy Chief of the Air Staff that the time had come for a monumental assault on an East German city to give the appearance of "a close coordination in planning between the Russians and ourselves". On 25 January Prime Minister Winston Churchill asked the Secretary of State for Air what was being done to hit the Germans retreating before the Russians. Two days later, after some departmental panic, he was promised operations against Berlin, Dresden, Chemnitz and Leipzig.

And this is how the death of Dresden came about.

In July 1944 the British Chiefs of Staff had considered the feasibility of an all-out blow against German civilian morale to end the war. After consultations between the Air Staff, the Foreign Office, the Political Warfare Executive and the Ministry of Economic Warfare, Portal put in a memorandum declaring that, in order to persuade the German High Command to surrender rather than continue a long guerrilla warfare, an unprecedently massive bombing attack on Berlin might break the morale of both the German leaders and the German civilians. This should not take place until the Nazi system was collapsing and defeat was imminent. Devastation by 20,000 tons of bombs dropped by day and night over four days was estimated as likely to produce "a sufficiently catastrophic effect" that would cause "at least a temporary breakdown in the morale of the people of Berlin". As an alternative to an attack on heavily bombed Berlin "immense devastation could be produced if the entire attack was concentrated on a single big town other than Berlin and the effect would be especially great if the town was one hitherto relatively undamaged."

This proposal, code-named Thunderclap, had been shelved by the middle of August. But it was dusted off and reconsidered on 22 January in the Air Staff discussions regarding an operation which would have political value in showing the Russians and the Germans that the Allies were aiding the Russian advance into Germany.

On 25 January the Deputy Chief of Air Staff, Air Marshal Sir Norman Bottomley, discussed this with the Commander in Chief Bomber Command, Air Chief Marshal Sir Arthur Harris, who suggested that a disruption of communications, already strained by the vast tide of refugees fleeing from the Russians in East Germany, might be effected by catastrophic blows against Chemnitz, Leipzig and Dresden as well as Berlin. On the same night Churchill asked his Air Minister, Sir Archibald Sinclair, what plans the Royal Air Force had for "basting the Germans in the retreat from Breslau". After consultation with Portal next day, Sinclair reported to Churchill that the oil plan still took precedence in Air Staff calculations, but area attacks on Berlin,

Leipzig, Dresden and Chemnitz could be undertaken when the weather was too bad for precision bombing. Churchill peremptorily rejected the balanced minute giving this information as soon as he received it and asked urgently for action against the East German cities. Sinclair, after hasty consultation, replied that such action would be taken "as soon as the present moon has waned and favourable weather conditions allow. This is unlikely to be before about 4th February."

On 4 February the Yalta Conference was in full session. General Antonov, Deputy Chief of Staff of the Red Army, asked for Allied bombing attacks against communications, particularly to "paralyse" the centres of Berlin and Leipzig, to prevent the movement of German troops from west to east. The Allied plans for such action were already in operation. On 3 February nearly 1,000 Flying Fortresses of the United States Strategic Air Forces bombed "railway and administration" targets in Berlin, a theoretically uncharacteristic American "blind" radar attack which resulted, according to German reports, in the death of 25,000 people including many refugees.

When, on 27 January, in response to the Prime Minister's brusque rephrasing of his request to the Air Minister, Dresden was put on Bomber Command's target list, it was not at first accepted. This, in retrospect, is very surprising. Although Sir Arthur Harris had perhaps lightly tossed it across to Sir Charles Portal more than once as a future objective, Dresden had never yet appeared in an official target list and Bomber Command Intelligence Section had remarkably little information on its target points or on its defences. It is even more surprising that Harris himself asked his deputy, Air Marshal Sir Robert Saundby, to check the inclusion of Dresden on the list with the Air Staff. Sir Norman Bottomley could not confirm the target immediately.[1] The doubt was not settled in London, but the query was referred to Yalta, where both Portal and Churchill

1. Yet Tedder says Bottomley visited SHAEF at the end of January 1945 to decide, with Tedder and Spaatz, targets for the Strategic Air Forces. Synthetic oil plants were given first priority for precision bombing by day when the weather allowed. "The next targets in order of priority were Berlin, Leipzig, Dresden, and other cities where heavy attack would hasten civilian evacuation from the east, and the subsequent confusion hamper the movement of reinforcements from other fronts." Tedder, *With Prejudice.*

were attending the conference. Confirmation from Yalta of the approval, in the highest quarters, of Dresden as a bomber target settled the issue. Staff preparations were made for the attack on the city, preferably in a round-the-clock raid with the Eighth Air Force.

Early in the morning of 13 February 1945 a rare favourable meteorological forecast made the raid by Bomber Command possible that night. Supreme Headquarters Allied Expeditionary Force gave its more than formal approval – for the position of the advancing Russians had to be checked. The executive order was issued and VIII Bomber Command was informed. With a curious reluctance that was noted at the time 800 crews of Bomber Command prepared for an attack on a city within the Russian orbit about which they knew little, their intelligence officers imaginatively assuring them at the briefing that Dresden was, according to the squadron officer's fancy, the headquarters of a German army, of the Gestapo, and of poison gas production. Sir Robert Saundby, Harris's deputy, laid on the attack with the utmost efficiency but "with considerable misgivings".

Dresden, an ancient city with a distant industrial suburb, was a cultural centre which was given by its citizens a significance equivalent to Oxford in England : indeed, it was believed in Saxony that, by some "pairing" agreement, Dresden would never be bombed as long as Oxford was spared. By February 1945 Dresden had suffered only two attacks on its railway yards and light industries, both by the Americans. After the first, in October 1944, in which a number of American and Allied prisoners of war were killed at work in the railyards, motor coach proprietors ran sight-seeing tours to the bombed district. In the second attack, on 16 January 1945, a British prisoner, Private Norman Lea, was among the 376 killed and was given a full military funeral, the German garrison being paraded to pay honour and both British and German guards of honour awaiting the coffin at the military cemetery. After the third raid, the Bomber Command attack of 13 February, there were not enough able-bodied men surviving to bury the dead – perhaps the bleakest statistic by which the "conventration" of a city can be gauged – and the victims were cremated by the thousand in pyres in the public square.

The pressure of the Russian advance towards the end of January had broken up scores of prisoner of war camps, at least nineteen containing men of the Western Allies, and their inmates were set marching to the west. The number of Allied prisoners of war around Dresden by mid-February was in the order of 20,000, though this fact was not known to Bomber Command Intelligence. A far greater influx into the city was caused by the panic flight of five million civilians who blocked the roads of Saxony. By the night of the raid the population of Dresden had doubled to about 1,300,000 and most of the newcomers were homeless women and children, mainly peasants who had never heard an air-raid siren in their lives.

And so the catastrophic blow was struck. Other historic air raids, as at Hamburg, had fortuitously produced the unpremeditated fire storms, the great tornadoes of wind caused by the induction of temperatures as high as 1,000° C., which sucked solids towards the central furnace and deprived all humans in the area of oxygen for breathing. In Dresden the fire storm was *intended*, and was entrusted to 244 Lancasters of 5 Group, Royal Air Force, who were expert and accurate incendiarists. Harris planned not only that the fire storm should occur, but that it should attract the fire brigades of the great towns within 100 kilometres of Dresden : and, once the fire-fighters were engaged with the bait, a second force of over 550 Lancasters should bury them in the white hot stones of the city they had come to succour. The entire plan was successful. The fire storm embraced eight square miles of Dresden. The incinerating tempest, strong enough to overturn railway trucks on embankments, threw running victims and laden perambulators directly into the heart of fires, or knocked them to the ground, where humans shrivelled to half their size on the sizzling pavements.

Fourteen hundred Lancasters were out that night and lost only six aircraft in the action. Before the British crews had passed debriefing, 4,500 Americans were airborne in 450 Flying Fortresses of the 1st Air Division VIII Bomber Command to bomb the remains of Dresden. They bombed blind through ten-tenths cloud on the New Town, taking only eleven minutes for the operation. Then over 100 Mustangs made low-level attacks on the crowded roads leading out of the city. At the same time other American bombers attacked Chemnitz, the city to which Harris had already ordered 717 aircraft of Bomber Command that night, while about 400 made diversionary raids.

The night attack on Chemnitz was a failure, partly through the indifferent weather, partly through fatigue and lack of incentive which gained no boost from the inability of the Pathfinder Force, who led the attack that night, to start a fire storm which the main wave could bomb. The tactical failure at Chemnitz sealed the strategical failure of Thunderclap, the catastrophic blow. The extinction of Dresden did not significantly aid the Russians, and did not shorten the war. Though carried out with the perfection of tactical efficiency to which Harris and his diligent deputy Saundby had keyed their forces, it recoiled in particular on the head of Harris, who bore obloquy for the deed almost from the day it was done. Certainly there was small justice in saddling Harris with any guilt. Eighteen years after the attack Sir Robert Saundby declared[1] that he was still mystified why the raid on Dresden had been ordered. Harris said "the attack on Dresden was at the time considered a military necessity by much more important people than myself." Saundby composed what is perhaps the most pathetic epitaph on the city's dead :

That the bombing of Dresden was a great tragedy none can deny. That it was really a military necessity few . . . will believe. It was one of those terrible things that sometimes happen in wartime, brought about by an unfortunate combination of circumstances. Those who approved it were neither wicked nor cruel, though it may well be that they were too remote from the harsh realities of war to understand fully the appalling destructive power of air bombardment in the spring of 1945.

The world reacted with revulsion to the chronicle of Dresden. The waves of condemnation and guilt rolled on, even being given expression in an amazing submission by Churchill himself, who as much as any single individual must take the responsibility of having instigated the attack. On 28 March the Prime Minister addressed a minute to General Ismay and Marshal Portal which ran in part :

1. In David Irving's exhaustive account, *The Destruction of Dresden*, Kimber, London, 1963.

K

It seems to me that the moment has come when the question of bombing of German cities simply for the sake of increasing the terror, though under other pretexts, should be reviewed. . . . The destruction of Dresden remains a serious query against the conduct of Allied bombing. . . . I feel the need for more precise concentration upon military objectives, such as oil and communications behind the immediate battle-zone, rather than on mere acts of terror and wanton destruction, however impressive.[1]

Portal declined to accept this minute, with its writing into the record the implication that the British bombing policy had been wrenched by the air commanders out of the control of the political leaders and turned to wanton ends. Next day, Churchill agreed to withdraw the missive, and eventually substituted a milder communication which did not mention terror attacks or wanton destruction, but began : "It seems to me that the moment has come when the question of the so called 'area bombing' of German cities should be reviewed from the point of view of our own interests . . ."[2]

The truth was that "our own interests" had been served by other means. Tedder's bombing had knocked out Germany without direct reference to civilian morale. Tedder's bombing had been conducted alongside Harris's personal panacea policy, using Harris's own forces for much of the time, besides the more cooperative effort of Spaatz (wielding the Fifteenth Air Force based in Italy as well as the Eighth from the West), and using also the Tactical air Force – directly commanded by Tedder after October 1944, when Leigh-Mallory took the air command in the Far East.

While the war area still lay in France the combined air forces continued the attack on transport and on German production, in addition to daily intervention in the ground battle. In October 1944 the transportation assault was extended to German territory, particularly to the Rhine-Ruhr, and true chaos began to show. In November the priorities ordered for the newly autonomous Strategic Air Forces were oil and trans-

1. Withdrawn minute, Prime Minister to General Ismay (for Chiefs of Staff Committee) and Chief of the Air Staff, 28 March 1945, quoted by Webster and Frankland, *The Strategic Air Offensive Against Germany, 1939–1945.*

2. Minute, Prime Minister to General Ismay (for Chiefs of Staff Committee) and C.A.S., 1 April 1945.

portation, and even Harris, under protest, did direct precision bombing to these targets. By late November, with the Russian advance into Rumania, Germany had lost 75 per cent of her previous oil production. Rail and water communications were now being blasted up to 150 miles east of the Rhine. Speer, the German Minister of Munitions, had already reported to Hitler : "The Ruhr area can be completely written off as far as German economy is concerned except for goods still manufactured within the inner network." The oil situation was so critical by December that in the Ardennes offensive German transport operated on petrol diluted by 70 per cent with crude benzol. In January 1945 one spur of the air assault was directed at jet aircraft, jet pilot training centres and jet airfields. By February the communications attack was so fierce and detailed that, as Tedder put it, no German motor cyclist was safe. During the one day of 22 February 9,000 aircraft operating from Great Britain, France, Belgium, Holland and Italy bombed railways, canals and vehicles. In the middle of March Speer told Hitler : "The final collapse of the German economy can be counted on with certainty within four to eight weeks. . . . After this collapse, even military continuation of the war will be impossible." It was an accurate forecast.

Churchill's revised minute questioning further area bombing on German cities was dated 1 April. Five days later Harris called off his bombers saying "There are no worth-while targets left in Germany." On 10 April the Fortresses of the Eighth Air Force, some already under posting to the air war in Japan, raided Berlin for the last time. On that day, too, Reich Marshal Hermann Göring, almost suicidally depressed, offered a gesture of reconciliation to the fighter leader he had humiliated and dismissed, Lieutenant General Adolf Galland, now leading a force of jet aircraft. Göring said as they parted : "I envy you, Galland, for going into action. I wish I were a few years younger and less bulky. If I were, I would gladly put myself under your command. It would be marvellous to have nothing to worry about but a good fight, as it was in the old days."

Too much had happened to Marshal Göring for him to hope to recapture the open-cockpit romanticism of "the old days". After the plot of 20 July 1944 to assassinate Hitler – an attempt which had been postponed repeatedly in an effort

to include Göring – the Reich Marshal's influence had waned
even more markedly than before. In October 1944 Hitler had at
last consented to the operation of the Messerschmitt Me 262
as a jet fighter – but the persuasion had been applied by
Himmler, not Göring. The Marshal seemed useful only to serve
as Hitler's whipping boy during the Führer's frequent attacks
on the effectiveness of the Luftwaffe. Göring himself passed on
these attacks, redoubled in venom, to the fighter pilots, who
were thus made to suffer in the air and on the ground for the
patent superiority of the Allies. Göring actually had one of
his diatribes recorded and gave orders that the record should
be played to the pilots while at action stations. This insane
example of a spleen worthy of Hitler is the clear measure of
Göring's consistent and ruinous failure to manage men once
he was in defeat.

"It would be marvellous to have nothing to worry about but
a good fight." Instead, there was a constant preoccupation –
part selfish, part statesmanlike – to save something for the German nation out of its imminent wreck. Hitler was a grotesque
mummer in the final decay of paranoia, physically and mentally
damaged by the assassination explosion, storming with dragged
foot and shaking hands through the underground apartments
of the Chancellery, and telephoning for non-existent air fleets
and artillery barrages to erase the Russians from the approaches
to Berlin. Göring saw him for the last time on Hitler's birthday,
20 April, and went south to Berchtesgaden. Three days later
Göring received a first-hand account of remarks made by Hitler
about the succession to his leadership, for it was now known
that Hitler had determined to die in Berlin. "Göring can take
over the leadership down there" (that is, in the south), Hitler
had said, and when it was objected that no one would fight
for Göring he had sneered "There's precious little fighting to
be done! When it comes to negotiating for peace Göring can
do that better than I. Göring is much better at those things."

When he received this report, Göring radioed a message to
Hitler suggesting a formal declaration that he was to take over
forthwith the leadership of the German nation. He then made
plans to get in touch with Eisenhower to arrange a surrender.
These schemes came to nothing because, shortly after sending
the message to Hitler, Göring was arrested by the S.S.

Hitler's reaction to Göring's signal had been fierce. He rescinded a decree of June 1941 appointing Göring as his deputy or successor in all offices of State, Party or Army. He sent a radio message to this effect and informed Göring at the same time that he was guilty of high treason, that his life had been spared only because of his past service, and that he must voluntarily relinquish immediately all his offices and the right of succession. Martin Bormann sent a parallel message to his S.S. leaders on the Obersalzberg to arrest Göring. This was done at seven in the evening of 23 April. The next day Bormann, who could still control national broadcasting, announced to the German people and the world that Göring had resigned "for health reasons".

Göring was held in custody throughout an uneasy week of tense inactivity in the south, while Germany shambled through the last motions of defeat. In the dawn of 30 April Hitler dictated his testament before conducting the suicide he planned. "Before my death," he declared, "I expel former Reich Marshal Hermann Göring from the Party and withdraw from him all rights that were conferred on him by decree of 20 June 1941 . . ." Once the will was drawn up Hitler added a postscript in which he again denounced Göring but praised the bravery of the Luftwaffe and ascribed its final failure to the former marshal. On that day Hitler shot himself and his body was burned Bormann sent an instruction to the S.S. at Berchtesgaden ordering the execution of Göring. This order was, in fact, ignored, and on 5 May the S.S. connived at Göring's "rescue" by a Luftwaffe detachment.

As soon as he could, in the confusion of that time, Göring notified the nearest American troops that he was prepared to surrender. He was eventually discovered by a search party of the 36th Division, Seventh Army, trapped in a refugee traffic jam through which Göring's half-dozen cars and two trucks laden with baggage could make no progress. After a convivial evening with Spaatz – the only air general whom Göring ever met – he was quickly stripped of his decorations and his Marshal's baton and consigned to prison as "defendant Göring".

He had seventeen months more to live, and a concealed capsule of cyanide to ensure his death. He survived the triumphs and victory parades of Arnold and Portal and Tedder and Harris. He stood his trial in Nuremberg. He was charged with conspiracy to break treaties, to plan and wage wars of aggression, to murder the civilian populations of occupied countries or to deport them for slave labour, to murder and illtreat prisoners of war, to murder and persecute populations on racial and religious grounds, to murder and torture in concentration camps, to plunder property and art, and to perpetrate the wanton destruction of cities, towns and villages, all on a scale unwarranted by any military necessity.

Göring received the 24,000 word indictment and began to read it. He remarked jovially that if he had won the war, no doubt he would be serving similar documents on the other marshals. "The victor will always be the judge," he said, "and the vanquished the accused."

CHAPTER THIRTEEN

THE RECKONING

> I refused to read histories of my own wars, because I
> might be tempted to reply, and I will have nothing
> to do with writing a book.
>
> THE DUKE OF WELLINGTON

Marshals train for as long as possible with only dummy casualties, but they learn best how to fight in the course of actual war. In the Second World War they had their first opportunity to test the theories regarding victory through air power which had been mainly developed since the First World War and never fully applied during the sporadic engagements of the intervening minor campaigns. The principal arms of air power were – in the order of their development and their acceptance by military thought – reconnaissance aircraft, tactical bombers and fighters used as sophisticated field artillery, strategic bombers directed at the sources of enemy power, the fighters which attacked the bombers, the fighters which supported their bombers, and transport aircraft used first to support any army and later to support an air force. Victory passes to the combatant who achieves the most effective combination of these forces to suit the fluid demands of his war. How did the air marshals approach and adapt to these requirements?

Göring conceived, designed and commanded in being the first comprehensive independent air force in the world. Arnold tardily followed and surpassed him. The British, having not balanced their pre-war production to make proper provision for air transport, never caught up; and, with the exception of the savage example of Tedder's devotedly professional armoured car crews and fighting ground staff in the Western Desert – who preserved an air force and therefore an army during two precipitate retreats – the Royal Air Force rarely operated as an integrated self-supporting, self-defending arm.

Göring began the war with a lithe and coordinated force

which, though its build favoured the sprint dash rather than the long distance event, was far more versatile than has sometimes been credited. The Luftwaffe was developed, after the cancellation of plans for the four-engined Ural bomber, theoretically as an army-support force. Yet it achieved brilliant strategic victories. The rapid emasculation of Poland, the knock-down occupation of Denmark, the swamping of Norway and the calculated ubiquitous violence of May 1940 which led to Dunkirk and the defeat of Holland, Belgium and France were brought about by a masterly use of air power which is not out of date in the nuclear age: Israel beat Egypt in 1967 by a Göring-type application of air strategy comparable to the beginning of the German defeat of Poland. In the Battle of Britain Göring applied an intensive air assault which, though it faltered in its concentration, was almost fatally effective in its precision assaults on airfields, fighter sector stations, and aircraft factories. Göring lost the Battle of Britain through faulty intelligence and unrealistic battle appreciation, but above all because of a shortage of fighters, which unbalanced his force and prevented him from using all his bombers most effectively. Under-appreciation of the power of fighters to interdict effective bombing, and therefore of the need to protect bombers with massive fighter cover from specialized aircraft, was a fault which Göring shared with all the air marshals except Dowding. The other common defect was slowness to give credence to and to adapt strategy to the inefficiency of the strategic bomber.

Precision strategic bombing materialized initially as a failure, the Germans proving the most accurate because their planned leap-frog war brought them bases nearer the target. The axiom on which the strategic thought had increasingly rested was shown to be false. The bomber did not "always get through". The resurgence of defensive power based on electronic warning devices, improved gun-laying and the high-performance fighter had been catastrophically disallowed. The concept of the self-defending bomber formation was a fiction, for insufficient attention had been paid to the armour and armament of the individual bomber. In addition, navigation training had been skimped to such a degree that a disturbingly high proportion of bomber crews could not reach a distant target even in daylight without trial and error for which the time/speed/range factor allied with even moderate defences allowed little margin. All day bomber formations, and particularly long-range bombers, needed defensive escorts, but for years they had to do without them.

All these defects were slowly remedied by the Royal Air Force and the United States Army Air Forces. Because the war was won, the tendency is to accept in retrospect the inevitability of the painful improvement and to assume a similar self-generating advance in a future war. This is a fallacious conclusion. When Bomber Command practice exposed the inadequacy of British Air Staff theory, taught and ramified for twenty years, two courses were open : to abandon the long-range strategic bomber or to improve its effect. The first alternative was not a flippancy. In Great Britain, for all strategic purposes except those of propaganda, the long-range bomber was non-functional for the first $2\frac{1}{2}$ years of war, and there were highly pressed self-justifying requisitions for the diversion of aircraft production entirely to tactical forms cooperating with the two senior services. In the United States the pressures on these fronts were even fiercer, and there was always the theoretical alternative to the strategic bomber – the disposable fleet of 500 pilotless aircraft or ballistic missiles, built for the price of one heavy bomber, conveying 500 tons of bombs and risking not one aircrew life. It cannot be lightly said even now that this project, with its potential for development, was correctly abandoned in 1941.

Yet we must judge the tree by the growth that is not pruned, and praise the forester accordingly. Arnold had been intimately concerned with the leadership of the United States air arm since the First World War. He exercised (and publicized) it to the limit in the civil mail runs of the thirties, and at GHQ Air Force he was testing the organization and tactics he put into use when war came. He built up the status of the Air Corps from being a second-class arm to the supreme service, and he gave it the back-up to maintain it there – in prestige based on understandable policy, production, logistics and ground strength.

In the West, strategic bombers were challenged by high-performance fighters and defended by long-range escorts. Göring failed in his control of the short-range fighters, Arnold

and Portal in their depreciation of the long-range fighters:
Churchill, always more realistic in battle detail than in strategic
theory, consistently championed long-range fighters even when
Portal declared that they were ineffective. Göring's failure was
the more significant, for it was due to him, and his unmilitary
subservience to Hitler, that the Allies were allowed to gain air
superiority over Germany. Hitler enlarged the role of the Luftwaffe as a strategic bombing force, in the Trenchard/Smuts
conception of a retaliatory arm. "I want bombers, bombers,
bombers," he screamed. What Germany needed – and had in
abundant potential – was fighters, fighters, fighters, including
the then supreme jet Messerschmitt 262. But by the time the
production balance had been righted, in 1944, the Allied
strategic offensive against oil allowed little fuel to fly them.
Göring's mental rigidity accepted Hitler's extension of Luftwaffe aggressiveness as a bomber force and repressed the recognition of the strategical requirements of defence at a time when
Germany needed an armada of fighters to protect her industries, which was the only way to ensure the re-creation of the
Luftwaffe. Göring, through defects of character and intelligence, accepted Hitler's incomprehension of the value of the
strategic retreat.

Because the Allied marshals – particularly Arnold – were less
rigid, the need for long-range fighters was tardily recognized
and then energetically pursued, and the Eighth Air Force, after
being ineffective for months, rocketed in potency along with the
Fifteenth Air Force. The Allied long-range fighters gained air
superiority over Europe. They sought out the German fighters
and destroyed them in the air while the bombers attacked the
fuel and fighter factories on which the home force depended.
In Bomber Command, Harris ignored the target of the German
fighter force. He had no plan to shoot it down, only to avoid
it, and in the end even his night bombing failed because the
German night fighter force achieved superiority.

The Air Staffs of Great Britain and the United States began
the war as convinced adherents of the power of strategic bombing, but differed in their theoretical application of the power.
Trenchard had laid down as the foundation of the Royal Air
Force thought that it was air force policy to attack, not the
enemy's army, but the civil population, to go straight to the

source of supply and to stop it : "The Army's policy was to defeat the enemy Army – ours to defeat the enemy nation." Mitchell also had urged on the Americans : "The hostile main army in the field is a false objective and the real objectives are the vital centers." But Trenchard, increasingly in later years, gave greater weight to the direct deterioration in enemy morale achieved by strategic bombing attacks. The Americans put firmer trust in eradicating sources of supply and lines of communication.

The "morale" objective of strategic bombing bedevilled the British High Command throughout the war. Trenchard, still an influential veteran, consistently advocated it, and it see-sawed irrationally in its acceptance by Churchill and the Chiefs of Staff. Early in his tenure of office Portal wrote, and got his fellow Chiefs tacitly to accept, that "the most vulnerable point in the German nation at war is the morale of her civilian population under air attack, and that until this morale has been broken it will not be possible to launch an army on the mainland of Europe with any prospect of success." The physical foundation of this mystical belief in the power of strategic bombing to achieve victory through shattering civilian morale was the unwelcome fact that, at the time, the Royal Air Force Bomber Command could not reliably hit anything more precise than civilian morale; and the temptation to exaggerate the impact was not withstood. With the amazing advance in bombing precision the cry tended to be damped by the Chiefs of Staff, but never by Harris, running Bomber Command with unprecedented independence. Yet even at the end of the war, when Bomber Command had shaped itself into an accurate laser of offence compared with its previous function as bludgeon, the theory of victory through civilian panic was revived by the Chiefs of Staff, and both the British and American air forces cooperated in the futile extinction of Dresden. Subsequent professional condemnation of that attack has not silenced the theory of the "Thunderclap" route to victory by selective obliteration. It was adopted, and indeed it worked at the highest political level, in the attack on Hiroshima, and the threat of similar treatment in the nuclear age has been promoted to become the supreme deterrent.

The air war in the west of 1939–45 was won by the disintegration, not of civilian morale, but of the vital centres, of the productive sources of military power, and of the communications by which production and power were conveyed. Churchill had denied that industrial destruction could effect military defeat : "Even if all the towns in Germany were rendered largely uninhabitable," he told Portal, "it does not follow that the military control would be weakened or even that war industry could not be carried on." He was answered in the end by Albert Speer, Reich Minister of Armaments and War Production : "The final collapse of the German economy can be counted on with certainty within four to eight weeks. . . . After this collapse, even military continuation of the war will be impossible."

That was an object which the Americans pursued far more single-mindedly than the British. Yet Tedder, the Briton who finally coordinated the strategy of victory, had to work almost as hard on Spaatz as on Harris to achieve it : Spaatz had, as what Harris may have called his "panacea", a sustained assault on German oil and German fighter production; they were both truly significant strategic objectives, but that fact alone was not enough; *some* air marshal needed the alertness of foresight to appreciate that an all-out diversion to communications at *this* moment and in *that* area was essential for quicker victory. The man who had this necessary fluidity of appreciation, who had the skill of correct assessment and the power and tact to impose his judgement, was Marshal Tedder.

These are the gifts of a great commander – adaptability, vision and leadership. Arnold used them to create an air force, but was thwarted when he tried to apply his vision to wage a quicker war, away from North Africa and Italy. Tedder used them to weld an *Allied* Air Force, the first and possibly the last in history, which was fully comprehensive in its impact, was not over-concerned with doctrinaire bickering against Army or Navy, and not irreparably damaged by prima-donna personality dissensions within its own ranks.

Tedder could not have achieved this without Portal, who sustained him and learned from him since the time Tedder commanded in the Mediterranean. Portal was Chief of the Air Staff for five years, until victory. He endured the weakness of the Royal Air Force as well as its ultimate strength, and accepted from Churchill the snarling reactions of defeat as well as the customary honours out of the victory bran tub. In the vortex of planning, and often of plotting, he remained the still centre from which the fundamental emphasis of the air war continued to be propagated. The war in the west was a committee war, directed in Great Britain by a Defence Minister, a War Cabinet and a Chiefs of Staff Committee in daily debate, powerfully affected even against their will by Ministers and Ministries, Parliament and Press, and having to dovetail many of their resolutions into the outcome of similar debates in the United States. Yet, whatever the pressure of political personalities, the men who made the decisions on operations and had to answer for them to posterity were the national Chiefs of Staff and the Anglo-American Combined Chiefs of Staff. In these committees Portal was anchor man. Of everyone else save Marshall it can be said that they were either extremists for their service point of view or poor diplomatists – which made them unsuccessful advocates. Of Portal's influence in the British Chiefs of Staff Committee Brooke, the Chief of the Imperial General Staff recorded his "greatest admiration for Peter's ability, not only in connection with the air where he was superb but in all the other matters we had to deal with. In debate with the Americans he was invaluable and had a wonderful way of clarifying complicated problems." A close observer, Lieutenant-General Sir Ian Jacob, Military Assistant Secretary to the War Cabinet, noted in his manuscript diary: "The Americans put their money on Portal. They would accept him as Commander in Chief over everything. They would put all the Allied Air Forces from Iceland to Bombay under his control. His great asset is his unshakeable honesty of thought and deed. They knew he knew his stuff and they trusted him one hundred per cent."

Yet this unshakable honesty had led him into a tortuous and humiliating deception, either of himself or others, at the beginning of his command. Playing a fearfully lonely game, aware that the past record of Bomber Command was about to crumble under the glare of its first competent clinical examination, he knew that faith was necessary to fortify facts in order to fashion the confidently-backed Royal Air Force that was to provide the straight left of victory. Portal fought Churchill tenaciously when the Prime Minister abandoned reliance on the war-winning potential of the Royal Air Force and reshaped production priorities on the basis of a personal promise to Stalin to open a second land front in Europe in 1943 : a political pressure which Portal doggedly withstood. He had to defend his Service from criticism that at times, especially from the Naval Staff, was vicious. He had to play a wily duel of wits with his friend Arnold in order to maintain the number of American-built aircraft in Britain. A declared believer in the general bombing of the German population long before Harris, Portal used Harris brilliantly, even although the retention of this crotchety commander meant occasional agonizing delays in getting policy adopted, occasional rough-riding, occasional backstairs intrigues. Through the long and difficult war he kept his temper although Churchill (who used his controlled – and occasionally uncontrolled – rages for intimidation) told him : "In war you don't have to be polite, you just have to be right." After the war he made no move to justify his work, to prove anyone right or wrong. He has made no claim, published no memoir, hit no one for six. He was the quiet man with the strong face at the centre. But perhaps, just as the Duke of Wellington was irreverently known to the common people as "that hook-nosed b— that licks the French," here, if anywhere in the military maelstrom of the Second World War, was, almost unknown to the common people, the hook-nosed b— who licked the Germans.

INDEX